Maximizing Business Performance and Efficiency Through Intelligent Systems

Om Prakash Rishi
University of Kota, India

Anukrati Sharma
University of Kota, India

A volume in the Advances in
Business Information Systems
and Analytics (ABISA) Book
Series

www.igi-global.com

Published in the United States of America by
    IGI Global
    Business Science Reference (an imprint of IGI Global)
    701 E. Chocolate Avenue
    Hershey PA 17033
    Tel: 717-533-8845
    Fax: 717-533-8661
    E-mail: cust@igi-global.com
    Web site: http://www.igi-global.com

Library of Congress Cataloging-in-Publication Data

Names: Rishi, Om Prakash, 1970- editor. | Sharma, Anukrati, 1981- editor.
Title: Maximizing business performance and efficiency through intelligent
  systems / Om Prakash Rishi and Anukrati Sharma, editors.
Description: Hershey, PA : Business Science Reference, [2017]
Identifiers: LCCN 2016056325| ISBN 9781522522348 (hardcover) | ISBN
  9781522522355 (ebook)
Subjects: LCSH: Information technology--Management. | Artificial
  intelligence--Industrial applications. | Management information systems.
Classification: LCC HD30.2 .M38348 2017 | DDC 658/.0563--dc23 LC record available at https://lccn.loc.gov/2016056325

This book is published in the IGI Global book series Advances in Business Information Systems and Analytics (ABISA) (ISSN: 2327-3275; eISSN: 2327-3283)

British Cataloguing in Publication Data
A Cataloguing in Publication record for this book is available from the British Library.

All work contributed to this book is new, previously-unpublished material. The views expressed in this book are those of the authors, but not necessarily of the publisher.

Advances in Business Information Systems and Analytics (ABISA) Book Series

ISSN:2327-3275
EISSN:2327-3283

MISSION

The successful development and management of information systems and business analytics is crucial to the success of an organization. New technological developments and methods for data analysis have allowed organizations to not only improve their processes and allow for greater productivity, but have also provided businesses with a venue through which to cut costs, plan for the future, and maintain competitive advantage in the information age.

The **Advances in Business Information Systems and Analytics (ABISA) Book Series** aims to present diverse and timely research in the development, deployment, and management of business information systems and business analytics for continued organizational development and improved business value.

COVERAGE

- Data Management
- Statistics
- Business Decision Making
- Business Process Management
- Strategic Information Systems
- Algorithms
- Forecasting
- Business Models
- Business Intelligence
- Management information systems

IGI Global is currently accepting manuscripts for publication within this series. To submit a proposal for a volume in this series, please contact our Acquisition Editors at Acquisitions@igi-global.com or visit: http://www.igi-global.com/publish/.

Titles in this Series

For a list of additional titles in this series, please visit: www.igi-global.com

Applying Predictive Analytics Within the Service Sector
Rajendra Sahu (ABV-Indian Institute of Information Technology and Management, India)
Manoj Dash (ABV-Indian Institute of Information Technology and Management, India) and
Anil Kumar (BML Munjal University, India)
Business Science Reference • copyright 2017 • 294pp • H/C (ISBN: 9781522521488) •
US $195.00 (our price)

Enterprise Information Systems and the Digitalization of Business Functions
Madjid Tavana (La Salle University, USA)
Business Science Reference • copyright 2017 • 497pp • H/C (ISBN: 9781522523826) •
US $215.00 (our price)

Strategic Information Systems and Technologies in Modern Organizations
Caroline Howard (HC Consulting, USA) and Kathleen Hargiss (Colorado Technical University, USA)
Information Science Reference • copyright 2017 • 366pp • H/C (ISBN: 9781522516804)
• US $205.00 (our price)

Business Analytics and Cyber Security Management in Organizations
Rajagopal (EGADE Business School, Tecnologico de Monterrey, Mexico City, Mexico
& Boston University, USA) and Ramesh Behl (International Management Institute, Bhubaneswar, India)
Business Science Reference • copyright 2017 • 346pp • H/C (ISBN: 9781522509028) •
US $215.00 (our price)

Handbook of Research on Intelligent Techniques and Modeling Applications in Marketing Analytics
Anil Kumar (BML Munjal University, India) Manoj Kumar Dash (ABV-Indian Institute of
Information Technology and Management, India) Shrawan Kumar Trivedi (BML Munjal
University, India) and Tapan Kumar Panda (BML Munjal University, India)
Business Science Reference • copyright 2017 • 428pp • H/C (ISBN: 9781522509974) •
US $275.00 (our price)

Applied Big Data Analytics in Operations Management
Manish Kumar (Indian Institute of Information Technology, Allahabad, India)
Business Science Reference • copyright 2017 • 251pp • H/C (ISBN: 9781522508861) •
US $160.00 (our price)

www.igi-global.com

701 E. Chocolate Ave., Hershey, PA 17033
Order online at www.igi-global.com or call 717-533-8845 x100
To place a standing order for titles released in this series,
contact: cust@igi-global.com
Mon-Fri 8:00 am - 5:00 pm (est) or fax 24 hours a day 717-533-8661

Table of Contents

Detailed Table of Contents

    Mahesh Kumar Singh, University of Kota, India
    Om Prakash Rishi, University of Kota, India
    Anukrati Sharma, University of Kota, India
    Zaved Akhtar, Vishveshwarya Institute of Engineering and Technology,
       India

Internet plays a vital role for doing the business. It provides platform for creating huge number of customers for ease of business. E-business organizations are growing rapidly and doubly in every minute; World Wide Web (WWW) provides huge information for the Internet users. The accesses of user's behavior are recorded in web logs. This information seems to be very helpful in an E-business environment for analysis and decision making. Mining of web data come across many new challenges with enlarged amount of information on data stored in web logs. The search engines play key role for retrieving the relevant information from huge information. Nowadays, the well-known search engines, like Google, MSN, Yahoo, etc. have provided the users with good search results worked on special search strategies. In web search services the web page ranker component plays the main factor of the Google. This paper discusses the new challenges faced by web mining techniques, ranking of web pages using page ranking algorithms and its application in E-business analysis to improve the business operations.

The aim of this research paper is to study the impact of Emerging Technologies and Social Media on different businesses, market and management. There is no doubt that business technology has revolutionized the way companies conduct business. The advent of the social media has brought tremendous changes and advancement in the marketing process. For marketers, this is a huge advantage because the rapid transition from mass to social media resents the opportunity to create impactful, relevant marketing messages. Social Media is fast evolving as one of the most reliable ways to connect and stay informed about the most recent developments in a particular industry. It offers a platform for discussions and information sharing about anything and everything, helping users build their online identity and reputation.

With the explosive increase in regular E Commerce users, online commerce companies must have more customer friendly websites to satisfy the personalized requirements of online customer to progress their market share over competition; Different individuals have different purchase requirements at different time intervals and hence novel approaches are often required to be deployed by online retailers in order to identify the latest purchase requirements of customer. This research work proposes a novel MR apriori algorithm and system design of a tool called IMSS-SE, which can be used to blend benefits of Apriori-based Map Reduce framework with Intelligent technologies for B2C E-commerce in order to assist the online user to easily search and rank various E Commerce websites which can satisfy his personalized online purchase requirement. An extensive experimental evaluation shows that proposed system can better satisfy the personalized search requirements of E Commerce users than generic search engines.

Agent technology has been suggested by experts to be a promising approach to address the challenges of the modern computer based education. Any agent satisfies four properties: autonomy, social ability, reactivity and pro-activeness. By using intelligent agents in an ITS architecture it is possible to obtain an individual tutoring system adapted to the needs and characteristics of every student. In this chapter, the authors are going to present a multiagent system i.e. named ABDITS which is distributed, dynamic, intelligent and adaptive with Pedagogy view for learners in intelligent system. This system is an integration of adaptive web-based learning with expert systems as well. A crucial feature of the ABDITS personal agent is that the case based reasoning approach for student modeling.

Role of computers are widely accepted and well known in the domain of Finance. Artificial Intelligence(AI) methods are extensively used in field of computer science for providing solution of unpredictable event in a frequent changing environment with utilization of neural network. Professionals are using AI framework into every field for reducing human interference to get better result from few decades. The main objective of the chapter is to point out the techniques of AI utilized in field of finance in broader perspective. The purpose of this chapter is to analyze the background of AI in finance and its role in Finance Market mainly as investment decision analysis tool.

Automated exploration of groups of customers to understand customer behavior from raw data is highly required to support strategic decision making given the pressure of competitive market. Several mathematical and statistical methods have been applied for autonomous model estimation from multivariate data. The current paper investigates employability of new generation of bio-inspired metaheuristic algorithms, named the artificial immune system (AIS), which in the current proposition, learn through density based kernels. As such the model simulates probabilistic behavior of the dendritic cells (DCs) during recognition of the antigens and danger signals, whose learning has been modeled with an infinite Gaussian mixture model. The unsupervised learning capability of the model has been found to be effective for multivariate data.

The purpose of this conceptual paper is to introduce one of the controversial issues in the business world which is labeled blue ocean strategy, this study also highlight blue ocean`s barriers like imitation and emulation. Brief comparison between competitive environment (Red Oceans) strategy and blue ocean strategy and also importance of role of management in using blue ocean strategy to increase return for the firms are issues that explained. The review of the research contains role of innovation and its value for this strategy to help the firms survive in competitive market. First movers and second fast imitators also are the issues that in this study explain about their advantages and disadvantages in brief comparison.

Recent computing world has seen rapid growth of the number of middle and large scale enterprises that deploy business processes sharing variety of services available over cloud environment. Due to the advantage of reduced cost and increased availability, the cloud technology has been gaining unbound popularity. However, because of existence of multiple cloud service providers on one hand and varying user requirements on the other hand, the task of appropriate service composition becomes challenging. The conception of this chapter is to consider the fact that different quality parameters related to various services might bear varied importance for different user. This chapter introduces a framework for QoS-based Cloud service selection to satisfy the end user needs. A hybrid algorithm based on genetic algorithm (GA) and Tabu Search methods has been developed, and its efficacy is analysed. Finally, this chapter includes the experimental analysis to present the performance of the algorithm.

New developments in the Information and Communications Technology industry have substantially increased the importance of the internet over the last decade. As a result, the finance sector has developed its technological capability to be able to compete in an online marketplace with other financial services providers and to be able to serve their customer. This chapter examines the use of technology in the financial industry and the various factors associated with it, as well as introducing the reader to the main types of project initiators-contributor business relations in online crowdfunding.

Chapter 10

Reshu Goyal, Banasthali Vidhyapeeth, India
Praveen Dhyani, Banasthali Vidhyapeeth, India
Om Prakash Rishi, University of Kota, India

Time has changed and so does the world. Today everything has become as a matter of one click. With this effort we are trying to explore the new opportunities features and capabilities of the new compeers of Internet applicability known as Social Media or Web 2.0. The effort has been put in to use the internet, social media or web 2.0 as the tool for marketing issues or the strategic business decision making. The main aim is to seek social media, web 2.0 internet applications as the tool for marketing.

Chapter 11

Supriyo Roy, Birla Institute of Technology, India
Kaushik Kumar, Birla Institute of Technology, India

Cold Chain addresses subset of supply chain involving production, storage and distribution of products that require 'level of temperature control' to retain 'key characteristics and associated value' in terms of life expectancy and perishability. Successful cold chain management is essential for pharmaceutical companies, transportation providers and health care practitioners. With growing population and their demand; especially in retail and pharmaceutical sectors drives Indian cold chain market and it has huge potential to grow in the near future. India's greatest need is for an effective and economically viable cold chain solution that will integrate the supply chains for all commodities from the production centers to the consumption centers; thereby reducing physical waste and loss of value of perishable commodities. This article highlights the importance of cold chain concepts with Indian business scenario. Strategic planning of cold supply chain and their real value towards good manufacturing practices are critically highlighted.

In the given study we have undertaken a comprehensive analysis on the simulation of different products emerging out from the assembly line. The study starts from collection of point of view of different authors from various studies. Then it has been found that the system of distributed manufacturing can be used to prepare a model that can be simultaneously simulated. The introduction of systems under a bigger system is introduced for accommodating the complete supply chain in a single diagram. The system is then implemented with the help of Petri NET software and the operational parameters are analysed by the output. The case study undertaken is of a cable manufacturing firm in which the methodology suggested is implemented and it is validated that such a methodology can help on controlling the different systems from a single point of control.

Foreword

The core of this book is an attempt to evaluate the blend between information technology and business practices. Intelligent systems have never been more important in business and management world. Fortunately the rapid growth of the businesses developed an urge for using intelligent systems in many functions of business enterprises. The era we live in cannot be imagined without using the intelligent systems. New invention of computing methods, generally known as "Intelligent Systems" is now effectively used in different functions of management, finance and business modelling. Performance of business(s) is dependent these days on the uses of intelligent systems in the enterprise(s). Direct marketing, stock market forecast, portfolio management, finance evaluations etc. are easier because of Intelligent systems. Without a doubt intelligent systems have supported business functions remarkably. The potential still have to be revealed in many other aspects of intelligent systems. Intelligent system applications are justified itself to the world of business in many ways.

The contributors tried to explore every bit and bite of intelligent systems relevance for business performance with logic, perception, reasoning and learning. The editors' unifying idea of maximising the business performance and efficiency through intelligent systems have been synthesize to explain each subfield of Intelligent systems applications which are useful in business functions. The good attribute of the book that the editors tried to avoid excessive formality in the appearance of these ideas while retaining exactness.

This book certainly provides such a conceptual framework for addressing the general problem, opportunities and challenges of using intelligent systems in business enterprise. It emphasizes that intelligent system works as a backbone for the business. It gives a boost in the performance of different functions of management, marketing, finance and production. The book covers such important topics as case based reasoning, blue ocean strategies, intelligent multi-agent systems etc. all of which are vital to intelligent systems and its applications. The chapters given in this book are quite significant, comprehensive and practically useful. Advanced uses of intelligent systems will definitely be a valuable reference for students and researchers. I believe most readers will find more surprise as they explore the pages of this combined effort of authors and editors.

M. M. Salunkhe
Symbiosis University of Applied Sciences (SUAS), India

Preface

Our major concern before editing this book was, would we read any book again and again? We believe that it is perfidious to write a book solely for others and it's always good if we join our hands for a task. What one single mind cannot do for the readers many brilliant minds can do that. That is the reason why we have decided to come out with an edited book of *Maximizing Business Performance and Efficiency Through Intelligent Systems*. We researched works of many academicians before proceeding for the title of the book. In fact the research in finalizing the topic took more time rather than the editing process of it. Our contributors and reviewers were committed about not wasting a single moment of readers on reading an invaluable sentence.

The book is meticulous effort of many minds. In the recent decade, the face of technology has vastly changed. Intelligent systems have opened new doors and have given opportunities to business(s) to perform better. The main focus of the book is to generate and extend the practical implications of intelligent systems which the readers can adopt especially in business functions. Instead of just unfolding the formal definitions, terms and steps each chapter of the book gives explicit suggestions that the business people should pursue.

Each chapter provides accessible information for beginners as well as theory and challenges for advanced students, serving both senior undergraduate students and researchers. The book is a blend of balance theory and experimentation, providing a thorough explication of the science of AI along with its engineering applications. This book encapsulates the latest results without being exhaustive and encyclopedic and provides principles and tools that allow readers to explore and learn on their own.

Assortment of specialization chapters such as Cloud Supply Chain, Blue Ocean Strategy, Applications of AI in Financial System, Intelligent Big Data Analytics: Adaptive E-Commerce Website Ranking Using Apriori Hadoop – BDAS-Based Cloud Framework have been given broad revelation in the book. The chapters of the book comprehensively organized and revised, yet considerably edited to focus attention on main issues. We see this book as a prime step towards association between the academicians and marketers. We planned to deal with many topics which were somehow were not the part of the present book. Most importantly we want this book to be benchmark for learning community.

Acknowledgment

From the many people who have been very supportive in the preparation of this book, *Maximizing Business Performance and Efficiency Through Intelligent Systems*, we are grateful to the contributors who have provided us invaluable chapters. We would like to thank the Hon'ble Vice Chancellor of our University Professor P.K. Dashora for providing us warm and healthy environment because of which we would be able to focus upon this book. Our thanks go to many of our colleagues and friends at the different Universities likewise University of Rajasthan and University of Kota.

We owe a great thanks to the authors of the book who have contributed to create our vision into reality. We especially like to thank those who read, reviewed and commented on the chapters for the improvements our book chapter reviewers Prof. P.K. Dyani, Prof. Ravinder Rena, Azizul Hassan.

We would like to sincerely acknowledge Jannie, Maria Rohde, Lindsay Johnston and the other team members of IGI Global publications who provided us this opportunity and supported us on every step. The encouragement given by them in the preparation of this book is speechless.

Finally, we would enormously thankful to all our Department's colleagues at University of Kota Department of Computer Science and Informatics & Department of Commerce and Management for their constant support.

Chapter 1
Knowledge Extraction Through Page Rank Using Web-Mining Techniques for E-Business:
A Review

Mahesh Kumar Singh
University of Kota, India

Anukrati Sharma
University of Kota, India

Om Prakash Rishi
University of Kota, India

Zaved Akhtar
*Vishveshwarya Institute of
Engineering and Technology, India*

ABSTRACT

Internet plays a vital role for doing the business. It provides platform for creating huge number of customers for ease of business. E-business organizations are growing rapidly and doubly in every minute; World Wide Web (WWW) provides huge information for the Internet users. The accesses of user's behavior are recorded in web logs. This information seems to be very helpful in an E-business environment for analysis and decision making. Mining of web data come across many new challenges with enlarged amount of information on data stored in web logs. The search engines play key role for retrieving the relevant information from huge information. Nowadays, the well-known search engines, like Google, MSN, Yahoo, etc. have provided the users with good search results worked on special search strategies. In web search services the web page ranker component plays the main factor of the Google. This paper discusses the new challenges faced by web mining techniques, ranking of web

DOI: 10.4018/978-1-5225-2234-8.ch001

pages using page ranking algorithms and its application in E-business analysis to improve the business operations.

1. INTRODUCTION

Today the Internet has changed the rules for doing businesses; this revolution towards E-business has changed the conventional way of doing businesses. This technique also faces some new challenges both for companies as well as customers. Customer confuse with multiple choice of specific product which results lost state. The big issue in front of the companies is to sustain their performance output in this competitive business environment. A promising solution to overcome this issue is recommended system which provides and guides the customer with the types of product he or she is buying or purchasing. If it is to be consider that each product or service have different page then page rank provide the rating of the similar product of different companies by using the ranking the page it can be calculated the popularity of the product or service.

Modern telecommunication technologies connect people distributed at different places in the world and ease the delivery of information. Therefore, users are enabled to share the knowledge with other people by available communication methods. However, it becomes very inefficient for a web surfer to navigate the sequence of web pages one by one due to the large amount of the unstructured web. Thus, search engines have been adopted as a solution to overcome from such problems over the past few years. Behind the search engine, web mining plays a key role since it can accelerate the exchange of knowledge hidden in volatile collections of data on the Internet.

1.1. Motivation

Nowadays the Internet has been well known as a big data repository consisting of different data types as well as a large amount of hidden informative knowledge, which can be discovered via a wide range of data mining techniques. All these kinds of techniques are based on intelligent computing approaches, or so-called computational intelligence, which is widely used in the research of web database, web data mining and information retrieval and so on. Although the progress of the web-based database management system research results in developments of different useful web applications or services, like Web search engines, users are still facing the problems of information overload and complexity due to the significant and rapid growth in the amount of information and the number of users. The web users usually experience from the difficulties of finding desirable and accurate information on the web due to low precision and low recall caused by the above reasons. For example, if a user wants to search the desired information by utilizing a web search engine such as Google, the search engine may provide to the user not only the information related to the query topic, but also a large amount of irrelevant /noisy information. The emerging of Internet has given research issues and challenges to web researchers for web-based information retrieval and information management. Web research academia is required to develop effective and efficient techniques to fulfill the increasing demands of web users, creating good quality Web communities (Zhang, Y., et.al.. 2006, and Kleinberg, J. 1998), extracting the informative knowledge from the available information (Craven, M., 1998, pp 509-516), capturing the underlying usage pattern from the Web observation data (Srivastava, J., et al. 2000, pp 12-23), recommending user customized information to offer better Internet service (Mobasher, B., et al., 2002, pp 61-82), and in addition mining valuable business information from the common or individual customer navigational behaviour as well (Ghani, R. & Fano, A,. 2002,pp 11-19).

Every relevant information is collected around the mining results which now represent actionable knowledge. These data are arranged according to different aspects, where each aspect represents a particular aspect of the objects represented in the web mining results. By using these information business analyst interprets the mining results and make informed business decisions.

2. WORLD WIDE WEB (WWW)

Terminology related to WWW as shown in figure 1.

- **WWW:** Is the collection of a large amount of distributed and interconnected data around the whole world. In other words the WWW is the set of all web Pages which are interconnected by hypertext links. What not all the people know is that this apparently heterogeneous source of information has some properties which I will explain in this section.
- **A Link:** Is relationships between two or more resources which expresses one or more (explicit or implicit). Links may also be established within a web page by using anchors.
- **A Web Page:** Is a collection of text information, images and other multimedia elements like audio video. Most important fact which is used to calculate importance of web pages in Page Rank calculation is Anchors/Keywords text or Hyperlinks contained in web page.

- **A Web Site:** Is a collection of interconnected web pages, including a homepage, residing at the similar location. Each web page of web site is identified by a single URL.
- A **Uniform Resource Locator (URL):** Is an identified for an abstract or physical resource, for example a server and a file path or index. URLs are location independent and each URL contains four distinct parts, namely the protocol types (usually http), the name of the Web server, the directory path and the file name. If a file name is not specified, index.html is assumed.
- **A Web Server:** Is a program which receives request from web browser and send web pages as response to browser.
- **A Web Browser:** Is a program which allows a person to view the contents of Web Pages, and navigating from one page to another.

2.1 Information Retrieval (IR)

Most of the concepts here described have been extracted from information retrieval (Pokorny, J. & Smizansky J.,). The problem of the information retrieval has always

Figure 1. Structure of the World-Wide Web

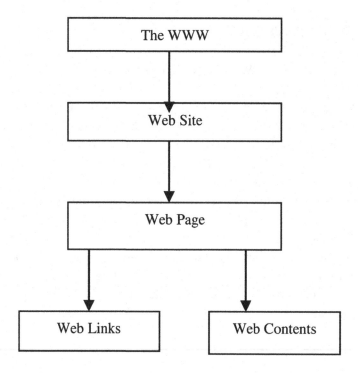

existed. In the past, vast amount of information were stored and to access this information accurately and speedily was really difficult. After the appearance of the computers this problem remains unsolved.

Imagine a store of documents. Imagine a user who creates a query and sends it to the system. He could retrieve the right answer reading all the documents in the store, filtering the documents he is interested in and discarding the rest. This is the "perfect" retrieval but of course this is impracticable. After this definition it seems to be necessary to define two new concepts:

- **Efficiency:** It is normally defined in terms of computer resources used such as core, backing store and processor time.
- **Effectiveness**: It is usually measured in terms of precision and recall. Where precision is the ratio of the number of relevant documents retrieved to the total number of documents retrieved.

Recall is the ratio of the number of relevant information retrieved to the total number of relevant information (both retrieved and not retrieved).

In the Figure 2 a typical Information Retrieval System Structure (Pokorny, J. & Smizansky J.,) is sketched. Information Retrieval System is composed of several basic components:

Figure 2. Information retrieval system

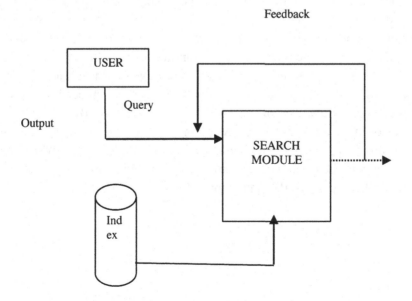

5

- **User Interactive Interfaces:** It needed to take the user query and make it user friendly. The whole and complex process behind should be transparent to the user.
- **Data Repository**: It is a database/repository with the data to be searched. Here a representation of each document is stored. It is not needed to have the whole document in the repository; many of the current information systems store only part of it (e.g. significant words, metadata, etc.).
- **Search Component:** It is the processor of the system. Some of the tasks it is in charge are:
  - Transform query to understandable format (e.g. from natural language to the computer understandable format)
  - Do matching with the index. In this case matching means "find relevant documents" because many times the match is not exact but the documents are still relevant to the user query.
  - Return the relevant documents as output. How to present the output and the order could be some tasks of this module.
- **Evaluation Component:** It takes care of the user behaviour with the results of the query. Many times systems can track what a user does after a transaction and take it into account in future interactions. For example, if a system shows some results found relevant to a query and the user refines the query and searches it again, the system can suppose that the previous results were unsatisfactory and it can remove them from the next output.

In order to satisfy the user's information needs, the IR system must find a way to interpret the contents of the information items and be able to rank them according to a degree of relevance to the user query. This interpretation involves how to extract information in syntactic and semantic ways. The goal of an IR system is to retrieve all the documents, which are relevant to a query while retrieving as few non-relevant documents as possible. To achieve this goal, IR needs users to provide a set of words which convey the semantics of the information need. Also, a document is represented by a set of keywords or index terms for IR to extract. These keywords or index terms can be derived from information experts or a computer through eliminating articles and connectives, the use of stemming (which reduces distinct words to their common grammatical root), and identifying nouns (which eliminates adjectives, adverbs, and verbs).

2.2 Crawlers and Search Engines

As it is known that the size of the whole World Wide Web is very large. This rapid evolution and exponential increase present a real challenge to web search engines because of several reasons:

- **Accessibility:** Not all the pages and all the information are accessible, users need a start point where they search for new pages. However, not all the pages are interconnected so crawlers will never visit some of them.
- **Crawling:** A crawler is only a program that retrieves Web pages, commonly for use by a search engine. It navigates in the WWW and jumps from one page to another retrieving information. This process takes time and periodically the crawler has to revisit the already crawled pages in order to maintain updated the information. Even if many crawlers work in parallel, it is not possible to visit all the available pages because there are limited resources (disk space, memory, time, bandwidth, etc.).
- **Storage:** Crawlers retrieve information from the pages they visit but this information has to be stored in our own repository. This repository has limited size.
- **Information Management:** Even if crawler reach to store all the information of the WWW, manage and manipulate this information is a big challenge. In the following sections some basic knowledge about this topic and some basic features of the World Wide Web are explained.

2.2.1 Architecture of Crawler

In the Figure 3 a typical crawler is sketched (Cho, J. Ya-Molina, H. G.and Page. L.,1998), Each module has different functions and communicates with each others as follows:

- **URL Listing Module:** It has a list (ordered or unordered) of URLs and gives them to the Retrieving module.
- **Retrieving Module:** It retrieves each document from the web and gives it to the Process module.
- **Process Module:** It realizes the following tasks over the document:
  - **Automatic Text Analysis:** Branching, removal of high frequency words or detecting equivalent branches are some examples.
  - **Indexing:** Finding of index terms from the document. A language that is used to describe documents and requests is called index.

Figure 3. Typical crawler structure

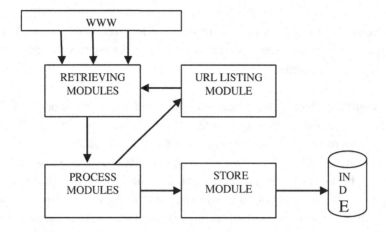

- ○ **Classification:** Use of thesauri, keyword clustering, document clustering...
- ○ **Filtering:** It is possible to filter the documents we are examining in order to store only some of them (regarding to the topic they belong to, the format they have, etc.).
- ○ **Link Extraction:** All the links a document has are extracted and sent to the URL Listing module in order to be crawled in the future.
- ○ After these tasks, it gives the result (data) to the Format and Store module.
- ● **Format and Store Module:** Converts data to an improved format and store it into the index.
- ● **Index/Repository**: Database/repository with the useful data retrieved. It will be used by the Search Engine.

2.2.2 Architecture of Search Engine

In the Figure 4 a typical search engine (Duhan,N, et.al, 2009), is sketched. Search engine provides user interface to user for information retrieval from the WWW. There are many components. Some of them work online i.e. when online user request a query, like Ranking, Query Parser. But some of them work offline like crawler, Indexer etc. These modules collect information from other web sites and store in warehouse for better performance. Web search engines arranging information about many web pages in some manner according to algorithm, which they retrieve from the html itself. A Web crawler (also known as a spider) is an automated web browser which follows every link on the site and retrieves these pages. The contents of each page are then analyzed to determine how it should be arranged in indexed form (for example, words are extracted from the titles, headings, or special fields called Meta tags. The web pages data are stored in an index database for use in later queries formed by users. The function of an indexing of the web page is to allow information to be found as quickly as possible. Some search engines, such as Google, store all or part of the source page in the cache as well as information about the web pages, whereas others, such as AltaVista, store every word of every page they find. This cached page always holds the actual search text because it is the one that was really sorted and arranged, hence it can be very useful when the content of the current page has been updated and the search terms are no longer in it.

When a user fires a query into a search engine (by using key words), the engine examines its index and provides a list of best-matched web pages according to its selection criteria, frequently with a short summary containing the document's title and occasionally parts of the text. The index is built from the information stored with the web data and the method by which applied for the information is indexed. Nowadays sorry to say, there are currently no known public search engines that allow documents to be searched by date. Most of the search engines use of the

Figure 4. Architecture of search engine

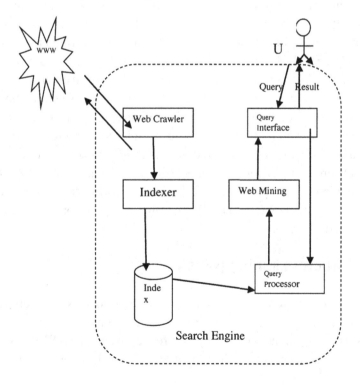

Boolean operators AND, OR and NOT to further specify the search query. Boolean operators are for literal searches that allow the user to refine and extend the terms of the search.

3. WEB MINING

Extraction of interesting information or patterns from large web databases is called web mining. Web Mining is an application of data mining techniques used to discover and retrieve relevant information and patterns (knowledge) from the WWW documents and services web mining can be divided into three categories(Broder,A, 2002).:

- Web Content Mining (WCM)
- Web Structure Mining (WSM)
- Web Usage Mining (WUM)

3.1 Web Content Mining (WCM)

It describes the automatic search of information resources available online, and involves mining web data content. It is prominence on the content of the web page not its links. It can be applied on web pages itself or on the result pages obtained from a web search engine. WCM is categorized from two different points of view: Information Retrieval (IR) View and Database View. In information retrieval view, most of the researches use collection of words, which is based on the statistics about isolated single word in collection of words, to represent unstructured text. For the semi-structured data, the scanner utilized HTML structures insides the documents. For database view, web mining always tries to infer the structure of the web site to convert a web site to become a database. Text mining and its application to web content has been the most widely researched. Research activities in this field also used the techniques from Artificial Intelligent such as Information Retrieval [IR], Image Processing, Natural Language Processing [NLP] and computer vision are the techniques used in content mining.

3.2 Web Structure Mining (WSM)

It is used to generate structural summary about the web sites and web pages. The structure of a typical web graph contains a set of web pages as nodes and a set of hyperlinks as edges connecting to any two related web pages. Web Content Mining techniques mainly focus on the structure of inner-document of the web page,

Figure 5. Taxonomy of Web Mining

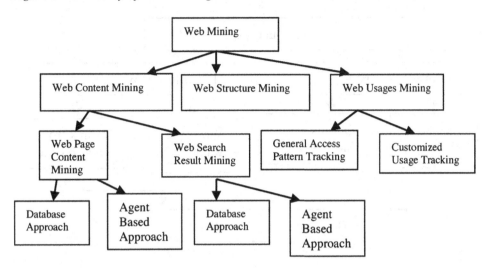

while Web Structure Mining (WSM) techniques discover the link structure of the hyperlinks at the inter-document level of the web page.

3.2.1 Inlinks and Outlinks of Web-Page

Inlinks are the web-links that come from other web page to the current web page that is the web-page is re-directed by other web pages; and, Outlinks are those web-links of current web-page which are direct to another web-pages. The web-page rank of the web page depends on number of inlinked and outlinked web-pages as shown in Figure 6.

The 'Decisive Factor' is calculated based on following formula

$$Inlink - Outlink\,Dicisive\,Factor\left(D_{pio}\left(A\right) = \left(\Sigma\left(PR\left(T_i\right)\right) + O(T_i))\right)X(\Sigma(O\left(Ti\right) + PR\left(To\right)\right)\right)$$

where,

DFio(A) = Inlink-outlink Decisive Factor of the Web-page 'A';
A = Current Web-page whose Decisive Factor would be calculated;
Ti = Web-pages which have a Web-link to Web-page A; i.e., inbound Web-pages
    or inlinked Web-pages;
To = Web-pages which are redirected from Web-page A; i.e., outbound Web-pages
    or outlinked Web-pages;

Figure 6. Operational flowchart of inlink and outlink decisive factor calculation

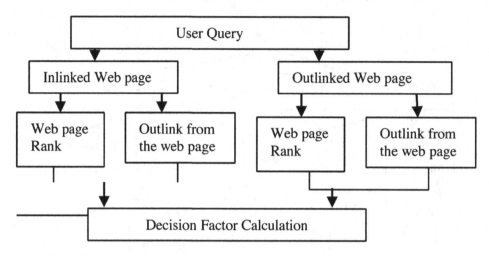

PR(Ti) = Web-page rank of the inbound Web-page Ti in Web-page A; O(Ti) = Number of outbound links from Web-page Ti;

PR(To) = Web-page rank of the outbound Web-page To from Web-page A; O(To) = Number of outbound links from Web-page To;

3.3 Web Usage Mining (WUM)

It focuses on the techniques that could predict user navigational behavior while the user interacts with web pages of particular site at particular time. Web usages mining technique allows for the collection of web access information for Web pages by the users. This usage data provides the paths leading to accessed web pages. This information is often gathered automatically into access web logs by the web server. Common Gateway Interface scripts give other useful information such as referrer logs, user subscription information and survey logs. Web usages mining are important to the overall use of web mining for companies and their internet/ intranet based applications and information access techniques. Usage data captures the identity or origin of web users along with their browsing behavior at a web site. Capturing, Modeling and analyzing of behavioral patterns of users are the main goal of this web mining category. Web usage mining consists of three phases, namely preprocessing, pattern discovery, and pattern analysis.

Web Usage Mining techniques can be used to expect the user behavior in real time by comparing the current navigational pattern of the online users with typical patterns which were extracted from past history stored in web log file. All recommendation systems could be developed to recommend the interesting links to products which could be matched with the user's interest. One of the major issues in web log mining is to group all the user's page requests so for identifying the paths that users followed during navigation through the web site. The most common approach is to use cookies to track the navigation sequence of users' page requests or by using some heuristic methods. Session reconstruction is very difficult from proxy server log file data and sometimes since not all users' navigation paths can be identified always.

3.3.1 Data Sources

The usage data collected from different sources represent the navigation patterns of different segments of the overall web traffic, varies from single user, single site browsing behavior to multi-user, multi-site access patterns. Web server log does not contain sufficient information for identifying the behavior at the client side as they relate to the pages served by the web server at the server side. Data may be collected from

- Web Servers
- Proxy Servers
- Web Clients
- **Web Server Data:** Web servers collect large amounts of information in their web log files databases are used instead of simple log files to store information so to improve querying of massive log repositories. They match to the user logs that are collected at web server as web log file. Some of the typical data collected at a web server include page references, IP addresses and access time of the users.
- **Application Server Data:** There are different commercial applications servers like Broad Vision, Web Logic, Story Server etc. which are widely used to enable the E-commerce applications to be built on top of them with little effort. The main feature is the ability to trail different kinds of business activities and log them in application server logs.
- **Application Level Data:** The new kinds of events can always be defined in an application, and sorting can be turned on for them generating histories of these specially defined events.
- The main issue on the server side is an aggregated picture of the usage of the services by all users, while on the client side there is complete picture usage of all services by a particular client, with the proxy side being somewhere in the middle.
- **Web Data Acquisition:** Data acquisition means collection of data for web mining purpose, and this is usually the first task in web mining application. The said data can be collected from three main sources which includes (i)

web server data (ii) proxy server data and (iii) web client data. The web server source was chosen for the fact that it is the richest and most important common data source; more so, it can be used to collect large amount of information from the log files and databases they represent. The user profile information, the access and navigation pattern are extracted from the historical access data recorded in the RSS reader site, users' address data base. The data are in huge volume and it contains so many complete information such as date, time, session in which activities occur, saver's name, IP address, user name, like pass word, dailies name, required feed, news headlines, and contents, as recorded in the database file.

- **Data Pre-Processing:** In the original database file extracted, not all the information are valid for web usage data mining only need entries that contain relevant information. The original file is usually made up of text files that contains large volume of information related queries made to the web server in which most of the instance contains irrelevant, incomplete, ambiguous and misleading information for mining purpose data preprocessing also evolved the cleansing, formatting and grouping of web log files into meaningful session for the sole aim of utilizing it for web usage mining.

- **Data Cleansing:** Data cleansing means eliminating irrelevant/noisy entries from the log file. There are following operations can be used for data cleansing: (i) Removal of entries with ''Error'' or ''Failure'' status. (ii) Removal of requests performed by automated programs such as some right to use records that are automatically generated by the search engine agent from access log file and proxies. (iii) Identification and removal of request for picture files associated with request for a page and request include Java scripts and style sheet file (iv) Removal of entries with unsuccessful HTTP status code, etc.

3.3.2 Pattern Discovery Techniques

Various data mining techniques have been investigated for mining web usage logs. They are statistical analysis, association rule mining, clustering, classification and sequential pattern mining.

3.3.2.1 Statistical Approach
The types of statistical information are usually generated periodically in reports and used by business administrators to improve the system performance and facilitate the site modification task, enhance the security of the system, and provide the support for marketing decisions.

3.3.2.2 Association Rule Mining

Association rule mining (Singh M. K, Akhtar Z. & Begam, N, 2012) finds interesting correlation relationships among a large set of data items. A typical example of association rule mining is E-market valet analysis. This process analyzes customer buying interest by finding associations between the different products that customers place in their "shopping volets". Such associations can help retailers to develop marketing strategies by gaining insight into which products are frequently purchased together by customers. For web usage mining, association rules can be used to find correlations between web pages (or products in an E-commerce website) accessed together during a server session. Such rules indicate the possible relationship between pages that are often viewed together even if they are not directly connected, and can be categorized into different groups of users with specific interests. Apart from being exploited for business applications, the associations are mainly used for web recommendation and personalization nowadays.

3.3.2.3 Clustering

Clustering is a special technique used for grouping a set of similar physical or abstract objects into classes of similar objects. A cluster is a collection of data objects that are similar to one another within the same cluster and are dissimilar to the objects in other clusters. A cluster of data objects can be used collectively as one group in practical applications. There exist a large number of clustering algorithms. The choice of a clustering algorithm depends both on the type of available data, and on its purpose and application that data.

In web usage mining, clustering techniques are mainly used to discover in two kinds of useful clusters, namely user clusters and page clusters. User clustering attempts to find groups of users with similar navigational behavior and habit, while the web page clustering required discovering groups of web pages that seem to be conceptually related according to the users' need. Such knowledge is useful for performing market segmentation in E-commerce and web personalization applications.

3.3.2.4 Sequential Pattern Mining

As mentioned earlier, web logs can be treated as a collection of sequences of access events from one user or session in timestamp ascending order. A web access pattern is a sequential pattern in a large set of pieces of web logs, which is pursued frequently by users. Such knowledge can be used for discovering useful user access trends and predicting future visit patterns, which is helpful for pre-fetching documents, recommending web pages, or placing advertisements aimed at certain user groups.

4. RANKING ALGORITHM

The web data is very large, diverse and has many must be related to the given query fired by the users. Therefore, efficient method/algorithm is used to arrange the entire pages in subject to the interest to a user's query during retrieval of required result called ranking algorithm. The collection of web pages are treated as a directed graph in which pages are denoted as nodes and links are denoted as edges.

Ranking algorithms can be based on various criteria such as link structure only, document property based only, and a combination of the former.

4.1 PageRank Algorithm (PR)

Surgey Brin and Larry Page developed a ranking algorithm used by Google, named PageRank after Larry Page (cofounder of Google search engine), that is based on link structure and content on the link of the web to determine the relevance of web pages (Page, L Brin, S.,Motwani, R. & Winograd. T., 1999), Google uses PageRank to order its search results in the form of link so that documents that are seem more important move up in the results of a search accordingly. This algorithm stated that if a page has some important incoming links to it than its outgoing links to other pages also become important. Therefore, it takes incoming links into account and propagates the ranking through links. Thus, the link of the web page gets a high rank if the sum of the ranks of its incoming links i.e backlink is high. It takes back links into account and propagates the ranking through links. In PageRank, the rank score of a web page (say R) is equally divided among its entire outgoing links from that web page. The values assigned to the outgoing links of page R are in turn used to calculate the ranks of the pages pointed to by R. An example showing the distribution of page ranks is illustrated in Figure 7.

Thus, a page has a high rank if the sum of the ranks of its back links is high. A simplified version of page rank is defined as follows

$$PR(p) = (1 - c) \sum_{q \in I(p)} \frac{PR(q)}{O(q)} \qquad (4.1.1)$$

In the calculation of PageRank a factor c is used for normalization. Note that $0 < c < 1$ because there are pages without incoming links and their weight is lost .

Later PageRank was modified observing that not all users follow the direct links on WWW

Figure 7. Distribution of page rank score

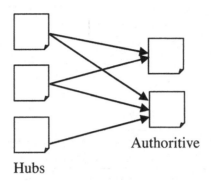

Hubs   Authoritive

$$PR(p) = (1-d) + d \sum_{q \in I(p)} \frac{PR(q)}{O(q)} \qquad (4.1.2)$$

where d is a dampening factor that is usually set to 0.85 (any value between 0 and 1), d can be thought of as the probability of users' following the links and could regard (1 − d) as the page rank distribution from non-directly linked pages. Consider the Figure 8 directed graph (Duhan,N, Sharma, A. K., & Bhatia, K. K, 2009).

4.1.1. Working of PR

To explain the working consider example hyperlinked structure shown in Figure 8, where A, B and C are three web pages. The PageRanks for pages A, B and C can be calculated by using Eq. 4.1.2.

PR(A)=(1-d)+d((PR(B)/2+PR(C)/1)   (4.1.2(a))

PR(B)=(1-d)+d(PR(A)/2+PR(C)/1)   (4.1.2(b))

PR(C)=(1-d)+d(PR(B)/2)   (4.1.2(c))

The PageRanks for pages A, B, C are calculated with d=0.5, the page ranks of pages A, B and C becomes: *PR(A)=1.2, PR(B)=1.2, PR(C)=0.8.*

4.1.2 Iterative Method of Page Rank

It is easy to solve the equations of the system, for determining the page rank values, for a small set of pages but if the web consists of billions of documents and it is not

Figure 8. Example graph

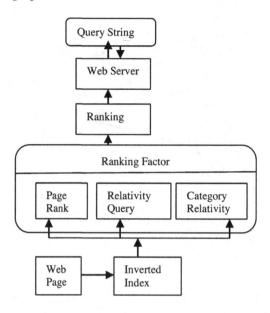

Table 1. Iteration method of Page Rank

Iteration	PR(A)	PR(B)	PR(C)
0	1	1	1
1	1	1.25	0.81
2	1.21	1.2	0.8
3	1.2	1.2	0.8
4	1.2	1.2	0.8
..	..	..	...

possible to find a solution by inspection method. In iterative calculation, each page is assigned a starting page rank value of 1 as shown in Table 1.

These rank values are iteratively substituted in page rank equations to find the final values. In general, much iteration could be followed to normalize the page ranks.

4.2 Weighted Page Rank Algorithm (WPR)

Wenpu Xing and Ali Ghorbani (Xing, W. & Ghorbani, A, 2004) proposed an extension to standard PageRank called Weighted PageRank (WPR). It rank pages according to their importance not only consider link structure of web graph. This algorithm assigns larger rank values to more important pages instead of dividing the rank value of a page evenly among its outgoing linked pages. Each outlink page gets a value proportional to its popularity. The popularity is measured by its number of inlinks and outlinks (Page, Brin, Motwani, & Winograd. 1999).

$$WPR(p) = (1 - d) + d \sum_{q \in I(P)} WPR(q) W_{(q,p)}^{in} W_{(q,p)}^{out} \qquad (4.2.1)$$

where Win (q,p) and Wout (q,p), for inlinks and outlins is given as

$$W_{(q,p)}^{in} = \frac{I_p}{\sum_{v \in R(q)} I_v} \qquad (4.2.2)$$

$$W_{(q,p)}^{out} = \frac{O_p}{\sum_{v \in R(q)} O_v} \qquad (4.2.3)$$

where Iv, Ip and Ov, Op represent the number of inlinks and outlinks of page v and page p respectively.

4.2.1 Working of WPR

Consider the directed graph Figure 8.

$$WPR(A) = (1 - d) + d(WPR(B) W_{(B,A)}^{in} W_{(B,A)}^{out} + WPR(C) W_{(C,A)}^{in} W_{(C,A)}^{out}$$
$$(4.2.1(a))$$

$$WPR(B) = (1 - d) + d(WPR(A) W_{(A,B)}^{in} W_{(A,B)}^{out} + WPR(C) W_{(C,B)}^{in} W_{(C,B)}^{out}$$
$$(4.2.1(b))$$

$$WPR(C) = (1 - d) + d(WPR(B) W_{(B,C)}^{in} W_{(B,C)}^{out} \qquad (4.2.1(c))$$

The weights of incominglinks and outgoinglinks can be calculated as:

W^{in} (B,A)=I_A/(I_A+I_C)=2/(2+1)= 2/3

$W^{out} (B,A)= O_A/(O_A+O_C)= 1/(1+2)= 1/3$

Similarly other values after calculation are:

$W^{in} (C,A)= 1/2$ $W^{out} (C,A)=1/3$

$W^{in} (A,B)= 1$ $W^{out} (A,B)=1$

$W^{in} (C,B)= 1/2$ $W^{out} (C,B)=2/3$

$W^{in} (B,C)= 1/3$ $W^{out} (B,C)=2/3$

The Page Ranks for pages A, B, C are calculated by using (4.2.1) with d=0.5, the page ranks of pages A, B and C are PR (A)=0.65, PR (B)=0.93, PR(C)=0.60. Here WPR(B)>WPR(A)>WPR(C).

4.2.2. Comparison of WPR and PR

To compare the WPR with standard Page Rank, the authors categorized the resultant pages of a query into four categories based on their relevancy to the given query:

- **Very Relevant Pages (VR):** Pages containing very important information related to the given query.
- **Relevant Pages (R):** Pages having relevant, not important information about the given query.
- **Weak Relevant Pages (WR):** Pages which do not have relevant information about the given query but contain the query keywords.
- **Irrelevant Pages (IR):** Pages neither containing the query keywords nor relevant information about it.

The WPR and the standard PR algorithms both provide sorted lists to users based on the given query. The following rule has been adopted to calculate the relevance score of each page in the list of pages, which differentiates WPR with PR.

4.2.3. Relevancy Rule

The relevancy of a page depends on its category and its position in the result list. The larger the relevancy value of result list, better it is ordered. The relevancy K is given in (4.2.2):

$$k = \sum_{I \in R(P)} (n - i) * W_i \qquad\qquad (4.2.2)$$

where i denotes the ith page in the resultant page list R(p), n represents the first n pages chosen from the list and W_i is the weight of ith page as given below:

$$W_j = \{V_1, V_2, V_3, V_4\}$$

where V_1, V_2, V_3 and V_4 are the values assigned to a page if the page is VR, R, WR and IR respectively. Also the values are chosen in such a way so that $V_1 > V_2 > V_3 > V_4$.

4.3 Page Content Rank Algorithm (PCR)

Jaroslav Pokorny and Jozef Smizansky (Pokorny, J. & Smizansky J.), gave a ranking method of page relevance ranking using WCM technique, called Page Content Rank (PCR). This method combined a number of heuristics process that is used for analyzing the content of web pages. The page importance can be determined on the basis of the importance of keywords, which the page contains. The importance of a term is specified with respect to a given query q. PCR uses a neural network as its inner classification structure.

In PCR, let for a given query q and a usual search engine, a set R_q of ranked pages is resulted, which are in turn classified according to their importance. Here a page is represented in a similar way as in the vector model and frequencies of terms in the page are used.

4.3.1 Working of PCR

There are four basic Steps.

4.3.1.1 Term Extraction

An HTML parser extracts terms from each page in R_q. An inverted list is built in this step which is used in step (iv).

4.3.1.2 Term Extraction

Statistical parameters such as a Term Frequency (TF) and occurrence positions; as well as linguistic parameters such as frequency of words in the natural language are calculated and synonym classes are identified.

4.3.1.3 Term Classification

Based on parameter calculations in step (ii), the importance of each term is determined. A neural network is used as a classifier that is learnt on a training set of terms. Each parameter corresponds to excitation of one neuron in the input level and the importance of a term is given by excitation of the output neuron in the time of termination of propagation.

4.3.1.4 Relevance Calculation

Page relevance scores are determined on the basis of importance of in terms of page, which have been calculated in step (iii). The new score of a page P is equal to the average importance of terms in P.

PCR asserts that the importance of a page P is proportional to the importance of all terms in P. This algorithm uses the usual aggregation functions like Sum, Min, Max, Average, Count and also a function called Sec_ moment given in Eq. 4.3.1.

$$\text{Sec \_ moment}(S) = \sum_{i=1}^{n} \frac{x_i^2}{n} \tag{4.3.1}$$

where $S = \{x_i \; i = 1..n\}$, $n = |S|$. Sec_moment is used in PCR reason being that it increases the influence of extreme values in the result in contrast to Average function.

4.3.2 Symbols Used in PCR

PCR algorithm considers the following symbols, which are used while discussing the parameter calculations in next section:

D: Set of all pages indexed by a search engine.
q: A conjunctive boolean query fired by the user.
Q: Set of all terms in query q.
$R_q \subseteq D$: Set of pages that are considered relevant by the search engine with respect to q.
$R_{q,n} \subseteq R_q$: Set of n top ranked pages from R_q. If $n > |R_q|$, then $R_{q,n} - R_q$
TF(P, t): Term frequency i.e. the number of occurrences of term t in page P.
DF(t): Document frequency i.e. the number of pages which contain the term t.
Pos(P, t): Set of positions of term t in page P.
Term(P, i): A function returning the term at the ith position in page P.

4.3.3 Parameter Calculations in PCR

The calculation of the importance of a term t, denoted by importance (t), is carried out on the basis of 5+(2*NEIB) parameters, where NEIB denotes the number of neighboring terms included into the calculation. The calculation depends on attributes such as database D, query q and the number n of pages considered. Further a classification function classify() is used with 5+(2*NEIB) parameters returning the importance of t The importance of a term t is considered to be influenced by the parameters described below:

Occurrence Frequency: It determines the total number of occurrences of term t in R_q by the equation (4.3.2)

$$\text{freq}(t) = \sum_{P \in Rq} \text{TF}(P, t) \qquad (4.3.2)$$

2. **Distances of Occurrences of T from Occurrences of Terms in Q:** If a term t occurs very often or close to the terms contained in Q, then it can be significant for the given topic.

Let QW (Eq. 4.3.3) is the set of all occurrence positions of terms from Q in all pages $P \in R_{q.n}$.

$$QW = \bigcup_{t \mu Q, P \in Rq,n} \text{Pos}(P, t) \qquad (4.3.3)$$

The distance of any term t from the query terms is the minimum of all distances of t from query terms, i.e.

$$\text{dist}(t) = \min(\{|r-s| : r \varepsilon \text{Pos}(P,t) \text{ and } s \varepsilon QW\}) \qquad (4.3.4)$$

Incidence of Pages: This value denoted by occur(t) is a ratio of the number of pages containing a term t to the total number of pages. Here a term having less DF regardless of its high TF is not considered important.

$$occur(t) = DF(t) / |R_{q,n}| \qquad (4.3.5)$$

Frequency in the Natural Language: In PCR, a database of frequent words is assumed and let F(t) be a function assigning to all these words an integer value representing its frequency in the given database. Then the frequency of t in the language can be defined as:

$$common(t) = F(t) \qquad (4.3.5)$$

Obviously, a term t is considered less important if it belongs to one of the frequent words of used natural language.

Term Importance: The importance of all terms from $R_{q,n}$ can be determined temporarily as:

$$importance(t)=classify(freq(t),\ dist(t),occur(t),common(t),O,0,.....,0) \qquad (4.3.6)$$

Synonym Classes: A database of synonym classes is used and for each synonym class S, an aggregate importance SC(S) is calculated as shown in Eq. 4.3.7

$$SC(S)=sec\_moment(\{importance(t\ '):t\ '\ \varepsilon S\}) \qquad (4.3.7)$$

A term becomes important if it is the synonym of an important term. This importance SC(S) is propagated to the term t by another aggregation over all its meanings:

$$synclass(t) = sec\_moment(\{SC(S_{t'}):\ t'\ \varepsilon\ SENSE(t)\}) \qquad (4.3.8)$$

where SENSE(t) contains all meanings t' of t.

Importance of neighboring term: The neighboring terms always affect the importance of a term i.e. if a term is surrounded by important terms, the term becomes important. It is described by (2 *NEIB) parameters, that is an aggregation of the importance of terms surrounding the term t. Let RelPosNeib(t, i), given in Eq. 4.3.9, be the set of terms which are the ith neighbour of term t in all pages Pε $R_{q,n}$, over all occurrences of t. If i < 0 left neighbours are got while i > 0 gives the right ones. The predicate Inside (P, n) is satisfied, if n is an index into the page P. Then,

$$relPosNeib(t,i) = \bigcup_{P\epsilon Rq,n} Term(P,j+1):\ j\epsilon Pos(P,t)\epsilon Inside(P,\ j+1)$$

$$(4.3.9)$$

The parameters *neib(t, i) for i:= -NEIB,-(NEIB-l), ... -1, 1, . NEIB* are defined as follows:

neib(t, i) = sec_ moment(RelPosNeib(t, i))

Based on these parameters the resultant importance of the term t is defined as:

importance(t)=classify(freq(t),dist(t),occur(t),common(t),

synclass(t),neib(t, -NEIB).,neib(t,NEIB)) (4.3.10)

4.3.4 Page Classification and Importance Calculation

In PCR, a layered neural network is used as a classification tool, which is denoted by NET. The NET has weights set up from previous experiments. Assuming that the network has $5+(2*NEIB)$ neurons in the input and one neuron in the output layer, let the calculation of a general neural network NET with the input vector v is denoted as NET(v) and NET[i] is an excitation of the ith neuron in the output layer of NET after terminating calculation. The classify() function can be defined as follows:

Classify $(P_1.,P_{5+(2*NEIB)}) = NET(P_1,P_{5+(2*NEIB)})$

The importance of a page P in PCR is calculated as an aggregate value of the importance of all terms that P contains. For a promotion of the significant term and a suppression of the others, the second moment is again used as an aggregate function [4.3.11].

Page_importance(P)=sec_moment({importance(t): t ε P}) (4.3.11)

The importance value of every page (Eq. 4.3.11) in $R_{q,n}$ m parts a new order to the n topped ranked pages in the result list of a search engine. This new order truly represents the pages according to their content scores in opposition to the PR and WPR.

4.4 Hyperlinked Induced Topic Search Algorithm (HITS)

This algorithm assumed that for every query topic, there is a set of "authoritative" or "authority" pages/sites (Borodin, A., Roberts, G.O., Rosenthal, J. S.& Tsaparas, P. 2001) that are relevant and popular focusing on the topic and there are "hub" pages/sites that contain useful links to relevant sites including links to many related authorities, for every query given by the user, there is a set of authority pages that are relevant and popular focusing on the query and a set of hub pages that contain useful links to relevant pages/sites including links to many authorities (see Figure 9).

Figure 9. Hubs and authorities

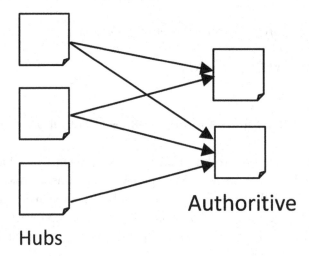

Authoritive

Hubs

HITS (Ding, C., He, X., Husbands, P. Zha, H. & Simon., H. 2001), assume that if the author of page p provides a link to page q, then p confers some authority on page q.

The HITS algorithm considers the WWW as a directed graph G(V,E), where V is a set of vertices representing pages and E is a set of edges that correspond to links. A directed edge (p, q) indicates a link from page p to page q. The search engine may not retrieve all relevant pages for the query; therefore the initial pages retrieved by the search engine are a good starting point to move further. But relying only on the initial pages does not guarantee that authority and hub pages are also retrieved efficiently. To remove this problem, HITS uses a proper method to find the relevant information regarding the user query.

4.4.1. Working of HITS (Algorithm)

The HITS works in two phases Sampling and Iterative in the Sampling phase a set of relevant pages for the given query are collected i.e. a sub-graph *S* of *G* is retrieved which is high in authority pages.

Step I: Sampling Step

In this step, a set of relevant pages for the given query are collected i.e. a subgraph S of G is retrieved which is rich in authority pages. The algorithm starts with a root set R (say, of 200-300 pages) selected from the result list of a usual search engine. Starting with R, a set S is obtained keeping in mind that S is relatively small, rich in relevant pages about the query and contains most of the strongest authorities. The pages in root set R must contain links to other authorities if there are any. HITS algorithm expands the root set R into a base set S by using the algorithm.

Algorithm: (Borodin, A., Roberts, G.O., Rosenthal, J. S.& Tsaparas, P., 2001)
Input: Root set R; Output: Base set S
Let S =R

    i.   For each page p E S, do Steps 3 to 5
    ii.   Let Tbe the set of all pages S points to.
    iii.   Let F be the set of all pages that point to S.
    iv.   LetS=S+T+some or all of F.
    v.   Delete all links with the same domain name.
    vi.   Return S.

One simple approach for finding hubs and authorities from set S is ordering them by the count of their outgoing and incoming links. This works well in some situations but does not work well always. Before starting the second step of the algorithm, HITS removes all links between pages on the same web site or same domain in Step 5 of algorithm, reasoning being that links between pages on the same site are for navigational purposes, not for contributing authority. Furthermore, if many links from a domain are pointing to a single page outside the domain then only a small number of these links are counted instead of all.

Step 2: Iterative Step
This step finds hubs and authorities using the output of sampling step.

Input: Base set S, Output:A set of hubs and a set of authorities.

    i.   Let a page p have a non-negative authority weight Hp and hub weight Ap. Pages with relatively large weights Hp will be classified to be the authorities, similarly hubs with large weights Ap.
    ii.   The weights are normalized so the squared sum for each type of weight is 1.
    iii.   For a page p, the value of xp is updated to be the sum of Yq over all pages q linking top.
    iv.   The value of yp is updated to be the sum of Xq over all pages q linked to by p.
    v.   Continue with step 2 unless a termination condition has been reached.
    Output the set of pages with the largest Hp weights i.e. authorities and those with the largest Ap weights i.e. hubs.

$$H_p = \sum_{q \in I(p)} A_q \qquad\qquad (4.4.1)$$

$$A_p = \sum_{q \in B(p)} H_q \qquad\qquad (4.4.2)$$

where Hp is the hub weight, Ap is the Authority weight, $I\,(p)$ and $B(p)$ denotes the set of reference and referrer pages of page p.

4.5 Distributed Page Ranking

Distributed Page Ranking (Shi, S. M., Yu, J., Yang, G.W.& Wang, D.X.., 2003) means how to perform page ranking in a peer-to-peer environment. Assume there are K nodes (called page rankers) participating in page ranking, and each of them is in charge of a subset of the whole web pages to be ranked. Pages crawled by crawler(s) are partitioned into K groups and mapped onto K page rankers according to some strategy. Each page ranker runs a page ranking algorithm on it. Since there have links between pages of different page groups, page rankers need to communicate periodically to exchange updated ranking values.

4.5.1 Web Page Partitioning

Different strategies can be adopted to divide web pages among page rankers: divide pages randomly, divide by the hash code of page URLs, or divide by the hash code of websites. As crawler(s) may revisit pages in order to detect changes and refresh the downloaded collection, one page may participate in dividing more than one time. The random dividing strategy doesn't fulfill this need for taking the risk of sending a page to different page rankers on different times. When performing page ranking, page scores may transmit between page rankers, causing communication overhead between nodes. Because number of inner-site links overcomes that of inter-site ones for a web site, divide at site granularity instead of page-granularity can reduce communication overhead greatly. To sum up, dividing pages by hash code of websites is a something better strategy

4.5.2 Distributed PageRank Algorithms

Two different algorithms, says as DPR1 and DPR2 (Shi, S. M., Yu, J., Yang, G.W.& Wang, D.X., 2003), are shown (see Algorithm 1 and 2) to performing distributed page ranking. Both of them contain a main loop, and in each loop, the algorithm first refreshes the value of X (for other groups may have sent new ranks by the afferent links of the group), and then compute vector R by one or more iteration steps, and lastly, compute new Y and send it to other nodes.

Note that each node runs the algorithm asynchronously, in other words, ranking programs in all the nodes can start at different time, execute at different 'speed', sleep for some time, suspend itself as its wish, or even shutdown. In fact, we can insert some delays before or after any instructions.

The difference between algorithm DPR1 and DPR2 lies in the style and frequency of refreshing input vector X and updating output vector Y. In each loop of algorithm DPR1, new value of R is computed iteratively (by algorithm 2) until converge before updating and sending Y to other groups. While with DPR2, each node always uses the latest X it can be acquired to compute R and update the value of Y eagerly.

4.6 Page Ranking Algorithm Based on Number of Links Visit (PRNLV)

PRNLV (Page Ranking based on Links Visit) (Singh, M. K. & Sharma, D. K., 2012) based on Web Structure Mining and Usage Mining, it takes the user visits of pages/links into account with the aim to determine the importance and relevance score of the web pages. To accomplish the complete task from gathering the usage characterization till final rank determination many subtasks are performed such as

- Storage of user's access information (hits) on an outgoing link of a page in related server log files.
- Fetching of pages and their access information by the targeted web crawler.
- For each page link, computation of weights based on the probabilities of their being visited by the users.
- Final rank computation of pages based on the weights of their incoming links.
- Retrieval of ranked pages corresponding to user queries.

4.6.1 Calculation of Visit (Hits) of Links

If p is a page with outgoing-link set O(p) and each outgoing link is associated with a numerical integer indicating visit-count (VC), then the weight of each outgoing link connecting to page p to page o is calculated by[Proposed]

$$Weight_{link}(p,q) = \frac{VC(p,q)}{\sum\limits_{q' \in O(p)} VC(p,q')} \tag{4.6.1}$$

4.6.2 Page Rank Based on Numbers Link Visit (PRNLV)

If p is a page having inbound-linked pages in set B(p), then the rank (PRNLV) is given by[Proposed]:

$$PRLV(p) = (1-d) + d(\sum_{b \in B(p)} PRLV(b).Weight_{link}(b,p)) \qquad (4.6.2)$$

where d is the damping factor as is used in PageRank, Weightlink() is the weight of the link calculated by (4.7.1). The iteration method is used for the calculation of page rank. Example fig 4.1 Taking d=0.5, these equations can easily be solved using iteration method the final results obtained are:

PRNLV(A)= 1.08, PRNLV(B)= 1.26, PRNLV(C)= 0.66

5. CHALLENGES AND ISSUES IN WEB MINING

Web mining is a technique for finding the relevant information from the huge web data. Web data is a collection of rich dynamic changes every instant, multi-relational or multidimensional and heterogeneous data. Since it huge set of information hence there are a number of challenges or issues in web mining, finding the relevant information from the web is not very easy task. Web mining process is divided into many steps like resource finding, data selection and pre-processing, generalization and analysis. Web analytics are one of the key challenges in web mining. The web analytics factors are link hits, web page views, and user sessions to find the identity of regularly visitors. The major challenges (Vijiyarani, S., & Suganya, E., 2015) of web mining is listed as

- Storage web data sets can be very large, it takes ten to hundreds of terabytes to store on the database.
- It cannot mine on a single server so it needs large number of server.
- Proper organization of hardware and software to mine multi-terabyte data sets.
- Limited customization, limited coverage, and limited query interface to individual users.
- Automated data cleaning.
- Over fitting and Under fitting of data.

- Over sampling of data.
- Scaling up for high dimensional data.
- Mining sequence and time series data.
- Difficulty in finding relevant information.
- Extracting new knowledge from the web.
- Data / Information Extraction concentrate on extraction of structured data from web pages such as products and search results.
- Integration of web information and matching of WWW schema. Data discovery from similar web sites is the main problem with lots of realistic applications since multiple web sites have similar data in different representations.
- Prediction from online sources i.e. customer always confident about the products, forums, blogs and chat rooms. Mining predictions are of big significance for marketing intelligence and product specification.
- Reducing unwanted/noisy search results. Significance of search information becomes unorganized due to the problem search engines often only tolerate for low precision criteria.
- Indexing information on the web. This causes low amount of recall with content mining.
- Session identification.
- Handling Common Gateway Interface data.
- Catching.
- Maintaining dynamic pages.
- Robot detection and filtering.
- Transaction identification.

6. IMPACT OF PAGE RANKING ON E- BUSINESS

Due to the huge amount of information existing in the web, when a user sends a query about a topic there exist an incredible number of pages related to this query but only a few part of such huge amount of information will be interesting for the user. That is why the search engines used ranking algorithms in order to sort the huge results.

6.1 Role of Page Ranking in Information Retrieval

The Web Information Retrieval System (Zhang, Y., Yu, J.X. & Hou, J., 2006) has three main components (see Figure 10), the Inverted index module, the Web Server, and the ranking module. The working flow describe as follows: firstly put query string into Web Server, the Web Server accept the query request and disassembles

Figure 10. Role of page ranking in information retrieval

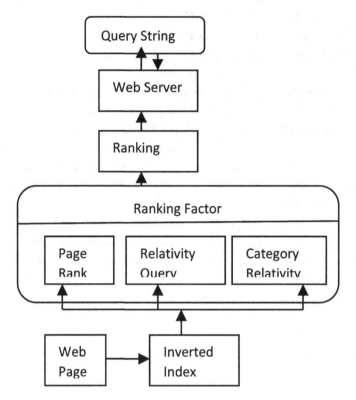

the query string into terms, Secondly lookup the web pages which are related to query terms, we choose the intersection set of web pages, and calculate the score of web pages, during calculating the score we must judge the category the web pages belong to. If the page belongs to one category we only calculate the score based on traditional algorithm, if the web page belongs to not only one category, we must check the categories it belongs to, and calculate its synthetically score.

6.2 Role of Page Ranking in E-Business Analysis

Page rank can define the popularity of the product or service associated with the page. The business analyst can use this information analyzing the product or service for business purpose. There's an enormous diversity of algorithms and approaches that facilitate making user interest recommendations. Some of them became very popular: the content-based filtering, collaborative filtering and cooperative filtering. They are used as a base of latest recommender systems.

The content based filtering approach in which the profiles are users and things by distinguishing their characteristic options, such as demographic information for user identification, and product information or descriptions for item profiling.

The collaboration filtering is used to track customers whose interests are identical to those of the current customer, and recommend list of products that similar customers have previously liked.

The cooperative filtering is commonly utilized in general product recommender systems, and consists of the subsequent stages. The foremost stage in cooperative filtering is to investigate users purchase histories so as to extract user teams that have similar purchase patterns. Then recommended the products that are really most popular within the user's cluster.

6.3 Role of Page Ranking in Recommendation System

This strategy is mainly based on the assumption that the users with implicit identical interests can be brought together to help each other obtain the preferred web pages. With considering the usage patterns discovered from the Web logs, the hidden web pages preferred by the users can be implied accurately and efficiently.

However, the existing web recommendation systems are always puts the prominence on localized recommendation, but neglects bridging global interests and local preferences. As a result, it is very difficult that, if the users want to browse the local interested web pages, they have to search by clicking the websites through citing the related results found by search engines.

6.3.1 Recommendation Strategy

Typically, in traditional search engines, a cited search result can be viewed as a product and a query containing several cited products stands for a transaction. That is, the cited products occurring together on the cited list frequently and can be defined as frequent products. To enhance the results of search engines re-rank the search results by discovering the relationships among the cited products. Based on association mining, the frequent itemset, which has no frequent predecessor of the products lattice, is called Maximum Frequent Itemset (products group).

6.3.2 Local Recommendation Strategy

To help the users those find the desired web pages without searching the local websites page by page embed the local recommendation list in search engines so that they can easily search the local result with global sites. In this stage, the individual web logs have to be generated from different websites at different locations first.

Then the usage patterns for each website are discovered independently. To make the recommendation more effective employ multi-support association rule mining permeated through the authority idea to assist the special recommendation. Hence, it is different from existing association-based web usage mining techniques since the different web pages have different minimum supports by their different prestige. Therefore, the web page with higher PageRank should have a high-value item in association mining. Hence, the contained high-value items with lower minimum supports can be searched easily.

The recommendation engine collects the navigational details of the active user and matches it to a similar user's group to generate a set of recommendation to the particular user at a quicker rate, therefore minimizing the problem of bottleneck caused by system computing load when dealing with listed web sites during peak visiting time.

The system will be provided a precise recommendation to the client based on his current navigation pattern, thereby overcoming time wastage in searching the right product or information caused by presentation of many irrelevant choices to the client at a time as it is in many existing systems.

7. CONCLUSION

Web Mining is a technique used to extract the useful information from very huge amount of web data. The usual search engines usually result in a large number of pages in response to users' queries, while the user always wants to get the best in a short span of time so he/she does not bother to navigate all the pages, page by page. The page ranking algorithms, which are an application of web mining, play a major role in making the user search navigation easier in the results of a search engine. Quickly discover frequent, time ordered event pattern since the heading is possible. Listing research issues of web mining and their solutions. Impact page ranking in the web business intelligence. Therefore, page ranking can improve the E-business operations in very efficient manner.

REFERENCES

Borodin, A., Roberts, G. O., Rosenthal, J. S., & Tsaparas, P. (2001). Finding authorities and hubs from link structures on the world wide web. World Wide Web, 415–429. doi:10.1145/371920.372096

Broder, A. (2002). *A taxonomy of web search, Technical report*. IBM Research.

Cho, J., Ya-Molina, H. G., & Page, L. (1998). Efficient crawling through URL ordering. *Computer Networks and ISDN Systems, 30*(1–7), 161–172.

Craven, M. (1998). Learning to Extract Symbolic Knowledge From the World Wide Web.*Proceedings of the Fifteenth National Conference on Artificial Intellligence (AAAI'98)*, 509-516.

Ding, C., He, X., Husbands, P., Zha, H., & Simon, H. (2001). *Link analysis: Hubs and authorities on the world*. Technical report:47847,

Duhan, N., Sharma, A. K., & Bhatia, K. K. (2009). Page Ranking Algorithms: A Survey. *IEEE International Advance Computing Conference (IACC 2009)*. doi:10.1109/IADCC.2009.4809246

Ghani, R., & Fano, A. (2002) Building Recommender Systems Using a Knowledge Base of Product Semantics.*Proceedings of the Workshop on Recommendation and Personalization in E-Commerce, at the 2nd International Conference on Adaptive Hypermedia and Adaptive Web Based Systems (AH2002)*, 11-19.

Kleinberg, J. (1998). Authoritative Sources in a Hyperlinked Environment.*Proceeding of 9th ACM-SIAM Symposium on Discrete Algorithms*, 668-677.

Mobasher, B., Dai, H., Luo, T., & Nakagawa, M. (2002). Discovery and Evaluation of Aggregate Usage Profiles for Web Personalization. *Data Mining and Knowledge Discovery, 6*(1), 61–82. doi:10.1023/A:1013232803866

Page, L., Brin, S., Motwani, R., & Winograd, T. (1999). *The pagerank citation ranking: Bringing order to the Web*. Technical report, Stanford Digital Libraries SIDL-WP- 1999- 0120.

Pokorny, J., & Smizansky J. (n.d.). *Page Content Rank: An Approach to the Web Content Mining*. Academic Press.

Ridings, C., & Shishigin, M. (2002). *Pagerank uncovered*. Technical report.

Shi, S. M., Yu, J., Yang, G. W., & Wang, D. X. (2003). Distributed Page Ranking in Structured P2P Networks. *Proceedings of the International Conference on Parallel Processing (ICPP'03)*.

Singh, M. K., Akhtar, Z., & Begam, N. (2012). Challenges and Research Issues in Association Rule Mining. IJECSE, 1(2), 767-774.

Singh, M. K., & Sharma, D. K. (2012). Page Ranking Algorithm based number of link visits: An implementation. *National Conference NCETIT-2012*.

Srivastava, J., Cooley, R., Deshpande, M., & Tan, P.-N. (2000). Web Usage Mining: Discovery and Applications of Usage Patterns from Web Data. *SIGKDD Explorations, 1*(2), 12–23. doi:10.1145/846183.846188

Su, J. H., Wang, B. W., & Tseng, V. S. (2008). Effective Ranking and Recommendation on Web Page Retrieval by Integrating Association Mining and PageRank. *IEEE/WIC/ACM International Conference on Web Intelligence and Intelligent Agent Technology*. doi:10.1109/WIIAT.2008.49

Vijiyarani, S., & Suganya, E. (2015). Research Issues in Web Mining. *International Journal of Computer-Aided Technologies, 2*(3), 55-64.

Xing, W., & Ghorbani, A. (2004). Weighted PageRank Algorithm. *Proceedings of the Second Annual Conference on Communication Networks and Services Research (CNSR'04)*. IEEE. doi:10.1109/DNSR.2004.1344743

Zhang, Y., Yu, J. X., & Hou, J. (2006). *Web Communities: Analysis and Construction*. Berlin: Springer.

ADDITIONAL READING

Andrew, Y. N., Zheng, A. X., & Jordan, M. I. (2001),Stable algorithms for link analysis. In *Proc. 24th Annual Intl. ACM SIGIR Conference*. ACM

Berners-Lee, T., Cailliau, R., Luotonen, A., Nielsen, H. F., & Secret, A. (1994). The World-Wide Web. *Communications of the ACM, 37*(8), 76–82. doi:10.1145/179606.179671

Bhushan, R., & Nath, R. (2013), Recommendation of optimized Web Pages to user using Web Log Mining Techniques, *3rd IEEE International Advance Computing Conference (IACC)*,pp 1030-1033. doi:10.1109/IAdCC.2013.6514368

Chakrabarti, S., Dom, S., Kumar, R., Raghavan, P., Rajagopalan, S., Tomkins, A., & Kleinberg, J. et al. (1999). Mining the Webs link structure. *Computer, 32*(8), 60–67. doi:10.1109/2.781636

Pinkerton, B. (1994) Finding what people want: Experiences with the web crawler. In The second Internation WWW Conference Chicago

Salton, G., & Buckley, C. (1998). Term Weighting Approaches in Automatic Text Retrieval. *Information Processing & Management, 24*(5), 513–523. doi:10.1016/0306-4573(88)90021-0

Chapter 2
The Impact of Emerging Technologies and Social Media on Different Business(es):
Marketing and Management

Smita Agrawal
Global Institute of Technology, India

ABSTRACT

The aim of this research paper is to study the impact of Emerging Technologies and Social Media on different businesses, market and management. There is no doubt that business technology has revolutionized the way companies conduct business. The advent of the social media has brought tremendous changes and advancement in the marketing process. For marketers, this is a huge advantage because the rapid transition from mass to social media resents the opportunity to create impactful, relevant marketing messages. Social Media is fast evolving as one of the most reliable ways to connect and stay informed about the most recent developments in a particular industry. It offers a platform for discussions and information sharing about anything and everything, helping users build their online identity and reputation.

DOI: 10.4018/978-1-5225-2234-8.ch002

INTRODUCTION

Several key advantages to how business will improve as a result of technological advances in business are as follows:

1. Reducing Business Costs

Due to the advancement in technology, business owners can use technology to reduce business costs. Business technology helps to automate back office functions, such as record keeping, accounting and payroll. Business owners can also use technology to create secure environments for maintaining sensitive business or consumer information ("Business Review Australia").

2. Improving Communication

Business technology can help small businesses to improve their communication processes through Emails, texting, websites and personal digital products applications, known as "apps,", which can help companies to improve communication with their consumers..

Companies may also receive more consumer feedback through these electronic communication methods. These methods also allow companies to reach consumers through mobile devices in a real-time format ("Business Review Australia").

3. Potential Increase in Business

Technology allows companies to reach in new economic markets. Rather than just selling consumer goods or services in the local market, small businesses can reach regional, national and international markets. Retail websites are the most common way, where small businesses can sell their products in several different economic markets ("Business Review Australia").

Websites represent a low-cost option that consumers can access 24/7 when needing to purchase goods or services ("Business Review Australia"). With the invent of Internet advertising small business owners are able to reach in new markets and customers through carefully placed web banners or ads .

4. Considerations

Business technology allows companies to outsource business function to other businesses in the national and international business environment. Outsourcing can help company's lower costs and focus on completing the business function they do best. Technical support and customer service are two common function companies outsource ("Business Review Australia").

Small business owners may consider outsourcing function if they do not have the proper facilities or available manpower. Technology allows businesses to outsource function to the cheapest areas possible, including foreign countries ("Business Review Australia").

TECHNOLOGICAL ADVANCES AND THEIR IMPACT ON BUSINESS

The age of electronics and more specifically, computers, has caused a tremendous paradigm shift in the way people do business today. Just 15 years ago, innovations such as the Facsimile (FAX) machine, and the Personal Computer (PC) were state-of-the-art and considered cutting edge. Today, many business people wouldn't be able to function efficiently without these tools ("Novel Guide").

A major challenge for the government and business sectors is that these new jobs demand highly skilled, adaptable, innovative workers who are constantly upgrading and learning new skills. In addition to the World Wide Web, the Internet offers other services including Newsgroups where people can post and reply to messages that are grouped by subject matter and Electronic Mail (E-mail). E-mail over the Internet provides extremely quick correspondence and helps to further the growth of the global market ("Novel Guide").

Communication is an example of one of these business processes that have grown in parallel with the computer and like the computer, this growth has been exponential. The global market has created the need for fast communications over a great distance. Teleconferencing and E-mail are two excellent examples of technologies that have met these needs and have literally transformed the way the business world operates.

- **Teleconferencing:** In some companies, Teleconferencing has all but replaced "physical" meetings, thereby drastically reducing travel costs and the loss of productivity as a result of the travel time required to attend the meetings
- **Electronic Mail (E-mail):** E-mail has transformed business communication drastically. E-mail has helped to advance the global market and provides immediate information transfer. In the modern business world, E-mail has all but replaced conventional postal mail for simple communications and has put a significant dent into the overnight delivery services. In addition, although the telephone is an immediate means of communication, some people would still prefer to communicate via E-mail. Their logic is E-mail gives them an opportunity to better articulate themselves and expound on their thoughts.

This is particularly effective for technical communications where specific details are important and would be prohibitively tedious to transcribe over the phone. E-mail also tends to reduce encoding when forwarding communications through a workflow ("Novel Guide").

Computer Aided Design

The methods for producing technical drawings has evolved from using drafting tables, ink and Mylar to using high-tech Computer Aided Design (CAD) applications. CAD provides an environment in which the user can produce technical documents three to four times faster than was done previously with manual methods. In addition, the CAD drawings are far more accurate, flexible and manageable. Since CAD drawings are in electronic format, they can be attached to E-mails and passed though a workflow to initiate an approval process. With the proper software, engineers required to review drawings, add their remarks and attach these "redlines" to the drawing so these comments can be included in the next revision. Historically, CAD drawings were produced as 2D orthographic representations of real-life 3D elements ("Novel Guide").

New technologies, in their diverse forms, are revolutionizing the world of work, how organizations function, change and evolve and the nature of leadership, managerial roles and professional careers. They have become integral elements of business, industry and commerce throughout the world, driving the growth of the two most powerful forces in the global economy—cyberspace and computing power ("Novel Guide").

Many see emerging technologies as a solution vector for the global challenges of the twenty first century. Today's emerging technologies include: computational sciences; nanotechnology; micro electro mechanical systems (MEMS); bio fuels; mobile technologies and a host of others. Yet an adequate understanding of their commercial, policy, and environmental, ethical and societal implications lags far behind the development of their science and technology ("Novel Guide").

Impact of Technology on Marketing

Communication helps businesses grow and prosper, creates relationships, strengthens the effectiveness of organizations, and allows people to learn about one another. Technologies, such as the Internet, mobile phones, social media, and customer relationship management systems greatly affect the way companies communicate with prospective customers. These new forms of communication are changing the media landscape ("Impact of Technology" 2016).

Many consumers and business professionals seek information and connect with other people and businesses from their computers and phones. With access to many sources of information and an interest in interactive media, consumers may collect more product information on their own. Work environments are also changing, with more people having virtual offices, texting on their cell phones, or communicating through social media sites such as Face book, LinkedIn and Twitter. As the media landscape changes, the money that organizations spend on different types of communication will change as well. Once companies have developed products and services, they must communicate the values and benefits of the offerings to current and potential customers ("Impact of Technology" 2016).

Integrated marketing communications (IMC) provide an approach designed to deliver one consistent message to buyers through an organization's promotions that may span all different types of media - such as TV, radio, magazines, the Internet, mobile phones, and social media. Delivering consistent information about a brand or an organization helps establish it in the minds of consumers and potential customers across target markets. With IMC, organizations can coordinate their messages to build the brand and develop strong customer relationships while also helping customers satisfy their needs ("Impact of Technology" 2016).

The use of business intelligence, predictive analytics, and Customer Relationship Management systems and other software applications and programs are all inherent in this new marketing approach. These technologies allow companies to quickly sort analyze and translate the variety of data they access from the increasing touch points with their customers ("Impact of Technology" 2016).

Young people today are part of the millennial generation, and it is consumers from this generation who are driving the change toward new communication technologies. A young consumer might opt to get promotions via mobile marketing - say, from stores on your cell phone as you walk by them or via a mobile gaming device that allows you to connect to the Web. Likewise, advertisements on Face book are popular as businesses continue to utilize more social media. Traditional media (magazines, newspapers, television) compete with media such as the Internet, texting, mobile phones, social media, user-generated content such as blogs, and YouTube as well as out-of-home advertising such as billboards and movable promotions.

Therefore, all forms of marketing media have been forced to come up with new innovations to remain relevant ("Impact of Technology" 2016).

Development and innovation in the technology sector has changed the business and personal landscape for all consumers. The rise in technology usage over the past decade has had a significant impact on the buyer/seller relationship ("Impact of Technology" 2016).

The Emerging Technologies in Marketing seeks to identify new technology trends which impact the discipline of Marketing. Currently the Initiative encompasses technologies such as social media marketing, ecommerce, Business Geographic Information Systems (GIS), location-based services, Web design, multimedia production and publishing, online and mobile advertising, electronic survey research, and mobile marketing tools ("Impact of Technology" 2016).

In industry, value can be derived in a number of ways. Professionals should be looking to technology to streamline work functions, reduce costs, and maximize return. Smart phones, applications, and Cloud-based services provide users with access to data, colleagues, and clients, among others, irrespective of location. Video-conferencing technologies minimize the time and expense of travel - across the world or even across town - to engage in face-to-face meetings. Internet marketing, social media and blogs empower salespeople to manage their personal "brand" through various channels in the marketplace. In relation to information, customer relationship building, and lead generation, there is an important opportunity professional to take advantage of all available benefits of technology("Impact of Technology" 2016).

These days, technology provides consumers with a comprehensive information solution. Technology provides consumers with near perfect information - no longer does a customer need to contact the salesperson for each and every request. Instead, they can often get answers by perusing a website or getting an automatic out-of-office reply by email. And, in fact, some customers wish to maximize their self-service approach to the home-buying and home-selling processes ("Impact of Technology" 2016).

Even when these technology-savvy customers do want to communicate with their agent, they do not reach for their phone to dial up the agent first. Instead, they are probably more inclined to send an email or a text message or a message through social media or perhaps even chat/video-chat by Skype ("Impact of Technology" 2016).

Technology and Social Media - for Business

Social media is continuing to have a huge influence on business, marketing and on how businesses engage with their target market. The use of social media to share and engage with others continues to grow at an astounding rate, so it would be wise for any business to develop and implement a sustainable social media strategy in order to successfully take advantage of this rapidly changing environment ("Impact of Technology" 2016).

The use of social media is growing at an astronomical rate. Social media websites such as Face book, Twitter, LinkedIn represent a huge opportunity for businesses to grab the attention of customers while simultaneously building a brand image. There are plenty of tactics that businesses can employ to do this including the creation of brand profiles on social networks such as Face book fan pages and creative advertising via branded podcasts and applications, also known as apps ("Impact of Technology" 2016).

Social media platforms provide the perfect opportunity to take advantage of word of mouth and to see it spread. Social media is growing at its fastest rate in developing countries. People are connected on a global scale and casually participate in each other's lives through online observation. Something as simple as "Liking" a brand on Face book can spread virally very quickly throughout the various social media channels. It is worth noting that individuals trust the opinions of their peers far more than a glossy magazine advert. Millions of people review products and services directly via social media sites using video through YouTube, which in many cases is then shared and disseminated via various other social media websites. As a consequence, the public increasingly look to social media to find reviews on various products and services to help them to make buying decisions. As a result, companies can and do provide products to popular YouTube users to review for their subscribers as well as create their own branded YouTube channels with branded videos about their products ("Impact of Technology" 2016).

Social media can assist greatly in the pre-call planning and prospecting phases. Sites such as LinkedIn and Face book empower the salesperson to customize his sales pitch to each individual client. Such sites may carry information on where she went to school, where she works, what social circles she runs in, etc. Armed with this information, a salesperson can tailor his entire selling approach for each client, providing a systematic and strategic way to build relationships ("Impact of Technology" 2016).

Blogging, for example, can be a powerful tool for an agent to brand himself in a specific area of expertise through social media. Blogging must be done consistently and provide quality, pertinent information. This means dedicating time to the process of research and writing. A blog that caters to a specific niche will go a long way in delivering value to potential consumers ("Impact of Technology" 2016).

The three main social media websites that dominate most discussions are LinkedIn, Face book, and Twitter. At a business-level, LinkedIn seems to gain the most traction for productivity by providing tools such as "recommendations" and "skill endorsements" for building-out the agent's profile for a potential customer. With LinkedIn, a current client can recommend or endorse her agent using all of the information (company, title) visible on the profile. The visible information combined with recommendations and endorsements allows potential clients to view and consider a prospective agent. Company pages with discussion boards allow clients and employees to connect ("Impact of Technology" 2016).

While Facebook has many similar capabilities, especially in the company page and interaction categories, it may be more difficult to discern and segment one's time spent on Facebook. There appears to be a real gray area between times spent

Figure 1. Types of social media ("Impact of Technology" 2016)

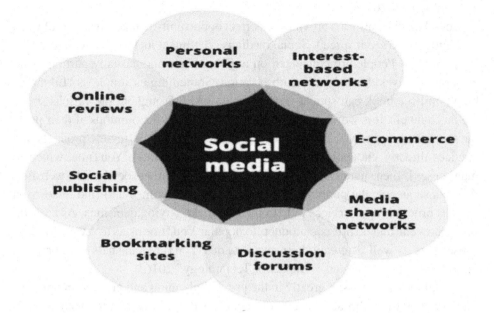

on Face book for personal versus business use. While connecting with prospective or past customers, there can be peripheral clutter that clouds an agent's ability to be as productive as possible while online. Similarly on Twitter, real estate professionals may find it difficult to make the distinction between personal time and business time. Using Face book or Twitter to post home listings, conduct client research, or announce open houses are all effective business activities ("Impact of Technology" 2016).

Types of Social Media

1. Relationship Networks

Relationship networks allowed keeping all communications in one place, on Walls, Timelines or private messages, and sharing updates with entire networks in one click. They vary from professional relationship networks that help to find work, connect with other professionals in the field, and share recommendations ("Impact of Technology" 2016).

2. Media Sharing Networks

This type of social network is defined by the primary type of media shared among users. Face book and Twitter have amazing video and image-sharing capabilities; however, the majority of posts shared on these channels contain text. For channels such as Flicker or Instagram, however, images are the main focus—users have to choose, upload and edit image files before proceeding with anything else, such as captions or mentions of other users. Similarly, with sites such as YouTube and Vimeo, or apps like Vine and Snapchat, video is the primary mode of communication ("Impact of Technology" 2016).

3. Online Reviews

Location-based review services such as Yelp and Urban spoon are getting more traction as personal social networks adopt geolocation, and more users choose to consult the Internet along with their friends for recommendations of best dining spots. There are sites to review anything from hotels, restaurant or your latest employer—and user reviews have more weight than ever before. Sites like Airbnb and Uber, the biggest service providers in the emerging sharing economy, rely largely on host and driver reviews, respectively, to determine who benefits from the service ("Impact of Technology" 2016).

4. Discussion Forums

Discussion forums are one of the oldest types of social media. Before we connected to our first university friends on The Face book, we discussed pop culture, current affairs, and asked for help on forums ("Impact of Technology" 2016).

5. Social Publishing Platforms

Social publishing platforms consist of blogs and micro blogs, where long and short-form written content can be shared with other users. These platforms range from real-time interaction networks such as Twitter—which, while still officially placed in the category of microblogging platforms, is not normally included in the blogging category by most users— to Medium and Tumblr, which are battling it out for the title of the best interactive social publishing; to more traditional blogging platforms, such as WordPress and Blogger ("Impact of Technology" 2016).

6. Bookmarking Sites

In the early days of the Internet (think "Hosting your own site on Geocities" era), content discovery online was a difficult task. Nowadays, there is a plethora of interesting, useful and enlightening content online, and sifting through all of it on your own is simply impossible. Of course, search engines like Google come in very handy when you know what to look for, but when you only have a vague idea of content you'd like to read or watch, there's bookmarking sites. These are web services like StumbleUpon, Pinterest, and Flipboard, where users collect content from elsewhere on the Internet, and save it to their account on the platform ("Impact of Technology" 2016).

Role of Social Media in Marketing

Social media has become a requirement for digital marketing because research shows that most consumers have a habit of spending a minimum of half an hour per day in various social media sites. This goes especially for small/medium businesses that arc looking to create a niche in the market. Proper use of social media sites will give businesses the opportunity to offer tough competition to popular brands ("Nielsen").

Social media plays an important role in how consumers discover, research, and share information about brands and products. In fact 60 percent of consumers re-searching products through multiple online sources learned about a specific brand or retailer through social networking sites. Active social media users are more likely to read product reviews online, and 3 out of 5 create their own reviews of products and services. Women are more likely than men to tell others about products that they like (81% of females vs. 72% of males). Overall, consumergenerated reviews and product ratings are the most preferred sources of product information among social media users ("Nielsen").

Research shows that social media is increasingly a platform consumers use to express their loyalty to their favorite brands and products, and many seek to reap benefits from brands for helping promote their products. Among those who share their brand experiences through social media, at least 41 percent say they do so to receive discounts. When researching products, social media users are likely to trust the recommendations of their friends and family most, and results from Nielsen's Global Online Survey indicate that 2 out of 3 respondents said they were either highly or somewhat influenced by advertising with a social context ("Nielsen").

Social Media also plays a key role in protecting brands: 58 percent of social media users say they write product reviews to protect others from bad experiences, and nearly 1 in 4 say they share their negative experiences to "punish companies". Many customers also use social media to engage with brands on a customer service level, with 42 percent of 18- to 34-year-olds acknowledging that they expect customer support within 12 hours of a complaint ("Nielsen").

Another interesting trend is the interest of consumers to act as ambassadors and advocates for brands through social media. A majority of active social networkers (53%) follow brands. These brands are increasingly recruiting their fans and followers to spread word-ofmouth recommendations about their products and services, and among consumers who write product reviews online, a majority say their share their experiences to "give recognition for a job well done" by the company. Social media users are also interested in collaborating with their favorite brands, with 60 percent of 18- to 34-year-olds saying they want to give product improvement recommendations and another 64 percent who want to customize their products ("Nielsen").

Online Social Media and Networks

Online Social Media and Networks have a growing role in marketing, which has important implications for how consumers, channels, and companies perform. In social media settings, consumers provide online feedback about products, and this feedback is visible to other agents, including other consumers, channel partners, competitors, and investors. Moreover, there is inherent variety in the way the feedback is received and processed (e.g., ratings, reviews) and the forums in which it is provided. The myriad characteristics of online social media environments have effects on outcomes of interest to marketers and implications for managerial practice ("Social Media Today").

Figure 2. Social media and digital marketing ("Social Media Today")

Social Media and Digital Marketing

The growth of social media marketing platforms has become a major part of building social signals that are very important in any SEO digital marketing campaign. People are unaware that emergence of different social media channels offers internet marketers a wider marketing opportunities in building brand visibility over the web. How website of any company rank on the search engine can make a big impact regarding customer and lead acquisition and conversion rate for site ("Social Media Today").

Social media marketing integrated with search engine optimization strategies is effective in building a website organic traffic. There are different social media marketing trends that will definitely affect the way digital marketers will undertake their search engine optimization campaign to boost their lead generation process and website conversion rates ("Social Media Today").

Investing in Social Media Marketing

Online marketers now view the value of social media marketing for their business on a different perspective. There is a significant explosion in the number of consumers who are using socials as a means of finding products and services that they need. According to prestigious social consumer statistics [6]:

Email marketing is viewed by digital marketers as one of the pillars for a successful lead conversion. The widespread use of email marketing remains to be prevalent despite the latest trend in digital marketing and marketers are taking the initiative of integrating social media marketing to further strengthen their business lead conversions. By using social media, your leads will find it easier to make a buying decision if they see your brand within their friends' social feeds. Social media marketers usually employ the process of updating their email marketing content in their social media status updates which effective in promoting brand marketing updates ("Social Media Today").

REFERENCES

Business Review Australia. (n.d.). Retrieved from: http://www.businessreviewaustralia.com

Impact of Technology on Marketing. (2016, May 26). Boundless Marketing. *Boundless*.

Nielsen, D. (n.d.). Retrieved from: http://www.nielsen.com/us/en/insights/news/2011/how-social-media-impacts-brandmarketing.html

Novel Guide. (n.d.) Retrieved from: http://www.novelguide.com

Social Media Today. (n.d.). Retrieved from: http://www.socialmediatoday.com/content/impact-social-media-marketing-trendsdigital-marketing

Chapter 3
Intelligent Big Data Analytics:
Adaptive E-Commerce Website Ranking Using Apriori Hadoop – BDAS-Based Cloud Framework

Dheeraj Malhotra
University of Kota, India

Om Prakash Rishi
University of Kota, India

Neha Verma
I. K. Gujral Punjab Technical University, India

Jatinder Singh
DAV University, India

ABSTRACT

With the explosive increase in regular E Commerce users, online commerce companies must have more customer friendly websites to satisfy the personalized requirements of online customer to progress their market share over competition; Different individuals have different purchase requirements at different time intervals and hence novel approaches are often required to be deployed by online retailers in order to identify the latest purchase requirements of customer. This research work proposes a novel MR apriori algorithm and system design of a tool called IMSS-SE, which can be used to blend benefits of Apriori-based Map Reduce framework with Intelligent technologies for B2C E-commerce in order to assist the online user to easily search and rank various E Commerce websites which can satisfy his personalized online purchase requirement. An extensive experimental evaluation shows that proposed system can better satisfy the personalized search requirements of E Commerce users than generic search engines.

DOI: 10.4018/978-1-5225-2234-8.ch003

INTRODUCTION

In a short span, less than 10 years, the shopping process has become modified enormously. This is largely due to the magnificent growth in web based shopping portals and websites, Modern customers prefer to shop online because of busy life style, easy availability of Internet, high computer literacy rate. Other attractive offers like easy exchange, cash back, cash on delivery and feedback availability like reliable offers are frequently available. However searching for an appropriate E-Commerce websites which best suits the customer requirements are still not so easy. Most of the online users are dependent on search engines to search for E-Commerce web site. When the same query is searched by different users, even a state of art search engine returns the same result, irrespective of the user submitting query. The search engines tends to return the results by interpreting the customer's query in all possible ways, the situation gets worse, if the query is incomplete or ambiguous, For example, for the incomplete search query *Orange*, some users may be interested in links to buy a new postpaid connection of *Orange* company, while others may be interested in searching documents for a fruit. Hence adaptive search system is required, which may intermediately modify the search query by keeping track of customer's preferences over a period of time and return results in correct order of ranking of output links to best match a customer's requirements.

Online generated data is explosively increasing on daily basis in the scale of many Giga Bytes. This is due to increased web traffic. For example to purchase an item online, user explores many links to search for good E-Commerce website which provides branded quality material at best possible discounted price. As a result, many shopping portals getting bulky data on daily basis like *Wal-Mart*, which handles more than 1 million customer transaction logs per hour, resulting into PB of data generated each day. This inordinate online generated data may be called as '*Big Data*' with emphasis on high values of 5 V's i.e. Volume, Variety, Velocity, Veracity and Value. Big Data is a term applied to those data sets having size, range of data sources and speeds of in/out beyond the capabilities of traditional relational databases to process and manages. This '*Big Data*' contains useful patterns which are never explored and advanced analytics is required to unhide these patterns. These extracted patterns are helpful for E -Commerce websites which they may apply in useful decision making process like market basket analysis to increase sales by exploring customer purchase patterns, improved inventory management to avoid situations like out of stock or overstock. This may be done by identifying unexpected sales trends from various sources like social media, previous transactions etc. For example a company named *Tesco* (British multinational grocery, United Kingdom) has implemented effective strategies to promote Market Basket Analysis i.e. Association Mining by Loyalty Card Program, under this program, Tesco mines shopping habits of millions of families which helps company in taking various important decisions like which items to be put at sale, BOGO (Buy One, Get One) offers and assortment of number of items to be offered as a discounted package etc.

Big Data analysis for market basket analysis on E-Commerce website data can be easily accomplished by employing Apriori-Hadoop–BDAS (Berkley Data Analysis Stack) framework, which is a popular, scalable and robust open source platform for processing Big Data. Hadoop can be used for writing efficient applications to process huge amount of data. Hadoop cluster has many parallel machines which can easily store and process huge data sets. Different clients may submit their jobs to distributed Hadoop cluster from distant locations. MapReduce programming model may be used to process data in Hadoop cluster with the help of two functions known as Map and Reduce to process Big Data in (Key, Value) pair format. Hadoop and Map Reduce based cloud framework may be used for deployment of Big Data based personalized E-Commerce website ranking system.

The overall objective of this chapter is to assist the customer while carrying out online purchase transactions to buy authentic and rationally priced products and E-Commerce website organization to optimize the structure of its website as to take advantage over its competitor E-Commerce websites.

Keeping this in mind the specific objectives are:

- To make comparative analysis of various traditional personalized search systems.
- To make comparative analysis of cloud deployment frameworks i.e. First Generation HDFS, Second Generation HDFS and BDAS.
- To develop Apriori-Hadoop-BDAS based website ranking model supported by Intelligent technologies like neural networks and semantic web for E-commerce website search and ranking system. They do not require customer efforts in the form of explicit ratings/feedback for extracting personalized search information from web.
- To develop Map Reduce based Apriori algorithm i.e. MR-Apriori algorithm which will overcome the limitations of conventional Apriori algorithm and can determine the relevancy of E- Commerce web site with respect to customer search query.
- To Design Intelligent Meta Search System for Simplified E-Commerce i.e. *IMSS-SE* tool which will accept E Commerce query from customer/ website owner. This tool will search and rank the listed websites on various factors such as page loading speed etc.
- To evaluate the effectiveness and efficiency of proposed *IMSS-SE* tool through experiment and graphical analysis.

BACKGROUND

Personalized search when supported by machine learning intelligent technologies like neural networks, semantic web etc. is termed as adaptive search which leads to easy & efficient analysis of Big Data available on Social media, customer purchase history etc. to retrieve personalized E-Commerce website search and ranking patterns. There are various types of conventional personalized search systems as discussed by various authors time to time through published literature and are discussed as follows:

Review of Personalized Search Systems Based on Hyperlinks

In general, Hyperlink structure of the web plays an important role in information retrieval from WWW. E-Commerce applications usually employ hyperlink personalization to assist the customer by recommending websites that are more relevant to user based on feedback obtained through customer purchase history and explicit ratings. It is usually assumed that customers who gave similar ratings to similar products have similar preferences and accordingly site recommend various product links to user that are most popular in his/her category of previous customers. E Commerce websites like Amazon, Jabong etc. follow hyperlink personalization to assist their customers in easily searching and purchasing relevant products.(Aoki, Koshijima & Toyama, 2015) proposed architecture of a hyperlink generation system Web index (WIX) system that can be used for replacement of keywords in web documents into links to web pages close to User's choice and hence to reduce the user burden to go through all the web pages presented by a search engine. However whenever there are multiple links that can be paired with keyword then there is requirement to search for web page to satisfy user requirement and also computing relevance takes time which is the limitation of proposed system. (Alam & Sadafa, 2014) discussed that fetching relevant information from web is quite complicated as search engines may return million of web pages in response to some query and the result becomes larger if the query is ambiguous as search engines retrieve documents corresponding to all possible meanings of a query. They proposed heuristic search method to label cluster of documents to assist user to locate his information easily. They deduced relevant label of cluster from title of documents sharing hyperlinks using Apriori algorithm. However effectiveness of proposed labeling method using title information only is not assured on various types of data sets.(Verma, Malhotra & Singh, 2015) proposed SNEC algorithm based on intelligent technologies like semantic web and neural networks to implement E-Commerce website priority tool for better evaluation of product search queries and to obtain correct ranking of websites. The proposed tool may be used to obtain E Commerce website rank with respect to its competitive web sites .However the tool may further be personalized if provided with various capabilities such as Security Comparison, Page Loading Speed and Ease of Navigation etc. to rank the websites as required by modern customer.

Review of Content Personalized Search Systems

Content personalization on web means to present dissimilar content to different customers/users on same web site. (Sugiyama, Hatano & Yoshikawa, 2004) explained that portals like My Yahoo present the information to users in which they may be interested. User may explicitly mention the tabs of his choice on such portals that may include Hollywood / Bollywood news, latest fashion updates, weather forecast etc. Users may create their preferred page layout as per their necessity on content personalized web sites. However such systems suffer from limitations like continuous effort from user is required as such systems are dependent on user inputs. Moreover these sites cannot automatically adapt with change in user needs unless user explicitly changes his formerly registered preferences. (Kuppusamy & Aghila, 2013) discussed a general purpose adaptive web page change detection model "CaSePer" to help the users who frequently visit a web page and are interested in knowing the latest changes rather than seeing the whole content of the web page. This model necessitates being adapted as a personalized search system. Moreover experimental effectiveness of such a search system is necessary to be evaluated.

Review of Recommender Based Search System

In this present era of Big Data, we get the overwhelmed feeling of continuously growing information on the WWW. Recommender systems have been emerged to deal with this problem of 'information explosion'.(Wasid & Kant, 2015) explained that Recommender Systems help users by recommending entertainment material like movies etc. to utilize their free time, E Commerce portals to make online purchase decision, matrimonial and financial services etc. They discussed a technique called particle swarm optimization to find priorities of different customers/users and generate accurately personalized recommendations for users. They discussed various filtering techniques that can be employed by Recommender System i.e. content based filtering, collaborative filtering, demographic filtering and hybrid filtering techniques. (Adamopoulos, 2014) discussed *Probabilistic Neighborhood* method to overcome the common problems of improvement of K nearest Neighbors approach. They also suggested the concept of *unexpectedness* in Recommender systems for specifying and satisfying the expectations of user.(Cacheda, Carneiro, Fernandez & Formso, 2011) proposed an efficient approach of collaborative filtering based on the differences between users and items rather than their similarities. They also proposed new metrics, GIM and GPIM to measure the prediction accuracy and undesirable biased prediction of Recommendation system. They compared various collaborative filtering algorithms to notice their strengths and weakness in diverse conditions. (Guy et al., 2010) discussed that RS will be integrated into search engines for smart and personalized search and also search may be viewed as a special case of RS. They also suggested that user experience is more important than algorithms and performance to the success of RS systems.(Jung, Harris, Webster & Herlocker, 2004) proposed a prototype SERF designed and developed for university library. This system learns from user what documents are relevant corresponding to a search query. It motivates user to enter more informative and longer queries and then asks for ratings of search system to indicate the level up to which system satisfy their information needs. However success of such systems depends heavily that how easily it can compel the user to provide the ratings. So, still substantial research and development is required to be done for Recommender Systems usage as a personalized search system.

Review of Search Systems Based on Contextual Relevance Feedback

In general, contextual system utilizes user's explicit and implicit data to build a shared contextual knowledge base by collecting various users' contextual profiles. (Limbu, Conor, Pears & Donell, 2006) discussed an approach to modify/expand queries so as to more accurately reflect the user's interest and hence to retrieve contextually personalized results using search engine. The proposed approach improves the precision and recall by disambiguating the query terms using a linguistic/thesaurus approach and due to addition of Meta keyword to original search query respectively. (Tanapaiankit, Versterre & Song, 2012) proposed a personalized search system QIC (Query In Context) which enhances search query by incorporating user preferences and ranking search results with context enrichment to reduce the number of contextually inaccurate search results . This is accomplished by allowing query terms with multiple meanings to get weighted towards appropriate contexts more frequently.(Vinay, Wood, Frayling & Cox, 2005) evaluated three different relevance feedback algorithms using target testing experimental procedure and found that the Bayesian algorithm performs better than Rocchio and RSJ algorithms. They also discussed that modern search engines do not provide the Relevance Feedback option to the user and also users are often dissatisfied with the returned results and is required to manually alter their query so as to retrieve relevant results for their search query.

Review of Search Systems Based on Intelligent Technologies

(Singh & Velez, 2014) suggested the design of a search engine Simha to proficiently search over various cloud based platforms for structured and unstructured data using Elastic search engine at backend. They also explained the importance of carefully designed processes i.e. Transform, Extraction and Load while indexing huge data sets. (Malhotra, 2014) discussed that huge size of WWW and interference by SEO leads to difficulty in extracting significant information from web using search engines. However, back propagation neural network can be easily trained to improve search engine page ranking process using supervised learning. (Li, Zhang & Xing, 2012) proposed framework of cloud based semantic++ search engine to search for results from social networks. They discussed inability of general search engines to handle the relationships built between people, objects and web pages by various social network applications such as twitter, face book etc. (Wang, Xu & Zhang, 2011) used an approach for search engine optimization based on user feedback which may be explicit or implicit and Back propagation neural networks and their use in implementation of unbiased ranking model of websites.

Problem Definition

The availability of data on WWW is quite vast. Such an enormous repository of data may be termed as Big Data. In this scenario, it becomes very difficult for online customers to find information about relevant E-Commerce website from the Internet. One of the frequently followed approaches is to use search engine. However, none of the search engine can completely solve the problem of relevant E Commerce website information retrieval as each search engine can index only a subset of information available on WWW. Moreover, traditional search engines also suffer from various limitations such as low recall, low precision and incorrect page ranking, (Mei & Bo, 2014). A typical search engine returns the same result corresponding to the same query, regardless of preferences or current requirements of specific user who submitted the query. This is not suitable for users with different information needs, for example, a frequent tourist searching for "World Trade Centre in New York" on Google in January 2015 found a news article on top, explaining what had happened in World Trade Centre during 9/11 Terrorist attack. However tourist wanted to search for information like shopping and various tourist attractions near World Trade Centre and hence page retrieved was not relevant to frequently travelling user due to lack of personalized search provision. Some of the modern search engines provide personalized search option. However they fail to adapt to changing user's requirement over time, (Wang & Wong, 2014). Even with popular search engines like Google, users are often required to alter their search query number of times to retrieve relevant documents, (Vinay, Wood, Frayling & Cox, 2005).

Alternatively, meta search engines may be used to address partial indexing problem of search engines to some extent, these search engine are built to retrieve their results from number of search engines, Whenever a query is submitted to meta search engine, it will search the query on all of its backend search engines followed by merging and ranking of results obtained from each of the search engine to display more satisfactory search result by improving precision and recall. However, meta search engine has its own associated challenges. The number of web documents returned in response to E-Commerce query by each of the backend search engine is very large. Moreover, if the query is incomplete or ambiguous, result becomes even larger as search engines try to retrieve documents corresponding to all possible meanings of query, (Alama & Sadafa, 2014). Therefore, merging and correctly ranking such a huge amount of this retrieved Big Data about E-Commerce websites require lot of efforts. Above all, web site searching and ranking systems using traditional data mining techniques are required to deal with many issues like:

- Trustworthiness of various E-Commerce websites appeared to have declined somewhat as online customer is not able to find the appropriate and authentic product at reasonable price, For instance, some of the E-Commerce websites are selling products without taking approval from the maker of the product at irrational prices. This leads to various difficulties for customer while taking warranty services from the manufacturer. Moreover, business analysts also find it difficult to compare their E-Commerce website with competitor websites and to find their strength and weaknesses respectively. (Verma & Singh, 2015).
- Traditional E-Commerce website search and ranking systems do not seem to focus on application and infrastructure scalability, partial failure support, component recovery, data recoverability and ability to respond in real time as required by modern Meta Search Systems or search engines to search in today's frequently mounting Big Data environment.
- Most of the popular search engines perform syntactic search of E-Commerce websites. This means they implement searching and ranking process in terms of keyword frequency count, proximity etc. between customer's product query and candidate website. This syntactic matching lack semantics. As a result, the product queries which can be interpreted in various contexts are likely to produce wrong results. Subsequently, the customer usually ends up either with thousands or even more website URLs and sometimes not even a single URL in the output.

- Unlike the previous research studies as discussed in the background section, proposed approach is novel in following ways (i) Proposed E-Commerce website search system can easily adapt with change in customer's preferences and current requirements by monitoring his/her long term and short term preferences using his/ her purchase history and browsing history. Moreover system can update customer's profile without requiring any periodic ratings/feedback. (ii) Proposed E-Commerce website search system is based on BDAS framework and hence will be future ready to take care of the requirements of the next generation of Big Data and possess capabilities like Scaling, ability to respond in real time etc.

COMPARISON OF PLATFORMS FOR BIG DATA ANALYTICS

Various Existing Deployment Paradigms are explained as follows, (Khurana, 2014):

- In the first type, clusters use blob store as a primary storage such as S3 or Azure blob store. Here clusters are transient in nature and exist till duration of workflow execution. The important key is blob store which is a source and destination of workflow. Here virtual machines are thought of as task execution containers.
- The second type uses first generation HDFS as primary storage. Here clusters are persistent in nature and are used for long term storage. Here virtual machines are persistent in nature and can perform execution as well as store data. This category may even use blob stores for periodic backups and to provide data to HDFS. This type of deployment paradigm is useful for workloads like Ad Hoc Batch, Ad Hoc Interactive and SLA Batch workloads due to requirement of persistent clusters, Interactive SLA workloads must be implemented on HDFS as they require blob stores as backup and virtual machines as servers.

Second Generation HDFS

With the changes in environmental trends and technological shifts, second generation Big Data systems not just require scalability, partial failure support etc but also need to support multiple analytic methods on varied data types, as well as the ability to respond in near real time as shown in figure 1, depicting Big Data Evolution, (Gebara, Hofstee & Nowka, 2015):

Figure 1. Comparison between First Generation and Second Generation HDFS

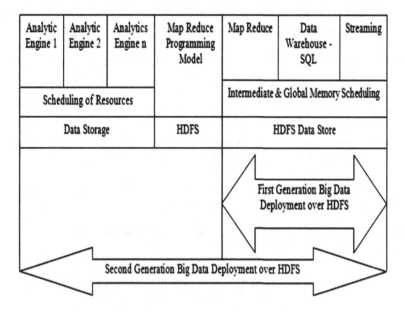

There are two significant trends of Second Generation Big data Systems that are responsible for choosing HDFS as a preferable deployment framework, (Khurana, 2014).

- There is rapid growth in network bandwidth as compared to hard drive bandwidth.
- Development of In- memory computation models such as Spark allow intermediate results to be kept in memory and hence reduces overhead of iterative analytics

HDFS is now adapted as long term store from which applications read their initial data and write their final results. The data layer is divided into sub layers for consistent storage and for intermediate objects separately. However, one of the major drawbacks of HDFS lies in running iterative algorithms. Map function needs to read data in the start of each & every iteration and to write back the data to the disk at the end of iteration. This repeated access of disk in reading and writing is responsible for degradation of performance. (Singh & Reddy, 2014).

Figure 2. Components of BDAS

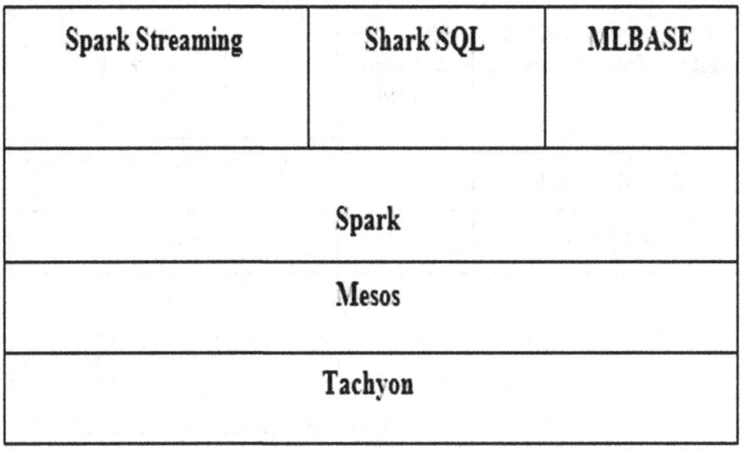

Spark Streaming	Shark SQL	MLBASE
Spark		
Mesos		
Tachyon		

BDAS: Next Generation Big Data Deployment Framework

BDAS i.e. Berkley Data Analysis Stack is a Spark and HDFS based data processing stack to overcome the limitations of generic Map Reduce Platform while running the iterative processes. Some of the important components of BDAS (Singh & Reddy, 2014) are discussed and shown below in Figure 2:

- **Tachyon:** It is the lowest level component of BDAS and is based on HDFS. MapReduce programs are compatible with Tachyon and can run without alterations. The advantage of Tachyon over HDFS is minimized Disk access by caching the frequently read files and enables files to be read at memory speed.
- **Mesos:** It serves the role of cluster manager which provides efficient resource allocation across distributed frameworks. It also supports HDFS and helps in improving horizontal scalability.
- **Spark:** It is the substitute for Map Reduce component of HDFS and allows memory caching to overcome the problem of iterative tasks processing.

The top most layers of BDAS consist of many applications that are still in the early stages of development. HDFS is the widely used distributed deployment framework for Big Data due to easy availability of large number of developed tools in the market, (Singh & Reddy, 2014).

Figure 3. Map Reduce Programming Model

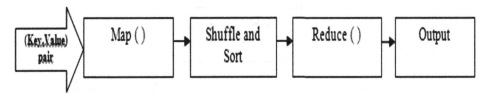

CLOUD ARCHITECTURE OF SYSTEM

Hadoop architecture is built for efficiently writing applications which process huge amount of data in-parallel on large clusters of commodity hardware in a reliable and fault tolerance manner with in a cloud environment. *Hadoop* is an open source implementation of Google MapReduce architecture, sponsored by the Apache Software Foundation. Hadoop consists of two core components: The Hadoop Distributed File System (HDFS) and Map Reduce. A Set of machines running HDFS and MapReduce is known as a Hadoop Cluster which is helpful for storing data. There are many other projects based around core Hadoop Often referred to as the "Hadoop Eco System" such as Pig, Hive, HBase, Flume, Oozie, Sqoop, Zookeeper etc.

The MapReduce Programming Model

MapReduce is a Programming Model used to process data in the Hadoop cluster. It is used for parallel computation of large scale data sets usually more than 1TB. MapReduce deals with large-scale data sets on a cluster mainly through the two steps i.e. Map Phase and Reduce Phase. Firstly, Map processes the input key/value pair to generate the intermediate results followed by shuffle and sort phase. Finally, Reduce phase is used to appropriately merge the processed results to obtain output. It is shown in the Figure 3.

Various components of the architecture of proposed system are shown in Figure.4. These components are explained as follows:

- **NameNode (NN):** In this architecture, NameNode is considered as master which directs commands to all Data Nodes (DN). These are considered as slaves. NN handles all book keeping tasks of HDFS. It serves file system metadata and information related to DN entirely from RAM for faster access and monitors overall health of distributed file system. NN is a node which is running all the time. However, there is a tradeoff, if NN fails which results in cluster becoming inaccessible. Hence system administrator will take care to ensure that NN hardware is reliable and available for smooth functioning.

61

Figure 4. BDAS based cloud architecture of proposed system

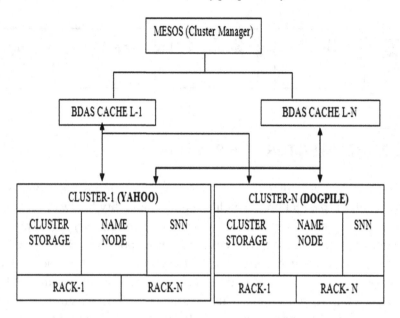

- **SecondaryNameNode (SNN):** SNN is not a backup of NN but it does some house-keeping tasks for it. SNN maintains Journaling or Editlog where incremental modifications are made to metadata. NN does not participate in Editlog or journaling activities as NN is already occupied in critical activities like rack placement strategy, block reading and writing etc. SNN communicates with NN to take snapshots of HDFS metadata at pre-defined time intervals as defined by Hadoop cluster for minimizing the downtime and loss of data. Hence, whenever NN fails then Editlog and image file can be used for back up for smooth conduct.
- **Mesos Cluster Manager:** It is a supervisor of Meta search tool architecture and is responsible for web page distribution, web page storage, inter cluster communication etc. Its design is crucial for efficient performance of Meta search tool.
- **DataNode (DN):** When you want to read or write a HDFS file, the file is broken into blocks and the NN will tell your Client which DN each block resides in. Client is a Java library or a service provided by Hadoop. DN's are constantly reporting to the NN. Upon initialization, each of the DN informs the NN of the blocks it is currently storing. After this mapping is complete, the DN's continually poll the NN to provide information regarding local changes as well as receive instructions to create, move or delete blocks from the local disk. The storage of blocks in DN's is governed by the concept of *Rack*

Placement Strategy, where First copy of block will be randomly placed on any rack. The second copy of block will always be in a different Rack, also known as off the rack. The third copy will be placed always in the same Rack as second rack but with different Data Node.

SYSTEM DESIGN

The proposed system design consists of following four phases and is shown in Figure 5:

- **Phase 1 Adaptive Query Expansion:** Accepts E Commerce query and expands this query by using customer's registered profile and browsing history. This phase will process the query to first remove the stem words like *an, a, the* etc. followed by query expansion with insertion of appropriate keywords by using information provided by customer during Sign Up/ Registration process and his search/browsing history in order to determine the customer preferences and current requirements. In this phase recommender system is used to extract ontological concepts to expand the customer's search query to more meaningful and unambiguous query.
- **Phase 2 Association Rules Generation:** Accepts expanded search query from previous phase and will search the expanded query on number of backend Search Engines and Meta Search Engines such as Google, Dogpile, Yahoo, Meta Crawler etc to retrieve various E Commerce websites This phase will first perform Data Collection, Data Preprocessing etc of data generated from E Commerce website. In order to determine Content Relevancy Vector(CRV) of each website, this phase will first calculate frequency of hits of various association rules generated from keywords of customer's query using Apriori association mining algorithm, supported by Map Reduce & BDAS based cloud framework.
- **Phase 3 Website Short Listing:** In this phase retrieved websites are shortlisted by using various criteria as mentioned by customer through the interface of SPESRS tool such as Transaction Security, Page Freshness, Page Loading Speed, and Response Time. Moreover, Time Relevancy Vector (TRV) i.e. time spent by previous user of candidate website is also taken into consideration to determine credibility of E Commerce website, Further Semantic Relevancy Vector (SRV) is also determined using OWL i.e. Web Ontology Language and Longest Common Subsequence (LCS) to determine precise proximity between customer purchase requirement and E Commerce website.
- **Phase 4 Website Ranking using Supervised Neural Networks:** This phase will determine rank of each of the E Commerce website by using Supervised

BPNN i.e. Back Propagation Neural Network. This phase first normalize all the vector inputs from previous phase i.e. TRV,CRV, SRV, Bias (B) and assign random weights IH1, IH2 and HO1, HO2 to input- hidden layer and hidden - output layer synapses respectively followed by training of neural network using linear activation function, Eventually, it will calculate the error rate by comparing calculated output with desired output using test data and will adjust the weights accordingly in backward stage of BPNN till the error rate is reduced than minimum tolerance and finally determine the output at hidden layer and output layer using sigmoidal function and summation function respectively.

Figure 5. Design of Proposed System

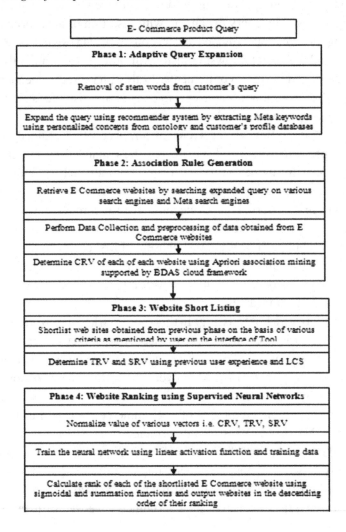

Apriori Association Rule Mining

Association Rule Mining is used to explore frequent patterns, associations and correlations among various itemsets in the transactional databases.

Apriori is one of the popular association mining algorithms. It was introduced by Srikant and Agarwal in 1994. It was an enhancement over one of the previous association mining algorithm i.e. AIS. AIS had limitation of multiple candidate item set generation and multiple scan over transactional databases, whereas Apriori works efficiently and effectively during candidate generation process and uses effective pruning technique.

During the process of finding frequent itemsets, Apriori avoid the calculation of counting infrequent itemsets. Candidate itemsets are generated through the self-join of frequent itemsets and are pruned by Apriori technique which leads to small number of frequent itemsets for comparison with *Support* and *Confidence* metrics, which leads to reduction in I/O overhead by avoiding additional computation. However Apriori suffers from the disadvantage of scanning the database multiple times which actually makes Apriori tedious.

Map Reduce Based Apriori Mining (MR- Apriori)

In order to overcome limitations of conventional Apriori mining algorithm, this chapter introduces map reduce based Apriori mining i.e. MR-Apriori which work as parallel mining algorithm rather than sequential mining algorithm. Here, Map functions follow a constraint of maximum allowed iterations in order to identify the candidate sets i.e. C_I. Reduce function is coded to work in parallel and accept output of Map function in order to calculate frequent item sets F_J. MR–Apriori algorithm is discussed as shown in Box 1.

IMSS- SE Tool

In order to assess the efficiency of proposed system design, IMSS- SE tool i.e. Intelligent Meta Search System for Simplified E Commerce is implemented using ASP. NET framework. The IMSS-SE possess simplified interface as well as designed for adaptive E Commerce search as compared to IMSS and IMSS-E Tool as proposed in our earlier research work. The interface of IMSS-SE tool is shown in Figure 6.The interface of tool allow customer/retailer to sign up and register his basic information such as age, gender, qualification, occupation etc along with optional preferred keywords to semantically determine his preferences while searching and ranking E Commerce websites. Here, search box in the interface of tool will allow customer or retailer to specify E Commerce specific search string as well as any or

Box 1.

```
Map () for Implementation of MR-Apriori Mining
Input: (K A = Offset, Val A)
Output: List (K B = Candidate Item set, Val B = 1 for each oc-
currence)
Algorithm of Map ():
 Map (KA, ValA) // For Key KA and Value ValAIf (max >= 1 && TI
 .Support>P) //P - Minimum Support
For each Candidate Item Set CIIf CI is a subset of ValAF[j] = TI
 // F [ ] - Frequent Item sets
             j++
             Return (CI, 1)
  End If
      End For
End If
End.
Reduce () for Implementation of MR-Apriori Mining
Input: (K B = Candidate Item Set, List (Val B = Individual Oc-
currence of Key))Output: (K C = K B, Val C = Total Occurrence of
Key)
Algorithm of Reduce ():
Reduce (K B, List (Val B))
Set Count[j] =0
For each Value in Val B
Count [j]= Count[j] + Value B
End For
If Count[j] >= C // C- Minimum Confidence
    Accept F[j] as Rule
Return (Key, Count[j])
End If
End.
```

all of the preference ranking tabs. IMSS-SE tool will assign personalized rank to the web sites retrieved from back end search engines like Google, Bing and meta search engines like Dogpile, Kartoo etc. IMSS-SE Tool will implement all the four phases as discussed in system design. The tool will return web links in the order of their ranking along with statistic of selected advanced search criterion, selected by customer/retailer on the interface of tool.

Figure 6. Interface of IMSS-SE Tool

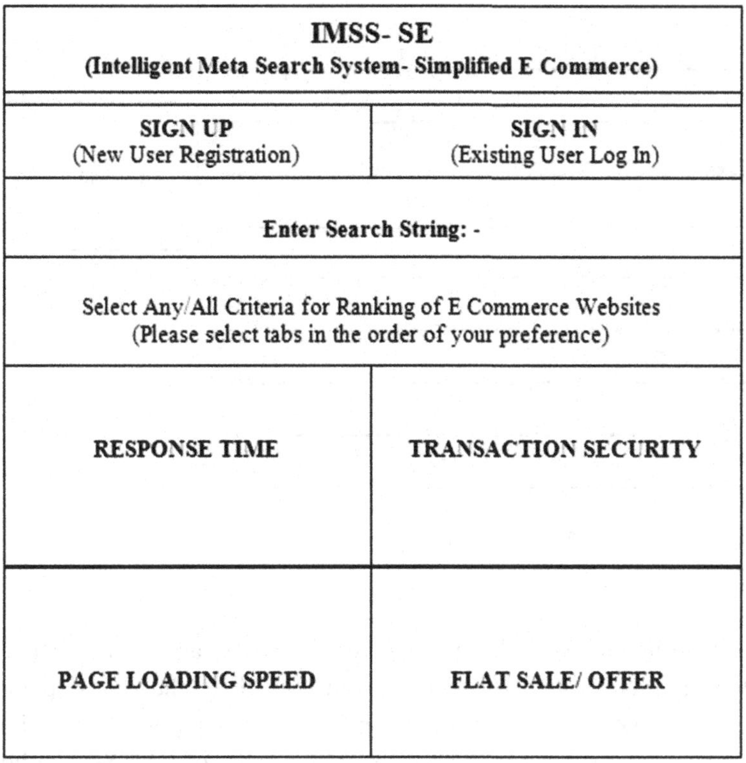

IMSS- SE
(Intelligent Meta Search System- Simplified E Commerce)

SIGN UP (New User Registration)	**SIGN IN** (Existing User Log In)
Enter Search String: -	
Select Any/All Criteria for Ranking of E Commerce Websites (Please select tabs in the order of your preference)	
RESPONSE TIME	**TRANSACTION SECURITY**
PAGE LOADING SPEED	**FLAT SALE/ OFFER**

EXPERIMENT AND GRAPHICAL ANALYSIS

The personalized relevancy of an E-Commerce web site to a specific customer for a given product query depends upon its position in output of search results. In order to compare the IMSS- SE Tool with a popular search engine i.e. Bing, Precision at Z metric is considered, which is being denoted by P (Z). For a given E – Commerce query, P (Z) reports how many fraction of results that are labelled as relevant are reported in the top Z results. Here it is assumed that a document ranked higher is considered as more relevant with respect to customer query and then the rank is compared with Human judgement to verify the relevancy reported by Tool as well as Bing and finally the difference in comparison of Precision of IMSS-SE Tool and Bing is plotted.

In order to carry out the experiment, 30 human volunteers were recruited in age group of 18 – 50 with minimum of 5 years' experience of carrying out E-Commerce transactions. We asked them to rank output of *IMSS-SE* and Bing for same E-Commerce transaction on the basis of various precision parameters such as response

Figure 7. Precision P(Z) Comparison of IMSS-SE and Bing Search Engine

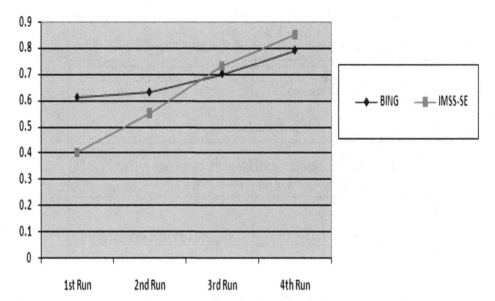

time, page loading speed etc. We normalized the values as assigned between 1-10 by volunteers to each of precision parameter and calculated the average personalized precision metric P(Z) . The graph shown in figure.7 compares the precision metric which is shown on vertical axis with respect to number of Item Sets on horizontal axis for Bing and *IMSS-SE* for the same product query. This graph initially shows the better precision of Bing, However, precision of *IMSS-SE* improves due to better learning by inherent supervised neural network with increase in trial runs. This simply proves the efficiency of proposed approach and MR-Apriori algorithm.

CONCLUSION AND FUTURE WORK

This chapter presents a novel MR-Apriori algorithm and a personalized E-Commerce website search and ranking tool, *IMSS-SE*. This tool supports online customers to easily locate suitable E-Commerce websites on top of ranked results while searching for a specific product. It also enables to assist retailer to well structure his/her E-Commerce website to satisfy the personalized purchase requirement of online customer. The proposed research work utilizes a novel Apriori- Hadoop-BDAS based Big Data analytics framework, supported by semantic web and supervised neural network to well adapt to personalized requirements of customer by learning from previous errors in ranking E-Commerce websites. The ranking effectiveness of proposed tool is justified by experimental evaluation, followed by comparison of personalized precision of *IMSS-SE* tool with popular search engine, Bing. The proposed tool can further be enhanced by including other advanced features such as capabilities to search for multimedia content like you tube, images etc., managing customer reviews and ratings history etc. to make intelligent recommendations to assist the customer in simply making online purchase decision.

REFERENCES

Adamopoulos, P. (2014). *On Discovering Non Obvious Recommendations: Using Unexpectedness and Neighborhood Selection Methods in Collaborative Filtering Systems.* ACM. doi:10.1145/2556195.2556204

Alama, M., & Sadafa, K. (2014). *Labeling of Web Search Result Clusters using Heuristic Search and Frequent Itemset. In ICICT, Procedia Computer Science, Science Direct* (pp. 216 222). Elsevier.

Aoki, Y., Koshijima, R., & Toyama, M. (2015). *Automatic Determination of Hyperlink Destination in Web Index.* ACM. doi:10.1145/2790755.2790784

Bo, C., & Mei, L. (2014). *Design and Development of Semantic based Search engine Model.* IEEE.

Cacheda, F., Carneiro, V., Fernandez, D., & Formso, V. (2011). Comparison of Collaborative Filtering Algorithms: Limitations of Current Techniques and Proposal for Scalable, High Performance Recommender Systems. *ACM Transactions*, *5*(1), 2:1-2:32.

Gebara, F., Hofstee, H., & Nowka, K. (2015). Second Generation Big Data Systems. *IEEE Computers & Society*, *48*(1), 36–41. doi:10.1109/MC.2015.25

Guy, I., Jaimes, A., Agullo, P., Moore, P., Nandy, P., Nastar, C., & Schinzel, H. (2010). *Will Recommenders Kill Search? Recommender Systems – An Industry Perspective.* ACM.

Jung, S., Harris, K., Webster, J., & Herlocker, J. (2004). *SERF: Integrating Human Recommendations with Search.* ACM. doi:10.1145/1031171.1031277

Khurana, A. (2014). Bringing Big Data Systems to the Cloud.what's trending? Column. *IEEE Computers & Society*, 72–75.

Kuppusamy, K. S., & Aghila, G. (2013). CaSePer: An Efficient Model for Personalized Web Page Change Detection Based on Segmentation. *Journal of King Saud University, 26*, 19–27.

Limbu, D., Conor, A., Pears, R., & Mac Donell, S. (2006). *Contextual Relevance Feedback in Web Information Retrieval*. ACM.

Malhotra, D. (2014). *Intelligent Web mining to Ameliorate Web Page Rank using Back propagation Neural Network. In Confluence: The Next Generation Information Technology Summit* (pp. 77–81). IEEE.

Malhotra, D., & Rishi, O. P. (2016, August). IMSS-E: An Intelligent Approach to Design of Adaptive Meta Search System for E Commerce Website Ranking. In *Proceedings of the International Conference on Advances in Information Communication Technology & Computing* (p. 3). ACM. doi:10.1145/2979779.2979782

Malhotra, D., & Verma, N. (2013). An Ingenious Pattern Matching Approach to Ameliorate Web Page Rank. *International Journal of Computer Applications,* 33-39.

Nieto, E., & Roman, F. (2013). Similarity Preserving Snippet Based Visualization of Web Search Results. *IEEE Transactions on Visualization and Computer Graphics*, 1–14.

Rasekh, I. (2015). *A New Competitive Intelligence based Strategy for Web Page Search*. IEEE.

Shou, G., Bai, K., Chan, K., & Chen, G. (2014). Supporting privacy protection in personalized web search. *IEEE Transactions on Knowledge and Data Engineering, 26*(2), 453–467. doi:10.1109/TKDE.2012.201

Singh, A., & Velez, H. (2014). Hierarchical Multi-Log Cloud-Based Search Engine. *IEEE International Conference on Complex, Intelligent and Software Intensive Systems, IEEE CPS* (pp. 212–219). IEEE.

Singh, D., & Reddy, C.K. (2014). A Survey on Platforms for Big Data Analytics. *Journal of Big Data,* 1-20.

Sugiyama, K., Hatano, K., & Yoshikawa, M. (2004). *Adaptive Web Search Based on User Profile Constructed without any Effort from Users*. ACM.

Tanapaiankit, P., Versterre, L., & Song, M. (2012). *Personalized Query Expansion in the QIC System*. ACM.

Tesai, C-W., Lai, C-F., Chao, H-C., & Vasilakos, A. V. (2015). Big Data Analytics: A Survey. *Journal of Big Data,* 1-32.

Verma, N., Malhotra, D., Malhotra, M., & Singh, J. (2015). E Commerce Web Site Ranking using Semantic Web Mining and Neural Computing. *Science Direct*, *45*, 42–51.

Verma, N., & Singh, J. (2015). Improved web mining for e-commerce website restructuring. In *Computational Intelligence & Communication Technology,2015 IEEE International Conference*. IEEE.

Vinay, V., Wood, K., Frayling, N., & Cox, I. (2005). *Comparing Relevance Feedback Algorithms for Web Search*. ACM.

Wang, H., & Wong, K. (2014). Personalized Search: An Interactive and Iterative Approach. *IEEE 10th World Congress on Services*, (pp. 3-10). IEEE.

Wang, Y., Xu, K., & Zhang, Y. (2011). Search engine optimization based on algorithm of BP neural networks. *IEEE International conference on computational intelligence and security* (pp. 390–394). IEEE.

Wasid, M., & Kant, V. (2015). A Particle Swarm Approach to Collaborative Filtering based Recommender Systems through Fuzzy Features. *Science Direct*, *54*, 440–448.

Youssif, A., Ghalwash, A., & Amer, E. (2011). *HSWS: Enhancing Efficiency of Web Search Engine Via Semantic Web*. ACM. doi:10.1145/2077489.2077530

Zhang, G., Li, C., & Xing, C. (2012). A Semantic++ Social Search Engine Framework in the Cloud. *IEEE International Conference on Semantics, Knowledge and Grids, IEEE CPS*, (pp. 277–278). IEEE. doi:10.1109/SKG.2012.9

KEY TERMS AND DEFINITIONS

Apriori Algorithm: A popular frequent item sets mining algorithm and is used to find association rule between the item sets.

Association Rule Mining: It involves exploring interesting customer habits by looking at associations between various products bought together. It is also known as Market Basket analysis.

Big Data: It is a huge collection of data sets possessing popular characteristics of V's i.e. Volume, Velocity and Variety, which are beyond the processing capabilities of tradition data mining systems.

Cloud Computing: It refers to Internet based computing that provide on demand access to sharable resources like software, OS platform, network infrastructure etc.

Hadoop: An open source framework based on Google Map Reduce architecture. It allows for distributed processing of large number of data sets using cluster of computers.

Map Reduce: It is a simple yet powerful programming model used for distributed and parallel processing of large data sets. A Map Reduce job consist of only two functions Map and Reduce which work on (Key, Value) pair.

Meta Search Engine: It refer to search engines which do not maintain their own database and crawler instead they retrieve output documents from number of search engines and rank them as per their algorithm.

Chapter 4
ABDITS Analysis, Design, and Working of Agents

Shweta Mahlawat
Banasthali University, India

Praveen Dhyani
Banasthali University, India

OmPrakash Rishi
University of Kota, India

ABSTRACT

Agent technology has been suggested by experts to be a promising approach to address the challenges of the modern computer based education. "An autonomous agent is a system situated within and a part of an environment that senses that environment and acts on it, over time, in pursuit of its own agenda and so as to effect what it senses in the future" (Franklin & Graesser, 1996). Any agent, in accordance with this definition, satisfies four properties: autonomy, social ability, reactivity and pro-activeness. By using intelligent agents in an ITS architecture it is possible to obtain an individual tutoring system adapted to the needs and characteristics of every student. In this chapter, the authors are going to present a multiagent system i.e. named ABDITS which is distributed, dynamic, intelligent and adaptive with Pedagogy view for learners in intelligent system. This system is an integration of adaptive web-based learning with expert systems as well. A crucial feature of the ABDITS personal agent is that the case based reasoning approach for student modeling.

DOI: 10.4018/978-1-5225-2234-8.ch004

INTRODUCTION

Agent based Distributed ITS is a Web-based, distributed, multi-agent learning system. The system ties the Web users (for students) and therefore the underlying data servers (for courseware and student profiles) in conjunction with the multi-agent resource management. The data and agents are supported by a distributed system consisting of workstations and storage devices connected via high-bandwidth networks. ABDITS is enforced using the current technologies of the net, World Wide Web and software system agents.

Several characteristics specific to asynchronous learning create multi-agent systems enticing. First, the scholars of a virtual category on the net are widely distributed, and therefore the variety of potential participants is massive. This renders static and centralized systems inadequate. A distributed multi-agent system with personalized agents for every student is incredibly enticing. Secondly, the classes are dynamic in nature. The background, knowledge, and ability of active students can modification over time. The training materials and teaching methodologies of the courses can modification too. Thirdly, students have completely different background and temperament.

Teaching methodology ought to be tailored toward every student's interest and data to create teaching and learning more practical. Moreover, students usually enter in many courses at constant time. Coordination of learning on completely different topics for every student can enrich the training expertise. Finally, students tend to induce along to debate study topics and share common interests. Smooth communications, as well as visualizing and sharing common contexts, have to be compelled to be supported. Hence, multi-agent systems became a promising paradigm in education.

ABDITS consists of variety of specialized agents with completely different experience. In ABDITS, every student is appointed a singular personal agent that manages the student's personal profile (with the assistance of Profile Agent and Evaluation Agent) as well as data background, learning designs, interests, courses listed in, etc. the personal agent talks to different agents within the system through numerous communication channels. A web course is supported by a set of teaching and course agents. The course agents (with the assistance of Test Agent and Exercise Agent) manage course materials and course-specific teaching techniques for a course. Multiple course agents exist on distributed sites to produce higher potency, flexibility, and handiness. The teaching agents will consult with any course agent of a course and infrequently select one near for higher performance (See below Figure1).

Figure 1. Communication among agents

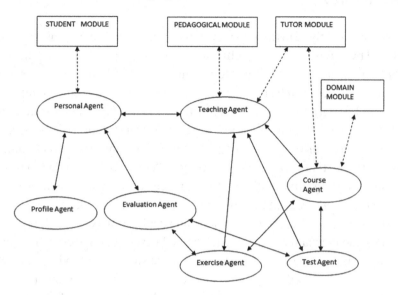

A teaching agent interacts with a student associate degree is an intelligent tutor of a course. Every teaching agent obtains course materials and course-specific teaching techniques from a course agent then tries to show the materials within the most applicable kind and pace supported the background and learning kind of the scholar. The teaching agents could adopt varied psychological feature skills like natural language understanding, voice communication, natural language generation, learning, and social aspects. These skills create it easier for college students to move with the teaching agents through natural styles of voice communication and expression. Multimedia presentations like graphics and animation create tough ideas and operations easier to know.

The basic elements of a teaching agent are a tutor module, a pedagogical module, and a student modeler. The tutor module creates exercises and queries consistent with the student's background and learning status, provides solutions, and explains the ideas and solutions to remedy student's misconceptions. It contains a problem generator, a problem solver, an explanation generator, and a domain knowledge base. The pedagogical module determines the timing, style, and content of the teaching agent's interventions. It's a case-based production system that uses the scholar model and education data to see the suitable actions. The scholar modeler provides a model of a student supported her learning style, data background, and interests. It should additionally incorporate the data gathered through dialogues with the scholar and therefore the student's learning profile like the actions the scholar performed and therefore the explanations he/she asked for.

BACKGROUND

Intelligent Tutoring Systems are interactive learning environments based on instruction assisted by computers. The intelligence of these systems is largely attributed to their ability to adapt to a specific student during the teaching process. In general, the adaptation process can be described by three phases: (i) getting the information about the student, (ii) processing the information to initialize and update a student model, and (iii) using the student model to provide the adaptation (Gonzalez, 2000).

Current research efforts have shifted from the development of intelligent tutoring systems (ITSs) that focus on the teaching of "content" knowledge to those that focus on teaching cognitive skills. This shift is seen as necessary because cognitive skills are increasingly recognized by educational establishments as the foundation for knowledge acquisition, comprehension, and application (Goh & Quek, 2007) so that ITS provide mechanisms for the design and development of system interfaces for tutoring/training, those are effective and at the same time modular, structured, configurable, flexible and adaptable(Oswaldo Vélez-Langs & Xiomara Argüello, 2007) during the development of real time ITS. But researchers felt some key issues involved in building an intelligent tutoring system for the ill-defined domain of interpersonal and intercultural skill acquisition. In such systems the tutor provides guidance in two forms: (1) as a coach that gives hints and feedback during an engagement with a virtual character, and (2) during an after-action review to help the learner reflect on their choices. Learner activities are mapped to learning objectives, which include whether the actions represent positive or negative evidence of learning. These underlie an expert model, student model, and models of coaching and reflective tutoring that support the learner (Lane & VenLehn, 2005). Whereas Kinshuk et. al., (2002) pronounced that no ITSs are found in an actual learning environment and there is no evidence that commercial organizations are rushing to turn their research into profitable products.

Recently, the research on agent-oriented programming has begun because the intelligent agent technique has developed rapidly. For example, Roda et.al [2003] presented an agent-based system designed to support the adoption of knowledge sharing practices within communities. The system is based on a conceptual framework that, by modeling the adoption of knowledge management practices as a change process, identifies the pedagogical strategies best suited to support users through the various stages of the adoption process. The resulting community-based system provides each member of the community with an artificial personal change-management agent capable of guiding users in the acquisition and adoption of new knowledge sharing practices by activating personalized and contextualized intervention. Bobin [2005] incorporated the theory of organizational influence to demonstrate the structural influence index within a network KMS. The benefits of structural indexing are identifying knowledge agents, evaluating knowledge sharing among organizational members, and objectively assessing the contribution of knowledge agents. The topology affects the agents' ability to share knowledge, integrate knowledge, and make efficient use of knowledge in multi-agent system. Zhu [2006] presented an overview of four major multi-agent system topologic models, assesses their advantages and disadvantages in terms of agent autonomy adaptation, scalability, and efficiency of cooperation. Su et. al [2006] provided customized course according to individual learning characteristics and capabilities based on analyzing portfolio information of learner and Chen et. al [2006] proposed scheme to help teachers to assess individual learners precisely utilizing only the learning portfolios in a web-based learning environment.

In the literature, very few authors have written on the use of agents with CBR for distributed teaching & learning. Web based Learning Environment are grounded on an interdisciplinary frame that includes: cognitive, psychology, philosophy, pedagogy and communication sciences. The core of Web based Learning Environment is fixed by the following branches: adaptive hypermedia, such as adaptive navigation and adaptive presentation; adaptive information filtering, as content-based filtering and collaborative filtering; intelligent collaborative learning, by adaptive collaboration, adaptive group formation and virtual students; intelligent tutoring, through curriculum sequencing, intelligent solution analysis and problem solving support; and intelligent class monitoring, like a remote teacher.

The author contribution consists in proposing an adaptive system to ensure an automatic and a continuous monitoring of the learner. This monitoring is based on cases (dropping out, difficulties met, etc.) past and similar. Moreover, the ABDITS system is open, scalable and generic to support any learning subject.

DESIGN OF ABDITS

Based on the theory of Case based Reasoning and Multi Agent System, an Agent based Distributed Intelligent Tutoring System (ABDITS) has been designed. The ABDITS focuses on the student behavior, analyze the characteristics of the students, preferred style, and knowledge level and accordingly supplies the study material according to their requirement. Evaluation of learning is also an important consideration to improve the learning efficiency. Several Agents like Personal Agent and Teaching Agent are used in ABDITs and play active parts in the effective learning process.

There are eight main steps in the design of ABDITS model as follows:

1. **Analyzing the Type of a Case:** First, Personal Agent will activate and It checks the authorization of a user. If it is an existing user, communicate with Profile

Agent and try to find out the type of a case. PA will do search for a match in a case base scenario. If a case is matched (partially or fully), accordingly communicate with Teaching Agent and provide the study material. If a new case, then Teaching Agent will decide the strategy of teaching and provide the study material accordingly. Personal Agent will add a new case in case base scenario.

2.   **Registration of a User:** If it is new user, Personal Agent will communicate to Profile Agent. Profile Agent will provide a registration form and first the student registers for the system and store the personal information into Personal KB. Profile Agent try to find out the characteristics of a student, such as their preference style, and their learning background etc. and store into Profile KB.

3.   **Preliminary Work on Cases:** To know the knowledge level of a case, Teaching Agent will provide a preliminary questionnaire according to chosen topic or a subject. During this process, Profile Agent will judge the actual learning style. Evaluation Agent will judge the performance of a case. If it is up to mark, then Teaching Agent will provide the study material accordingly otherwise Teaching Agent will suggest a new strategy for the case.

4.   **Update the Case Base:** Personal Agent will update the case base scenario accordingly. If a case is matched fully, then the performance of a case. If it is expected then ok. If it is not, then what kind of (Excellent, Average or poor) because on the basis of this, Teaching Agent will take the decision how was the study material? Updating is required or not. Accordingly cases will be updated too.

5.   **Decision on Strategy of Teaching:** When a case is defined, Teaching Agent has to take the decision for strategy of teaching. Teaching Agent will communicate to Course Agent and provide the study material accordingly. If performance is not up to mark, Teaching Agent tries to find out the reason for that. A User is not in mood to do study or provided study material is not perfect for that user. Whatever the reason, Teaching Agent will find out accordingly the decision has to been taken and inform to Personal Agent as well. So Personal Agent can do update in case base scenario as well.

6.   **Reviewing:** When Teaching Agent supplies the study material, it is necessary to check the performance of user. According to performance of a user, we can take the decision on difficulty level of study material. Exercise Agent will provide some exercise on particular topic. Evaluation agent will watch on performance of a user. According to performance, teaching agent will take a decision for providing the contents of material like normal, with more examples or some advanced level etc.

7.   **Evaluating:** When a user finish the topic, it is necessary to examine the performance. On basis of that, Teaching Agent will be able to take decision,

he/ she is ready to go for next topic or he/ she require more studies(Remedial Contents). For that purpose, Test Agent will provide questionnaire. Evaluate Agent will watch on performance and report to Personal Agent and Teaching Agent. What type of mistakes he/ she is doing, on the basis of that, Teaching Agent will decide the strategy for next.

8. **Updating:** Automatically updating is required on each and every level here. Personal Agent will update on case base scenario. Profile Agent and Evaluation Agent will do update on profile and performance level. Teaching Agent will update the strategy of teaching of a particular case. Course Agent will update the course material whenever it is required. Same with Test Agent and Exercise Agent. Teaching Agent will do contact with tutor as well and inform that on which topic, where the updating is required. Which topic is not up to the mark? What the level of question and where the changes are required. Each and every aspect of learning need to be updating timely.

Design of Agents

ABDITS presents an environment for developing an agent primarily based ITS that works during a totally distributed mode with the assistance of variety of specialized agents with totally different experience, particularly profile agent, evaluation agent, exercise agent, test agent, personal agent, course agent and teaching agent. Figure 2 depicts action of an agent normally wherever it's shown that the agent interacts with the environment through sensors and effectors (Russel & Norvig, 2003).

In this context, the ABDITS agents are designed with the subsequent properties taken into account:

- **Reactivity:** Agents ought to maintain a nonstop relationship with their sur-roundings and answer the changes that happen in it.
- **Interactivity:** Agents ought to move with one another so as to attain the goals.
- **Autonomy:** Agents ought to understand once and the way to hold out the tasks assigned to them.
- **Pro Activity:** Agents have goals or express objectives (i.e. to seek out didactical contents in graphic media, to pick out structural navigation tools, etc.) and wish to act consequently associate degree in an autonomous manner to attain them.
- **Learning:** The User agent learns from student interactions so as to adapt the training surroundings to the scholar model (learning profile and student data state).

Figure 2. Actions of an agent

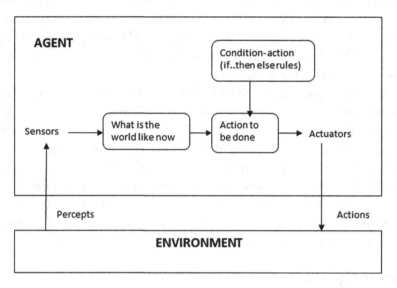

The agency and personalization model of this system follows the behavior shown in Figure 3. Students (rectangles) interact with an environment (USD platform) through agents (circles) that represent them. The agents have a double function: *interacting* with each other and with the habitat on behalf of the student and *filtering* the information (type and style of didactic contents, navigation tools and navigation techniques) that the students receive from other agents and the habitat. The agents are individuals (each student has his/her own agent) and they all have knowledge about the objectives and learning styles of the scholars they represent; they are also capable of learning from interactions with the environment.

Each of the agents is described below in the above context:

Analysis and Design of the *Profile* Agent

The aim of the Profile agent is to register student activity from the student learning atmosphere because the learning tasks are administrated. These monitoring tasks carries with it registering the student mouse-clicks on relevant buttons of the complete operating table throughout a learning session - once he/she studies a lesson, completes exercises or enters the system for the primary time. Therefore, the student model is updated by the personal agent performance that processes the collected data. The Evaluation agent improves its operation by giving some data to assist inspire the training expertise or to reinforce the information the student has acquired. The collected activity additionally permits the fine-tuning of the coed learning profile

Figure 3. ABDITS model of agency and personalization

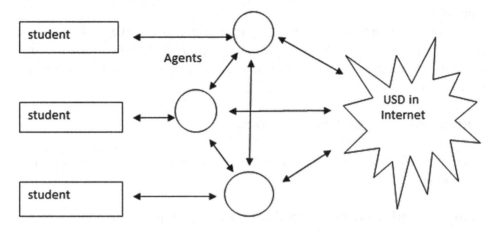

Table 1. Student activity data, collected by the Profile agent

Monitoring Area	Student Activity Data
Initial access to the system	Answers to the ILS questionnaire
The entire learning session	• Session beginning and ending: date and time • Number of mouse-clicks on the chat button Number of mouse-clicks on the e-mail button • Number of mouse-clicks on the forum button • Number of mouse-clicks on the agent Evaluation button
The current learning lesson	• Number of mouse-clicks on the navigation tree links • Number of mouse-clicks on the navigation arrows (backward and forward arrows) • Number of mouse-clicks on the glossary button • Number of mouse-clicks on the bibliography button • Number of mouse-clicks on the search button • Number of mouse-clicks on the SMIT agent button • Number of configurable exercises (on student preferences) for self assessment carried out • Number of exercises (adapted to the state of student knowledge) for self assessment carried out • Names of visited nodes • Number of visits per node • Time spent in visiting a node
The exercises carried out	• Number of Easy questions carried out • Number of Normal questions carried out • Number of Difficult questions carried out • Answers to questions • Time spent in completing exercises • Exercise qualification

by the agents. Table 1 summarizes the relevant information thought-about for every space of watching.

The first time students access the system, this action allows the *Profile* agent to ask the student to answer the ILS (Index of Learning Styles) questionnaire. The result of the evaluation of this questionnaire allows the initial student learning profile to be assigned.

Requirements: Use Case Diagram

Figure 4 shows the *use case diagram* of the Profile agent. Tables 2, summarize the description of its elements.

Analysis and Design of the *Exercise/Test* Agent

The aim of the Exercise /Test agent is that the construction of appropriate exercises for a student learning session. This method is distributed with the subsequent two options taken into account:

Figure 4. Use case diagram of the Profile agent

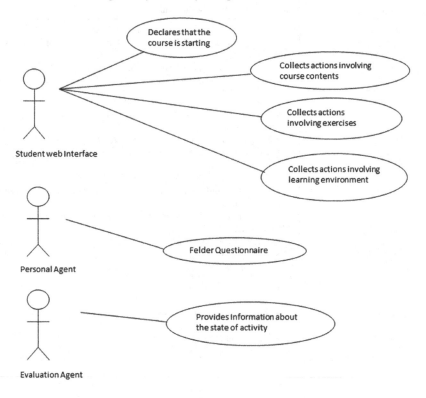

Table 2. Characteristics of the Profile agent use case diagram elements

Use Case	Functionality	Role Concerning Student Activity	Actors	Precondition	Postcondition
Declares that the course is starting.	Informs the Teaching and the Personal agents about the beginning of a lesson.	The information collected at this point is relevant to the functioning of the Teaching and Personal agents.	The student actions are collected from the virtual working desktop of the student Web interface.	The student should have begun to study a new lesson.	Data collected concerning the beginning of a new lesson should be coded using the corresponding agent ontology and should be sent to the Teaching and Personal agents.
Collects actions involving course contents.	Collects data concerning the lesson learned in the current session.	The student carries out activities, such as navigating the page contents, reviewing the recommended bibliography, completing self- assessment exercises, etc.	The student actions are collected from the virtual working desktop of the student Web interface.	The student should have begun to study a lesson.	Data collected from the learned lesson should be coded using the agent ontology and should be sent to the Personal agent. In this case, the Personal agent updates the temporary student model that it has in the memory. Mouse-clicks on the Evaluation agent button will wake the Evaluation agent to allow the student to check the history of the displayed messages.
Collects actions involving exercises.	Collects data concerning the exercises completed by the student.	The time spent when completing the exercise as well as the level of difficulty of the exercise and the answers given to the questions are relevant parameters for updating the student model by means of the Personal agent.	The student actions are collected from the virtual working desktop of the student Web interface.	The student should have completed a proposed exercise.	Data collected concerning the student activities carried out when completing exercises should be coded using the corresponding agent ontology and should be sent to the Personal agent. Feedback information is sent to the Evaluation agent if necessary.

continued on following page

Table 2. Continued

Use Case	Functionality	Role Concerning Student Activity	Actors	Precondition	Postcondition
Collects actions involving learning environment.	Collects data concerning the general actions carried out by the student during the entire learning session.	The mouse-clicks on available relevant buttons of the virtual desktop may represent particular student behavior tendencies that are important to detect. This collected data may be used to update the student model by means of the Personal agent.	The student actions are collected from the virtual working desktop of the student Web interface.	The student should have closed the current learning session.	Data collected general concerning the student actions in the learning environment should be coded using the corresponding agent ontology and should be sent to the Personal agent. The student is disconnected from the system.
Felder questionnaire	Collects the answers to the Felder questionnaire.	Allows the initial assignment of the student learning profile.	The information is requested by the Personal agent.	This is the first time that the student accesses the system.	Initialization of the student learning profile.
Provides information about the state of activity	Provides information about its activity state(test of survival).	There is no role concerning student activity. This case is just for the agent activity control	The information is requested by the Evaluation agent.	The monitor agent should have received a control test message.	The Profile agent response should be coded using the corresponding agent ontology and should be sent to the Evaluation agent.

- The student's preferences, within which case it's the student who configures the topics and therefore the kinds of queries that he/she desires to answer (configured exercise).
- The student's information level, within which case it's the agent who selects the topics and therefore the kinds of the queries that the student ought to answer in a very given moment (adapted exercise).

An exercise is actually a group of multiple selection queries. Each of those queries is related to a subject and grade of problem in line with the domain model structure. There are three levels of problem and they are described as 1- easy, 2- normal and 3- tough.

There are two kinds of exercises in a very lesson:

- **Mandatory Exercises:** These are described as necessity nodes within the navigation map. during this case, it's the teacher who determines the overall characteristics of the exercise that the agent ought to produce for the student, as an example, the amount of inquiries to complete, their level of problem, the amount of attainable makes an attempt at the exercise that the student is allowed, the overall time that the student could pay on the exercise, etc.

- **Optional Exercises or Self-Assessment Exercises:** During this case, the student could confirm the overall characteristics of the exercise to complete. The student can also request an adapted exercise from the Exercise /Test agent according to his/her level of information.

The use case diagram of this agent is described next.

Requirements: Use Case Diagram

See Figure 5 and Table 3.

Analysis and Design of the Evaluation Agent

Evaluation agent is introduced in the environment using an animated interface. Its goal is to calculate and show the performance of student time to time and inform the student the messages (i.e. warnings, motivation, feedback, etc.) coming from

Figure 5. Use case diagram of the Exercise/Test agent

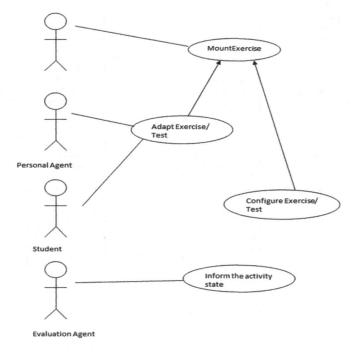

Table 3. Characteristics of the Exercise /Test agent use case diagram elements

Use Case	Functionality	Role Concerning Student Activity	Actors	Precondition	Postcondition
MountExercise.	Constructs an exercise and shows it to the student.	Enables evaluation of the student's knowledge (self assessment or from the teacher's point of view)	The basic characteristics of an exercise are handled by the Pedagogic agent from the pedagogic domain. For optional exercises, the student decides the exercise characteristics or allows the Exercise / Test agent to configure an exercise. From the student interface, it is the Course agent that requests this task for the lesson that has been learnt by the student.	A request to make an exercise should exist.	The Exercise / Test agent shows the exercise by means of the student interface and the student may begin to complete it.
Adapt Exercise	Chooses the exercise characteristics according to the student progress, applying some of the learning principles proposed by Gagne [Gag 1985].	Allows the student to do exercises adapted to his/her level of knowledge.	The student requests this type of exercise. The Personal agent provides information with data about the student model.	A request to make an adapted exercise should be made by the student.	The Exercise / Test agent presents the exercise via the student interface and the student may begin to complete it.
ConfigureExercise	Allows the student to configure an exercise according to his/her preferences.	Allows the student to do exercises adapted to his/her preferences.	The student requests this type of exercise.	A request to make a configured exercise should be made by the student.	The Exercise / Test agent shows the exercise by means of the student interface and the student may begin to complete it.
Informs about the activity state	Provides information on state of activity (test of survival).	There is no role concerning the student activity. This case is just for the agent activity control	The information is requested by the Evaluation agent.	The Exercise / Test agent should have received a control test message.	The Exercise / Test agent response should be coded using the corresponding agent ontology and should be sent to the Evaluation agent.

other agents in the environment. (e.g., to interrupt the student with a warning message from the Teaching agent). Each message representation demands the selection of certain animations and body movements to define the student behavior in any particular situation. The aim of using this agent is to "humanize' the learning environment and to make it user-friendlier and closer to the student. The messages that the Evaluation agent may show come from the Profile, Personal, Teaching and Exercise/Test agents.

Requirements: Use Case Diagram

Figure 6 shows the use case diagram of the Evaluation agent.
The characteristics of the elements of this diagram are shown in Table 4.

Analysis and Design of the *Personal* Agent

The student model represents the computer system's belief regarding the learner's information. So as to permit instruction to be separately tailored, it's initial necessary to capture the student's understanding of the topic. With this info, the issue of

Figure 6. Use case diagram of the Evaluation agent

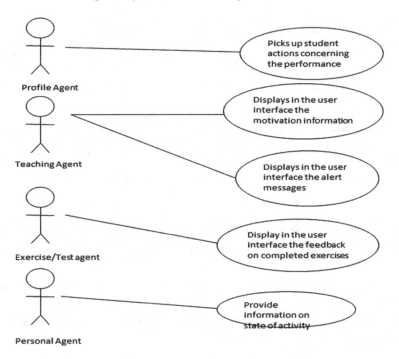

Table 4. Characteristics of the Evaluation agent use case diagram elements

Use Case	Functionality	Role Concerning The Student Activity	Actors	Precondition	Post-Condition
Picks up student actions concerning the Evaluation performance	Allows users to manage the Evaluation agent behavior in particular situations.	The student is able to interact with the Evaluation agent in order to consult the history of displayed messages.	The Profile agent which collects the student actions on the Evaluation interface.	The Evaluation agent should have displayed messages on the user interface.	The student may check the agent message history.
Displays in the user interface the motivation information	Displays to the student the motivation information sent by the Teaching agent.	The student is able to get advice on ways to do things if he/she has demonstrated particular behaviors when learning tasks are carried out.	The Teaching agent.	The Evaluation agent should have received from the Browsing agent, a request to display a motivation message.	The Evaluation agent selects from its internal knowledge base an action script to display the message using a life-like character.
Displays in the user interface the feedback on completed exercises	Displays the student the feedback information sent by the Exercise /Test agent concerning aspects of completed exercises	The student is able to receive feedback information concerning exercises he/she has completed.	The Exercise/ Test agent	The student should have completed an exercise.	The Evaluation agent selects from its internal knowledge base an action script to display the message using a life-like character.
Displays in the user interface the alert messages	Displays the student the alert messages prepared by Personal agent when the tasks for which it was programmed have been completed.	The student is able to receive the alert messages that he/she has programmed by means of the Personal agent.	The Personal agent	The tasks for which Personal agent was programmed should have been completed.	The Evaluation agent selects from its internal knowledge base an action script to display the message using a life-like character.
Provides information on state of activity	Provides information on state of activity (test of survival).	There is no role concerning the student activity. This case is just for the agent activity control	The information is requested by the Personal agent.	The Evaluation agent should have received a control test message.	The Evaluation agent response should be coded using the corresponding agent ontology

the material and any necessary rectification is controlled among the educational system. Building a student model involves defining:

- The "who", or the degree of specialization in decisive who is sculptural and what the learner history is;
- The "what", or the goals, plans, attitudes, capabilities, information and beliefs of the learner;

- "How" the model is to be acquired and maintained;
- And "When" to grant help to the learner, to supply feedback to the learner, or to interpret learner behavior.

In maintaining the scholar model, the factors that require to be thought-about embrace the fact that students don't perform systematically, they forget info haphazardly then exhibit giant leaps in understanding. The student model, which is that the essential part once providing personalized learning in e-learning systems, is that the one that builds and maintains the system's understanding of the scholar.

In the context of the ABDITS, it's the Personal agent that builds and maintains the student model - taking into thought the domain model (domain and pedagogical knowledge) and therefore the student performance. The Profile agents collect all the data regarding the scholar performance for the personal agent (see Table 5) and therefore the Teaching and therefore the Exercise / test agents consult the Personal agent for info regarding the student model so as to adapt the contents and therefore the navigation methods for a selected student.

In this section, we will discuss various aspects of the *Personal* agent design.

Table 5. Information that builds and maintains the system's understanding of the student

Type of Information	Description
Student learning profile	This information is assigned at the beginning of the course by means of the ILS (Index of Learning Styles) questionnaire evaluation. This profile is fine-tuned by using CBR techniques.

Student knowledge state(student progress during the learning session or during the study of the complete lesson)	Student progress in a course is measured by the evaluation of certain variables that may determine how well a topic is "learned". Some of these variables are:
	• The nodes visited for the studied concepts: which nodes were visited, and how much time was spent on the visit.
	  • The exercises completed (self-assessment or assessment):
	  o Number of exercises that were completed
	  o Levels of difficulty assessed
	  o Number of Easy- level questions that were answered correctly or incorrectly
	  o Number of Normal- level questions that were answered correctly or incorrectly
	  o Number of Difficult-level questions that were answered correctly or incorrectly
	   o Grading obtained for the best attempt at an exercise
	   o Time spent on doing the exercise
	   o Number of exercises that were configured by the student
	   o Number of exercises that were adapted by the Exercise/Test agent.
	  • Etc.

Requirements: Use Case Diagram

Figure 7 shows the *use case diagram* of the *Personal* agent.
    A description of the elements in this diagram is given in Table 6.

Analysis and Design of the *Teaching* Agent

In the context of the ABDITS, it's the Teaching agent that defines the navigation methods and therefore the content that a student could study increasingly in a very learning session consistent with the scholar case primarily based model (learning profile and information state) and therefore the structure of the domain. To hold out these accommodative tasks, the Teaching agent evaluates the choice rules of the pedagogical domain, requesting appropriate data regarding the scholar case primarily based model from the private agent. The knowledge that the scholar receives is conferred by the Course agent through a customized interface with technology navigation tools.

Figure 7. Use case diagram of the Personal agent

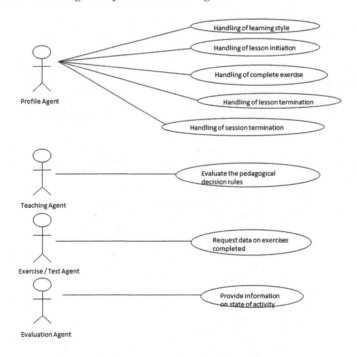

Table 6. Characteristics of the Personal agent use case diagram elements

Use Case	Functionality	Role Concerning Student Activity	Actors	Precondition	Postcondition
Handling of learning style	Requests the evaluation of the ILS questionnaire to assign the student learning profile.	If the student enters the system for the first time, he/she is assessed by the ILS questionnaire	The Profile agent presents the ILS questionnaire and collects the student answers.	The Personal agent should have sent a message to the Profile agent requesting the information to initialize the student learning profile.	The Personal agent updates the temporary student model in the memory
Handling of lesson initiation	Stores in the temporary student model base the information collected by the profile agent with respect to the moment (date, time and entry number) in which the student begins studying a lesson in a learning session.	The student lesson access is captured by the Profile agent because it represents relevant data for statistical analysis carried out by the Personal agent when building the student model.	The Profile agent picks up this information	The Profile agent should have sent a message regarding the beginning of a lesson (using the newUnit object of the ontology).	The User agent updates the temporary student model in the memory.
Handling of completed exercise	Stores in the temporary student model base the information collected by the Profile agent with respect to the student exercise performance.	The student performance when completing an exercise is captured by the Profile agent because it represents relevant data for statistical analysis carried out by the Personal agent when building the student model.	The Profile agent picks up this information.	The Profile agent should have sent a message regarding the student exercise performance(using the Exercise object of the ontology).	The Personal agent updates the temporary student model in the memory.
Handling of lesson termination	Stores in the permanent student model base (database) the information concerning the student performance during the lesson that was studied.	The information collected by the Profile agent at the end of the lesson will indicate to the Personal agent that it can update the permanent student model in the database.	The Profile agent picks up this information.	The Profile agent should have sent a message regarding the termination of the studied lesson in a learning session (using the Unit object of the ontology.)	The Personal agent updates the permanent student model in the database.

continued on following page

Table 6. Continued

Use Case	Functionality	Role Concerning Student Activity	Actors	Precondition	Postcondition
Handling of session termination	Stores, in the permanent student model base (database), the information concerning the student performance when using the tools that help the development of the learning activities (e-mail, chat, forum, and the Teaching agent)	The student performance using the general tools that may help learning is captured by the Profile agent because it represents relevant data for statistical analysis carried out by the User agent when building the student model (this information may reflect information about learning styles and may offer indicators to improve the tools for helping learning).	The Profile agent picks up this information	The Profile agent should have sent a message regarding the ending of the learning session (using the Session object of the ontology).	The Personal agent updates the permanent student model in the database.
Evaluates the pedagogical decision rules	Sends the necessary information that the teaching agent requires to evaluate a pedagogical decision rule concerning aspects of student behavior.	A pedagogical decision rule is evaluated when the student navigates through the learning contents. The result of this evaluation may lead to the discovery of new navigation paths for the student or may allow the reinforcement of what the student is currently learning.	The teaching agent makes the request.	The Teaching agent should have sent a message asking for specific information about the student model that may evaluate a pedagogic decision rule	The Personal agent sends the requested information.
Requests data on exercises completed	The Exercise Adapter agent needs to know the student performance in the exercise, in order to evaluate the rules for adapting exercises according to the student knowledge level.	This procedure lets the Exercise/Test agent know the development of the student's knowledge when completing exercises.	The Exercise/Test agent requests this information.	The Exercise/Test agent should have sent a message to the User agent requesting the information about the exercises that the student has completed.	The Personal agent responds to this request.

continued on following page

Table 6. Continued

Use Case	Functionality	Role Concerning Student Activity	Actors	Precondition	Postcondition
Provides information on state of activity	Provides information on state of activity (test of survival).	There is no role concerning student activity. This case is just for the agent activity control.	The information is requested by the Evaluation agent.	The Personal agent should have received a control test message.	The Personal agent response should be coded using the corresponding agent ontology and should be sent to the Evaluation agent.

Requirements: Use Case Diagram

Figure 8 shows the use case diagram of the Teaching agent. The description of its elements is shown in Table 7.

Figure 8. Use case diagram of the Teaching agent

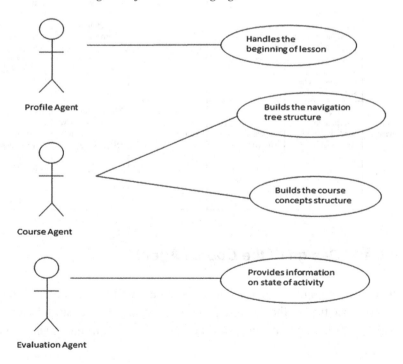

Table 7. Characteristics of the Teaching agent use case diagram elements

Use Case	Functionality	Role Concerning Student Activity	Actors	Precondition	Postcondition
Handles the beginning of the lesson	The course identifier that is sent by the Profile agent will allow the Teaching agent to choose suitable learning material for the student	The student begins to study a new lesson.	The Profile agent sends the information.	The student should have begun to study a lesson.	The Profile agent informs the event of the course beginning to the Teaching agent.
Builds the navigation tree structure	By means of this request, the Teaching agent evaluates the pedagogic decision rules (using information from the student and domain models) to select suitable materials and the conditions that will allow the course navigation tree to be adapted for the student.	*This procedure allows the student to navigate the course in an adaptive way.*	The Course agent	*The Teaching agent should have received a message requesting the information.*	The Teaching agent responds to the request with suitable information that will allow the navigation tree of the course for the particular student to be built.
Builds the course concepts structure	By means of this request, the Pedagogic agent consults the user agent for information about the knowledge state of the student on the concepts that he/she has learnt.	The concepts structure allows the student to find out his/her knowledge state on the concepts that compose the course.	The Course agent	The Teaching agent should have received a message requesting the information.	The Teaching agent responds to the request with suitable information that will allow the concepts state diagram for the particular student to be built.
Provides information on state of activity	Provides information on state of activity (test of survival).	There is no role concerning student activity. This case is just for the agent activity control	The information is requested by the Evaluation agent.	The Teaching agent should have received a control test message.	The Teaching agent response should be coded using the corresponding agent ontology and should be sent to the Evaluation agent

Analysis and Design of the *Course* Agent

The Course agent is an assistant agent that creates, within the student interface, the navigation structure of the training content (HTML pages) custom-made to the coed learning profile and to the coed level of data. The accommodative navigation techniques, like hidden link, direct steering and link annotation likewise because the choice of appropriate navigation tools, are applied to help the student in navigating the contents in an exceedingly customized means.

Because it operates, the Course agent communicates with:

- The Teaching agent (which builds and maintains the navigation tree and therefore the idea state diagram in step with the student model) so as to refresh the knowledge to be presented;
- The Teaching agent so as to point that nodes have specific info for review associated to them (i.e., list or exercises), on condition that the scholar has programmed it to produce such alerts.
- The Exercise/Test agent if the lesson has exercises assigned that ought to be drawn to the student in an exceedingly easy interface (to encourage or to strengthen behaviors).

In short, the Course agent is employed to adapt the options displayed within the interface to the wants of the learner

Requirements: Use Case Diagram

Figure 9 shows the use case diagram of the *Course* agent.

Figure 9. Use case diagram of the Course agent

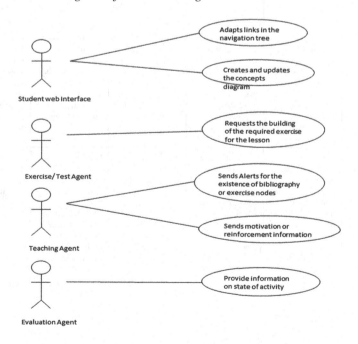

Table 8. Characteristics of the Course agent use case diagram elements

Use Case	Functionality	Role Concerning Student Activity	Actors	Precondition	Post-Condition
Adapts links in the navigation tree	Builds and shows in the student interface the learning contents applying techniques for adaptive navigation.	The student is able to navigate the content via the navigation tree or by using the complementary navigation tools.	The student web interface	The student should be studying a lesson in the learning environment	The Course agent allows the student to navigate the content.
Creates and updates the concepts diagram	According to the student knowledge state concerning the concepts of the course, it creates and updates, in the student interface, the concept state diagram. The information concerning the student knowledge state is updated by the Teaching agent.	The student is properly informed about his/her state of knowledge on the concepts of the course.	The student web interface.	The student should be studying a lesson in the learning environment	The Course agent allows the student to visualize his/her knowledge state on the concepts of the course by the concept state diagram that it has built in the interface.
Requests the building of the required exercises for the lesson	Requests the exercise /test agent to build the required exercises for the lesson.	The student may assess his/her knowledge by doing configurable or adapted exercises.	The Exercise / Test agent	The learning material should have associated exercises.	The Course agent asks the Exercise Adapter agent to build the corresponding exercises for the lesson and to present them via the student interface.
Sends alerts about the existence of bibliography or exercise nodes	Informs the Teaching agent if some nodes have bibliography or exercise nodes associated	The student is able to review the bibliographical references or to make exercises using the Teaching agent recommendation.	The Teaching agent	The student should have programmed the Teaching agent for alerts on the bibliography or exercise nodes	The Course agent sends the alert to the Teaching agent if the nodes associated with bibliography or exercises that the student should revise, exist.
Sends motivation or reinforcement information	Sends the Teaching agent the motivation or the reinforcement information that should be presented by a user-friendly (affective) interface.	The student may correct certain behavior by analyzing this information. The student feels assisted during his/her learning process.	The Teaching agent	Some particular behavior of the student during the development of his/her learning activities should have motivated the presentation of this type of information.	The Course agent sends the corresponding information to the Teaching agent.

continued on following page

Table 8. Continued

Use Case	Functionality	Role Concerning Student Activity	Actors	Precondition	Post-Condition
Provides information on state of activity	Provides information on state of activity (test of survival).	There is no role concerning student activity. This case is just for the agent activity control	The information is requested by the Evaluation agent.	The Course agent should have received a control test message.	The Course agent response should be coded using the corresponding agent ontology and should be sent to the Evaluation agent.

The description of the elements of this diagram is presented in Table 8.

WORKING OF AGENT

Personal Agent

1. Authorization of a user (with help of Profile Agent).
2. Maintain Student Index, Case Index.
3. If an existing user, search in case base scenario.
4. Communicate with Teaching Agent to decide the teaching strategy.
5. Interaction with Profile Agent and Evaluation Agent as well as to see the performance of a user and update into dbase as well.
6. Update into case base scenario as well for further cases.

Profile Agent

1. Student / User Registration.
2. Maintain the personal information dbase (Personal KB).
3. Manage the learning style, knowledge level, preference style, course enrolled etc.
4. Communicate with personal agent and find the type of user and define a case of particular user.
5. Update into dbase regarding personal and profile information.

Evaluation Agent

1. Watch on performance of a particular case on particular topic.
2. Report to Personal Agent.

3.   Update the dbase Performance KB.

Test Agent

1.   Communicate with Course Agent and Teaching Agent.
2.   Provide the questionnaire according to requirement.
3.   Evaluate the result and report to Evaluation agent via Teaching Agent.
4.   Update into Test KB.

Exercise Agent

1.   Communicate with Course Agent and Teaching Agent
2.   Provide the exercise on basis of current topic.
3.   Evaluate the performance and report to Evaluation Agent via Teaching Agent.
4.   Update into Exercise KB.

Course Agent

1.   Maintain Course Index and the dbases regarding Domain Module(Course Material).
2.   Update into Theory KB, Remedy KB, Test KB, Exercise KB etc.
3.   Communicate with Teaching Agent.
4.   Provide the study material decided by Teaching Agent.
5.   Interaction with Tutor Module.

Teaching Agent

1.   Communicate with Personal Agent and Course Agent.
2.   Decides the teaching strategy according to a case i.e. asked by Personal Agent.
3.   Provide the contents with the help of Course Agent, Exercise Agent and Test Agent.
4.   Examine the performance of a case and automatically update the strategy of teaching accordingly.
5.   Inform to Tutor Module, where the updation is required.

CONCLUSION

In this chapter, the ABDITS agent design and working were discussed. The author described how agents were designed to carry out flexible and autonomous actions in the environment of the USD platform in order to achieve adaptive presentation and navigation on the learning content using a user-friendly and assisted interface. Agent flexibility was provided by including features such as reactivity, proactivity, interactivity and learning. The complete ontology for agent communications was also defined.

REFERENCES

Aamodt, A., & Plaza, E. (1994). Case-based reasoning: Foundational issues, methodological variations, and system approaches. *AI Communications, 7*(1), 39–59.

Andreas, B., & Andreas, G. H. (2001). A Framework for Internet-Based Distributed Learning. Academic Press.

Badjonski, M., Ivanovic, M., & Budimac, Z. (1997). Intelligent tutoring system as multi-agent system. *IEEE International Conference on Intelligent Processing Systems (ICIPS '97), 1*, 871-875,

Brusilovski, P. (1999). Adaptive and Intelligent Technologies for Web-based Education. *Kustliche Intelligence, 4*, 19–25.

Brusilovsky, P., Schwarz, E., & Weber, G. (1996), ELM-ART: An Intelligent Tutoring System on World Wide Web. In C. Frasson, G. Gauthier,, & A Lesgold (Eds.), *Proc. of 3rd International Conference on Intelligent Tutoring Systems, ITS-96*. Springer Verlag. doi:10.1007/3-540-61327-7_123

Burger, C., & Rotherme, K. (2001). *A Framework to Support Teaching in Distributed Systems*. University of Stuttgart.

Burns, H. L., & Capps, C. G. (1988). Foundations of intelligent tutoring systems: an introduction. In M. C. Polson & J. J. Richardson (Eds.), *Foundations of Intelligent Tutoring Systems*. Hillsdale, NJ: Lawrence Frlbaum.

Chappell, A. R., & Mitchell, C. M. (1997). The Case Based Intelligent Tutoring System: An Architecture for Developing and Maintaining Operator Expertise. *Proceedings of the 1997 IEEE International Conference on Systems, Man, and Cybernetics*, 308-318. doi:10.1109/ICSMC.1997.638311

Corbett, K. (2005). *Anderson*. Intelligent Tutoring System.

Cristea, A., & Okamoto, T. (2002), Student model-based, agent-managed, adaptive Distance Learning Environment for Academic English Teaching. IWALT 2002 Proceedings, 159-162.

Fabiano, A., Dorca, C. R., Lopes, M. A., & Fernandez. (2003). A Multi agent architecture for Distance Education Systems. *Proceedings of the 3rd IEEE International Conference on Advanced Learning Technologies.*

Holt, P., Dubs, S., Jones, M., & Greer, J. (1991). The state of Student Modeling. In *Student Modelling: The Key to Individualizes Knowledge-Based Instruction, NATO ASI Series, 125* (pp. 3–35). London, UK: Springer verlag.

Jose, M., & Gascuena, A. F-C. (2005). *An Agent-based Intelligent Tutoring System for Enhancing E-Learning/ E-Teaching.* Academic Press.

Kolodner, J. L. (1993). *Case-Based Reasoning.* San Mateo, CA: Morgan Kaufmann. doi:10.1016/B978-1-55860-237-3.50005-4

Lin, F. O. (2005). Designing Distributed Learning Environments with Intelligent Software Agents. *Journal of Educational Technology & Society, 8*(1), 132–133.

McCalla, G. I., & Greer, J. E. (1991). *Granularity-Based Reasoning and Belief Revision in Student Models, In the Key to Individualised Knowledge-Based Instruction.* NATO ASI Series.

Riesbeck, C., & Schank, R. (1989). *Inside Case-Based Reasoning.* Hillsdale, NJ: Lawrence Erlbaum.

Rishi, Rekha, Govil, & Madhavi. (2007). Agent Based student Modeling in Distributed CBR based Intelligent Tutoring System. *Proceedings of the World Congress on Engineering and Computer Science.*

Safiye, T. (2005). *A Multi Agent system Approach For Distance Learning Architecture.* TOJET.

Self, J. A. (1991). Formal Approaches to Student Modelling.GREE91, 295-352.

Shang, Shi, & Chen. (2001). An Intelligent Distributed Environment for Active Learning. University of Missouri-Columbia.

Weiss, G. (1999). Multiagent Systems: A Modern Approach to Distributed Artificial Intelligence. Cambridge, MA: MIT Press.

Wenger, E. (1987). *Artificial Intelligence & Tutoring System.* Los Altos, CA: Morgen Kaufman. doi:10.1016/B978-0-934613-26-2.50013-X

Yazdani, M. (1987). Intelligent Tutoring Systems: An Overview. In R. Lawler (Ed.), *Artificial Intelligence and Education* (pp. 183–201). *Ablex Publishing Corp.*

Chapter 5
Applications of AI in Financial System

Santosh Kumar
IMS UNISON University, India

Roopali Sharma
Birla Institute of Technology, India

ABSTRACT

Role of computers are widely accepted and well known in the domain of Finance. Artificial Intelligence(AI) methods are extensively used in field of computer science for providing solution of unpredictable event in a frequent changing environment with utilization of neural network. Professionals are using AI framework into every field for reducing human interference to get better result from few decades. The main objective of the chapter is to point out the techniques of AI utilized in field of finance in broader perspective. The purpose of this chapter is to analyze the background of AI in finance and its role in Finance Market mainly as investment decision analysis tool.

OBJECTIVES

Role of computers are widely accepted and well known in the domain of Finance. Artificial Intelligence(AI) methods are extensively used in field of computer science for providing solution of unpredicted event in a frequent changing environment with utilization of neural network. Professionals are using AI framework into every field for reducing human interference to get better result from few decades.

DOI: 10.4018/978-1-5225-2234-8.ch005

The main objective of the chapter is to point out the techniques of AI utilized in field of finance in broader perspective. The purpose of this chapter is to analyze the background of AI in finance and its role in Finance Market, mainly in process of investment decision making from evolution and use of AI techniques in this respect.

INTRODUCTION OF ARTIFICIAL INTELLIGENCE

Few decades before, a computer program was only used for a numerical computation and computing the path of a bullet. Now a days, a computer programs are used in decision making in important decisions area, supported by a big database across global. As the tasks that computers perform are getting complex and intertwined with the daily life decisions, such behavior of decision making from the computer programs associate with intelligence. So these programs labeled as intelligence incorporated without human neural system, named Artificial Intelligence (AI). However experts are using AI and its concepts in every area of decision making still this branch is unexplored and not known to masses. AI as an academic discipline started from Dartmouth conference organized by John McCarthy from Stanford University and Marvin Minsky from MIT in the 1955 as "the science and engineering of making intelligent machines". Many researchers define AI, as branch of computer science concerned with making computers behave like humans. While some define AI as extension of human intelligence through use of computers.

Alan Turing undertook a test of a machine's ability to demonstrate intelligence, Turing Test, by judgment to distinguish between human and AI machine on natural language conversation .The AI approach can further divided into two major areas -Conventional AI and Computational AI .Conventional AI is based out on logic and rules to make decisions. Computational AI takes biological mechanisms. Computational AI are more advanced form and broadly used in decision making in economy and social sciences. Artificial Neural network (ANN), Expert system (ES), Fuzzy systems (FS), Genetic algorithms (GA) are examples of Computational AI used in field of Financial and Investment decision making.

We use AI every day, without knowing the facts, a simple conversational navigator's application like Google Voice for Android. Our smart phones are getting better day by day; remind us on simple things like birthday of friends, time to go to work, hands free searching and messaging and even telling us if we forget attachment in an email. Such automations are based on concept and application of AI. Currently IBM along with Google is working on AI research for creating a Super computer, WATSON that could change our future significantly. WATSON is learning everything related to human behavior, nature and other complexities in order to forecast and recommend on our future actions.

Concepts of AI has been used in every industry, from computers to pharmaceutical .After gain of trust in these field, professional are start using AI in financial services decision making as well.

HISTORY OF AI IN FIELD OF FINANCE

History of AI in Financial services domain can be traced back from Pacific National Bank of USA in 1987, set-up a Fraud Prevention Security Task force to check the unauthorized use of cards at ATM machines and vendor counters. The bank build a prototype on a regular office computer to perform as warning system for fraud prevention, modeled around the weather warning systems that warned before possible natural disasters like cyclones and earthquakes. This prototype was successful and paved the way for AI-based technology into consumer interactive products and services. Thus,AI has found a new home in financial industries and used as a valuable tool to many business applications for decision making.

In 2001, Wednesday, 8 August, BBC has flashed a new "Robots beat humans in trading battle". Technology giant IBM pitted robotic commodity trading agents, known as "bots", in opposition to humans in trading Commodities, pork bellies and gold. The bots made 7% more return than the human traders, reported in New Scientist magazine.

A book titled "Foundation of Investment Systems Using Artificial Intelligence and the Web" authored by Robert R. Trippi (2002), identify AI as Wall Street's most promising technologies. AI enabled systems can handle more information and react more quickly for consistent decisions than a group of human. Authors methodically explain how AI systems can help in higher investment returns, with real-life examples.

Sycara, Decker, Pannu, Williamson, & Zeng,(1996), researchers at Carnegie Mellon University, designed an integrated multi agent system that considers data of asset valuation, and risk management, named WARREN, which refers to the first name of the famous investor Warren Buffet .

The recent literature by Tsakonas, Dounias, Doumpos, & Zopounidis(2006) highlighted the role of neural network in investment by combination of knowledge based techniques, neural network and techniques of genetic algorithm .Bhattacharyya, Pictet, & Zumbach,(2002) have used knowledge-rich operators for investing in foreign exchange markets.

Many literatures supporting benefits of AI in investment and financial market has been published in last 2 decades. Thus different concept and use AI in different segments of finance market has been evolved. Kun Chang Lee, Namho Chung & Inwon Kang (2008), M. Uther & H. Haley (2008), Shun-Yao Tseng (2012), Rustam

Vahidov and Gregory E. Kersten etc are the major contributors in the research of this field.

APPLICATION OF AI IN FINANCIAL MARKET

Accurate and effective decisions are required in constantly changing financial market condition. There is a massive increase in use of information technologies for accurate decisions making in finance field. Conventional statistical methods are regularly complemented by application of machine learning in recent times. The area of applied machine learning also helps in discovering hidden facts in huge amounts of data. The major techniques of AI utilized in finance Markets are as follows.

Expert (Knowledge) Systems (ES)

An expert system (ES) is a AI enabled computer-based system that emulates the logic process of an expert within a particular domain of knowledge. ES are designed on explicitly formulated specific knowledge gathered from experts for decision making as explained by Feigenbaum et al.(1988). The aim of an ES is not to copy the mental processes of experts during a decision making process but attainment of high quality decision. ES have capacity to give recommendation even the sufficient required data is un- available by using database of alternative inferences.

The research by Armstrong and Collopy (1992), developed a role model for making an annual extrapolation forecasts for demographic and economic time series on data.

This rule based ES produced more accurate forecasts than the traditional random walk and statistical tools combined. They performed better, especially in long periods for series with major trends, high uncertainty and low stability.

The comparative study by Korczak and Lipinsky (2004) between two real time trading systems by use of Stochastic oscillators based on relative Strength index & Ease of Movement. The first trading system was based on 350 trading rules and other on 150 trading rules created in linear combination on data of Paris Stock Exchange . They concluded that reduction in trading rules decreased the computation time without change on expertise quality. This highlights the main advantages of ES as they combined knowledge from different sources for decision making process.

Artificial Neural Networks (ANNs)

Artificial neural networks (ANNs) are combination of simple neural elements in parallel arrangement and mesh like a human nervous system likened data source with explicit knowledge about target values . The functioning of ANNs is largely depend on values in the network, widely used to solve problems of prediction, classification, and control by adjusting the weights between connected elements

The major advantage of ANNs is their capabilities to capture nonlinearity without predefine information about relationships between variables. ANNs operate as "universal approximation systems" with the skill to imitate almost any function related to variables. In comparison to traditionally used econometric models ANNs provide results in very short period. The drawback in ANNs based applications is the non existences of a standard pattern to design the network .ANNs have been successfully applied to solve problems of generalization in prediction of corporate bond rating. ANNs are used by central banks across globe to forecast the interest rates and the monetary policy.

The result of an empirical research shown in Table 1, depicts the association between forecasting accuracy of ANN and ARIMA model using Mean Square Error(MSE) on data of the USA GDP deflator, 1st quarter 1960 to 3rd quarter 2003. The performance of ANN better than AIRMA models in the first two quarters on test set, while the advantage disappeared for longer horizon due to early stopping approach .

There has been abundance of studies attempting to forecast the price levels in exchange by using indicators of technical analysis as input variables in ANNs framework (Egeli et al., 2003); (Gençay, r.; Stengos, t., 1998); (Safer, 2003). (Chen et al., 2008); (Mizuno et al., 1998); (Nagarajan et al., 2005); (Yao et al., 2000). The results show that indicators as inputs into ANN framework improve the forecasting accuracy of stock prices. Figure 1 shows the data transformation process in ANN framework applied on Japanese stock exchange.

Fuzzy Systems

Fuzzy systems are a knowledge based expert system designed on Fuzzy logic concept. Fuzzy Logic calculates uncertainty from membership values in between the range of 0.0 to 1.0 with 0.0 indicates absolute failure and 1.0 represents absolute Success.

The fuzzy system is made up of three steps - Fuzzification, fuzzy inference and defuzzification . Fuzzification is the conversion of real to fuzzy data, and defuzzification is transformation of fuzzy data to real data after inference by fuzzy system, usually based on IF…THEN rules.

A fuzzy rule based neural networks have been used to predict stock market returns many times in various research. A stock trading system proposed by Ang and Quek (2006) on moving average rules achieved higher return than a traditional random trading system. Fuzzy neural network (FNN) based on general stock trading rules developed by Wong et.al achieved better return single ANNs and other traditional trading system in Taiwan stock Exchange.

Table 1. Ratio of ANN and AIRMA

	Forecast horizon (quarters)					Forecast horizon (quarters)			
	1	2	3	4		1	2	3	4
Ar1	0.84	0.77	0.98	1.20		0.85	0.77	0.77	0.72
Ar2	0.89	0.84	1.04	1.18		0.86	0.81	0.81	0.73
Ar3	0.90	0.83	1.01	1.15		0.90	0.85	0.81	0.73
Ar4	0.90	0.82	0.96	1.12		0.90	0.85	0.83	0.72
Ar5	0.93	0.80	0.94	1.07		0.90	0.87	0.82	0.72
Ar6	0.86	0.79	0.91	1.04		0.92	0.86	0.82	0.72
Ar7	0.77	0.75	0.84	0.98		0.94	0.87	0.84	0.74
Ar8	0.77	0.73	0.83	0.91		0.93	0.88	0.84	0.76

Note: Each cell shows the ratio of the Mean Square Error of the Neural Network model to the Mean Squared Error to the Auto Regression model.

Source: Nakamura, 2005.

Figure 1. System composed of ANNs and indicators of technical analysis as inputs into network

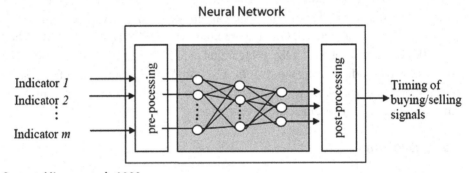

Source: Mizuno et al., 1998.

Agent-Based Computational Economics (ACE)

Agent based Computational Economics (ACE) is an example of AI enable agent (variables) based model, suitable for economy modeled based forecasting. Economics can be study as a complex adaptive system to adapt changes in the external agents (environment). Bruun (2006), ACE is a bottom up system forming models of agents and interaction rules which lead to setting up the whole system using simulations within this modeling approach the structure evolves without forcing any presumptions upon it. The resulting ACE models must be dynamically create a economic system solely on the basis of agents' interactions without further intervention from the other modeler.

Early researches of artificial agents are based on zero intelligent agents. Le Baron (2000) investigated the efficiency of zero intelligence traders on artificial foreign exchange markets and he found that budget allocation of these agents was similar to human agents.

In other studies simulations with more sophisticated agents have evolved. Raberto et al. (2003) set up a model where trading strategies of agents were based on technical trading rules and fundamental values. Kendall and Su (2003) utilized agent based approach on five selected stocks from London Stock Exchange, trading behavior of artificial agents was based on indicators of technical analysis. This research demonstrated stable and satisfactory learning abilities of artificial traders, different learning behavior related to the different stock price patterns was discovered, an important finding for further research in portfolio selection. Kumar and Bhattacharya (2009) used multi agent approach for portfolio selection and they achieved higher average returns across one month, two months and three months out-of-sample period than the FTSE 100 index.

The relative disadvantage of ACE modeling is that it requires detailed specification for agent data and methods determining structural attributes, behavioral dispositions and institutional arrangements. If the agent interactions induce sufficiently strong positive feedbacks, small changes in initial specifications could radically affect the types of outcomes that result.

COMPARATIVE STUDY IN PORTFOLIO PERFORMANCE

The investment and portfolio domain is changing in stochastic and random environment. Take the stock exchange as an example; there are more than five thousand securities available for selection by portfolio manager or individual investors. This creates a problem of filtering all those stocks to find the ones that are good for investment. There is also availability of enormous information that may affect the performance in market to some extent, as stock market is efficient. All above is making tremendously difficult for a portfolio manager to create the portfolio without relying on any tools.

An experiment has been conducted by department of commerce, Texas A&M University. In the experiments, commonly used AI systems - Bayesian network system, and a feed forward neural network system as shown in figure 2. The data of eight financial ratio mentioned below of the S&P 500 companies as the input variables these systems, from the period of 1987 to 1996.

- Debt to equity
- Market /book value

Figure 2. Artificial Intelligence systems for portfolio selection

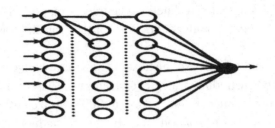

Feed Forward Neural Network System

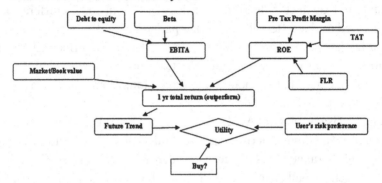

- EBIT
- Return on Equity (ROE)
- Pre-tax profit
- Total asset turn over (TAT)
- Financial leverage ratio (FLR) and
- Beta (β)

To test the performance, all these systems made the decision proposal on which of the S&P 500 stocks to be included in the portfolio. Compare the return output from selected portfolio by these AI system with return obtained from mutual funds, human portfolio selection, in same period.

Return from both AI systems outperforms the leading mutual fund by a large margin in 1997. They also ran these AI systems with the data from a negative return year (2000); the S&P 500 and the primary mutual fund houses produced negative return for the year while both AI systems produced a positive return.

By above experiment on real time data, we could conclude that the use of AI system for security selection in portfolio outperformed over the human portfolio manager.

SUMMARY

The chapter offers supportive evidence for suitability of use AI enabled systems in various financial applications according to their capacity to process non-linear variable relationships, ability to learn and evolve in time and also ability to make decisions at expert level.

AI algorithms are used for optimization problems - optimization of stock market timing and portfolio creation. These tools can be used for creation of quantitative tools for short-time prediction of exchange, inflation and interest rates. Expert systems try to make decisions on the expert level and they are applied in analysis of securities as well as in company assessment. If we have an uncertain notion of the methods for a decision (what is typical for human decision makers), fuzzy systems could be the appropriate solution. In last decades the Agent-based Computational Economics has emerged. Current ACE concentrates on financial market modeling. The approach of artificial neural networks is put into effect due to their ability to study the nonlinear relation between variables and their ability to work with uncertainty. They are frequently used for solving prediction problems, forecasting macroeconomic indicators and time series prediction on financial markets.

REFERENCES

Algoet, P. H., & Cover, T. M. (1991). Asymptotic optimality and asymptotic equip-partition properties of log-optimum investment. *Annals of Probability*, 876–898.

Chen, A., Hsu, Y., & Hu, K. A (2008). Hybrid Forecasting Model for Foreign Exchange rate Based on a Multi-neural network. *ICNC '08: Fourth International Conference on Natural Computation*. Jinan: IEEE.

Cover, T. M. (1991). Universal portfolios. *Mathematical Finance, 1*(1), 1–29. doi:10.1111/j.1467-9965.1991.tb00002.x

Trippi, R. R., & Lee, J. K. (1996). *Artificial Intelligence in Finance and Investing*. Irwin.

Chapter 6
Autonomous Market Segments Estimation Using Density Conscious Artificial Immune System Learner

Vishwambhar Pathak
BIT MESRA Jaipur, India

ABSTRACT

Automated exploration of groups of customers to understand customer behavior from raw data is highly required to support strategic decision making given the pressure of competitive market. Several mathematical and statistical methods have been applied for autonomous model estimation from multivariate data. The current paper investigates employability of new generation of bio-inspired metaheuristic algorithms, named the artificial immune system (AIS), which in the current proposition, learn through density based kernels. As such the model simulates probabilistic behavior of the dendritic cells (DCs) during recognition of the antigens and danger signals, whose learning has been modeled with an infinite Gaussian mixture model. The unsupervised learning capability of the model has been found to be effective for multivariate data.

DOI: 10.4018/978-1-5225-2234-8.ch006

INTRODUCTION

Across the rapidly emerging applications of computational intelligence, development of methods and techniques to explore interesting information without having any prior knowledge about data characteristics has been of paramount concern. Market segmentation refers to the field of active research and practice wherein customer's behavior is to be understood through computational models for digging out the hidden groups in the data collected though purchase entries or surveys for example. The problem thus narrows down to the task of segmentation of structured data. The problem is dealt with in detail with underlying issues and methods in this work. Modern clustering techniques have been developed vastly exploiting concepts from multiple disciplines, a comprehensive reading can be found in Jain (2009). The present chapter revisits earlier work (Pathak, Dhyani, & Mahanti, 2011) in which the AIS based learning model DCAIGMM was developed. The efficacy of the model has been investigated in comparison to contemporary autonomous segmentation model.

BACKGROUND

Market segmentation refers to the marketing strategy that seeks to divide a broad market perspective into subsets of consumers, locations, and businesses, in terms of common needs, interests, and priorities in a way to define their strategies to target potential customers. It is more so sought by small scale companies to optimize the cost to increase consumer penetration. The analysis covers a wide range including geographic segmentation, demographic segmentation, behavioral segmentation, psychographic segmentation, occasional segmentation, segmentation by benefits, emotive Segmentation, cultural segmentation, and multi-variable account segmentation. Computational tools have been proved of great help in the recent knowledge world, where accurate data analyses have been made possible due to huge amount of data about business operations being stored continuously. Several mathematical and statistical methods have been developed and successfully applied help the decision makers. Data mining and machine learning algorithms of wide range including the Decision Trees, Classification and Regression Trees, Rough Sets, Self organizing maps, Fuzzy inference engines, and vast range of bio-inspired algorithms have been reported in research literature (Prabha & Ilango, 2014; Mattila, 2008; Yao, 2013; Taylor, n.d.; Chulis, 2012); majority of which have been implemented in successful commercial tools for the task. The current work focuses on a bio-inspired algorithm based on natural immune system dynamics modeled using density based model estimation methods, applied to extracting segments from multivariate data.

- **Brief Introduction to Natural and Artificial Immune System:** The AIS algorithms are inspired from the robust protection mechanisms of the natural immune system (NIS) which involves recognition, discrimination of the harmful and the safe bio-organisms interacting with human bodies and corresponding remedial action. Classical theories of immune system function (Castro, Von Zuben, 1999) suggest three protection layers, divided as follows:
- **Physical and Physiological Barriers:** Initial resistance to the external invaders is created by the skin, the respiratory system, and the mucous membranes. The macrophages and antibodies present in the skin and the mucous membrane lining the respiratory and digestive tracts compose the initial defense. Most of the alien microorganisms are killed by the destructive enzymes present in saliva, sweat, and tears, or by the stomach acids. Some of the invaders are also destructed or deactivated by the pH and temperature of the body.
- **Innate Immune System and Adaptive Immune System:** THE authors of Janeway (1992, 1993) Janeway & Travers (1997), Fearon & Locksley (1996), Parish & O'Neill (1997), Carol & Prodeus (1998), Colaco (1998), and Medzhitov & Janeway (1998) discussed the division of the innate immune and the adaptive immune functional dynamics. Figure 1 represents the layers as given in (Castro & Von Zuben 1999).
  - The innate immune destroys many pathogens on first encounter. It consists of a class of blood proteins called *complement*, which assists, or complements, the activity of antibodies. The *pattern recognition receptors* (PRRs) encoded in the germinal centers recognize molecular *patterns associated with microbial pathogens* (PAMPs). The distinct structures of the immune recognition molecules and the host tissues make the innate immune system capable of distinguishing between *self* and *nonself*. The innate immune system induces co-stimulatory signals in *antigen presenting cells* (APC) that leads to T cell activation, starting the *adaptive immune response*.
  - The *adaptive immune system* consists of two types of *lymphocytes*: the B cells and T cells. B lymphocytes secrete specific antibodies that recognize and react to stimuli the T (killer) lymphocyte. The random process of generation of these antigen receptors is expressed through the *clonal selection* of receptors with particular specificity. The antibody molecules are formed by piecing together gene segments. Each cell adapts the available pieces differently to make a unique receptor, enabling the cells to collectively recognize the infectious organisms, even if one has never faced it before (Nasraoui, Gonzlez, Cardona, Rojas, & Dasgupta, 2003).

Figure 1. Multi-layer structure of the immune system (Castro 1999)
Source: Castro (1999)

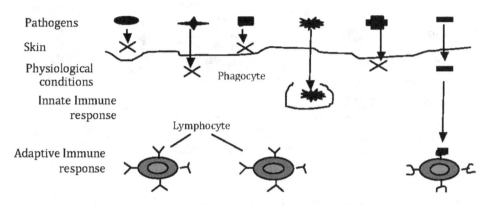

Danger Theory of Artificial Immune System: Matzinger (2002) contradicted the classical self-nonself recognition, and later Aickelin & Cayzer (2002) suggested that "instead of responding to foreignness, the immune system responds to danger". Figure 2 depicts the immune response as seen by this danger theory. Accordingly, a damaged cell dying an unnatural death sends out *distress* (or *danger*) *signal*, whereupon neighboring antigens are captured by *antigen-presenting cells* (APCs) such as macrophages or dendritic cells (DCs), which then travel to the local lymph node and present the antigen to lymphocytes; in effect, establishing a danger zone around a danger signal. Thus only the B cells producing antibodies that match antigens within the danger zone get stimulated. These B cells undergo clonal expansion process.

SUITABILITY OF AIS FOR APPLICATION TO DATA CLUSTERING

As can be observed from the Figure 3, adopted from Nasraoui et. al. (2003), antibodies in the natural immune system (NIS) interact and associate together. As such, the immune system works by identifying the non-like, either by self/non-self learning (*adaptive immunology*) or by identification of extremely unwanted (danger) elements (*innate immunology*). This association of similar antibodies is modeled in various AIS as the antigen recognition ball (ARBs) (Timmis, Neal & Hunt, 2000). These ARBs later attract evolving antigens, depending on the similarity of the later to one of the groups of antibodies. The intra-subset interactions contribute the internal binding of the ARB, and an overly stressed one may even split. Such interactions are responsible for splitting and merging of ARBs in due course. These features of natural immune system appear to have analogy with the needs of the task of clus-

Figure 2. Danger signal based immune mechanism (Aickelin & Cayzer, 2002)

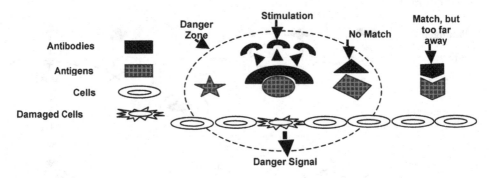

tering, resembling the splitting and merging of clusters. This is helpful in avoiding overfitting as well as in segregating outliers, indicated by antibody unbound by any antigen over a period.

In addition to the above observation, strength of NIS summarized by Nasraoui et. al. (2003) is remarkable: *Recognition* (Anomaly detection, Noise tolerance), *Robustness* (Noise tolerance), *Feature extraction, Diversity* (can face an entire repertoire of foreign invaders), *Reinforcement learning, Memory* (remembers past encounters: basis for vaccine), *Distributed Detection* (no single central system), *Multi layered* (defense mechanisms at multiple levels), and *Adaptive* (Self- regulated). Therefore, quite naturally, upcoming theories related to function of the NIS have been curiously analyzed and used to take inspiration for evolution of variety of AIS methods for clustering. These Artificial Immune Systems have been successfully applied to wide range of machine learning tasks. Many supervised and unsupervised learning algorithms based on adaptive immune metaphor have been implemented successfully Castro & Von Zuben (1999, 2000). The innate immune

Figure 3. Internal and external immune interactions

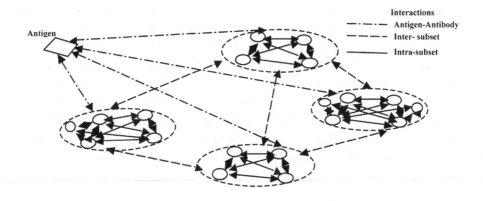

metaphor has been widely applied in task of anomaly detection (Kim, Bentley, Aickelin, Greensmith, Tedesco, & Twycross, 2007; Gonzalez, 2003). However, very few attempts have been made to use the features of innate immune system for the task of clustering. The innate immune system is defined to function on the basis of danger signals. Applicability of danger theory in pattern recognition tasks has been endorsed in work by authors of Nasraoui, Cerwinske, Rojas, & Gonzalez (2007) and Matzinger (2002) to be more applicable to low memory concerns. Moreover, in a relevant work by authors of Bentley, Greensmith, & Ujjin (2005), two algorithms for clustering based on innate immune metaphor have been successfully implemented and have been shown to be useful for the task of clustering.

Survey of Traditional Data Clustering Methods and Challenges

Major Clustering Approaches

Traditional partition-based clustering methods like k-means are limited by the need to specify the number of clusters. The hierarchical techniques are someway capable to answer the question "Which are the best clusters"? A statistical-probabilistic approach helps to overcome these limitations, wherein the goal is to find the most likely cluster for the given data, i.e. they associate a certain probability for belongingness to a cluster. This helps to eliminate the brittleness that is often associated with rather deterministic approaches. The concern of clustering high dimensional data has been addressed well by density concerned algorithms reported in literature. The basic idea of the density-based algorithms is to separate the set D into subsets of similar densities. In the ideal case they can determine the cluster number k automatically and detect clusters of arbitrary shape and size. The dynamics of the sets of lymphocytes/ antibodies/antigens as explained by Jerne has been investigated in terms of dynamical systems theory and subsequently probabilistic model for AIS have been tried (Stepney, Smith, Timmis, Tyrrell, Neal, & Hone, A. N. W., 2005; Tome 1996). The probabilistic cellular automaton model (Tome, 1996) associated a probability with the death process of the immune cells, which is measured on parameters depending on the type of neighboring cells and that on antigen density. These models are claimed to include the effect of fluctuations which are probabilistic in nature and play an important role in determining the critical behavior of the system. Artificial antibodies can be abstracted out in a probability vector which is updated (i.e. it learns) in a way which models how the population of antibodies would be changed. Such a method would base on the proportional cloning rule which makes the rate of change proportional to the expected difference in gain.

Comparison of Density Concerned Methods with Other Clustering Methods

Cluster analysis is the task of detecting groups of similar objects in large data sets, without having specified these groups by means of explicit features. The density-based clustering introduced above achieves a high flexibility with respect to cluster shapes and addresses the problem of noise detection by simultaneously examining several items. Therefore these algorithms count to the most advanced and robust approaches among the various cluster algorithms. The strength and weakness of clustering algorithms are largely observed with concern to dimensionality of the data. On this test-bed density based methods have scored well. For example, *DBSCAN*, using R-Tree structure, is good for low-dimensional data, whereas it finds application to high-dimensional data it with a step of multidimensional scaling to map into low-dimensional space. The work by authors of Stein & Busch (2005) introduced another density-based algorithm *MajorClust* to work well even in high-dimensional data application viz. document clustering. Another set of methods for data clustering, namely the hierarchical cluster algorithms work well to detect complex structures in the data however they are sensitive to noise. Iterative algorithms, e.g. *k-Means, Kohonen's ANN, Fuzzy k-Means* work robustly with respect to noise but mostly detect spherical clusters. Unlike "Distance" and "Partitioning" based methods, "Density" type methods directly seek dense areas of the data space, and can find more good clusters, while being robust to noise. Here, the criterion Density/distance/Partition refers to whether a density type of association (e.g. fitness/stimulation in AIS) measure is used or one that is based on distance/error. The runtime of the density based algorithms, viz. *DBSCAN*, *MajorClust*, and *Chameleon* is comparable to hierarchical algorithms, i, e., $O(n^2)$, or even $O(n \log(n))$ for low-dimensional data if efficient data structures are employed. By definition, the Meta-search based algorithms that see clustering as global optimization task, e.g. those based on Simulated Annealing or Genetic Algorithm methods, are supposed to perform best. However, in practice, their performance is badly affected due to heavy runtime, and sometimes difficult finding specification for a 'global goal criterion'. A simple graph-based algorithm given by Rinaldo & Wasserman (2010) has been shown to successfully approximate high-density clusters. They have proposed data-based methods for selection of bandwidth and have verified that accurate clustering is possible even in high-dimensions. Density estimation methods have also been successfully applied to the task of subspace-clustering. The later has played important role in the problem of handling multidimensional data space and other issues related to real life applications. Subspace clustering is to automatically find the units clustered in each subspace, i.e. with the combination of different dimensions. Three density-based subspace clustering algorithms, SUBCLU (density-connected *SUBspace CLUstering*) using concept of density in grid-based approach, FIRES (*FIlter REfinement Subspace clustering*) using pre-clustering and post-processing phases, and INSCY (*Indexing Subspace Clusters with in-process-removal of redundancY*) using recursive breadth first approach have been studied in (Sembiring & Zain, 2010).

Density Estimation Methods

Common approaches for estimation in mixture models can be found in (Dinov, 2008). The methods which influenced the model development in the present work are summarized below.

1. **Expectation Maximization Method:** It is an iterative algorithm with two steps: an expectation step and a maximization step. In the expectation step, initial guess for mixture model parameters, representing the partial membership of each data point in each constituent distribution, is computed by calculating expectation values for the membership variables of each data point. That is, for each data point x_j and distribution Y_i, the membership value $y_{i,j}$ is given by Equation 1:

$$\mu_i = \frac{\sum_j y_{ij} x_j}{\sum_j y_{ij}} \tag{1}$$

Then in the subsequent maximization steps with expectation values in hand for group membership, the membership values are recomputed for the distribution parameters. The mixing coefficients, a_i, defined by Equation 2 are the means of the membership values over the N data points:

$$a_j = \frac{1}{N} \sum_{j=1}^{N} y_{ij} \tag{2}$$

The component model parameters θ_i, or example mean μ, given as in Equation 3 are also calculated by expectation maximization using data points x_j that have been weighted using the membership values. For example, if θ is a mean μ, it would be computed using:

$$\mu_i = \frac{\sum_j y_{ij} x_j}{\sum_j y_{ij}} \tag{3}$$

With new estimates for a_i and the θ_i 's, the expectation step is repeated to re-compute new membership values. The entire procedure is repeated until model parameters converge. An excellent use of the EM method for clustering of breast cancer data has been provided in Fraley & Raftery (2000).

2. **Spectral Methods:** These methods are useful when data is high-dimensional, and the hidden distributions are known to be log-concave (such as Gaussian distribution or Exponential distribution). These methods use Singular Value Decomposition of a matrix containing data points. The top k singular vectors are considered, where k is the number of distributions to be learned. The projection of each data point to a linear subspace spanned by those vectors groups the points originating from the same distribution very close together, while points from different distributions stay far apart. A detailed discussion of theory and applications of these methods was found in (Stoica & Moses, 2005).

3. **Kernel Density Estimation:** Given a collection of n d−dimensional observations $x_1, x_2, ..., x_n \in x$ assumed to be independently and identically distributed (i.i.d.) and $x = R^d$, one method of estimation of probability density function p(x), which is attractive due to its non-parametric nature is kernel density estimation (also known as Parzen Window Estimation). This provides the following estimation for $\hat{p}(x)$, given in Equation 4 (Owens, Greensted, Timmis, & Tyrrell, 2009):

$$\hat{p}(x) = \frac{1}{nh^d} \sum_{d=1}^{n} K\left(\frac{x - x_i}{h}\right), K(x) \geq 0, \int_{-\infty}^{\infty} K(x)dx \qquad (4)$$

where K(.) is a kernel function with width h. Given the properties, that K(.) is always positive and integrates to one; then $\hat{p}(x)$ is also a probability density function. Further, if h = h(n) is a function of the number of samples n then $\hat{p}(x)$ will converge to p(x) if $\lim_{n\to\infty} h(n) = 0$ and $\lim_{n\to\infty} nh^d(n) = \infty$. Common choices for the kernel K(.) are the standard multivariate normal density function given in Equation 5:

$$K_n(x) = 2\pi^{-d/2} \exp(-x^T x / 2) \qquad (5)$$

Alternative choice is the bounded multivariate Epanechnikov kernel given by Equation 6 (Owens et. al. 2009), which may be computationally simpler to evaluate:

$$K(x) = \begin{cases} (2c_d)^{-1}(d+2)(1 - x^T x) & if \quad x^T x < 1 \\ 0 & otherwise \end{cases} \tag{6}$$

A complete discussion of the semi-parametric and non-parametric estimation models can be found in book (Härdle, Müller, Sperlich, & Werwatz 2004). Chapter 3.4 of the book details efficiency of various kernel functions, namely the uniform kernel, the triangle kernel, the Epanechnikov kernel the Quartic kernel, the Gaussian kernel. It concludes through the experiments, that for practical purposes, the choice of the kernel function is almost irrelevant for the efficiency of the estimate. Sometimes in solving a given data analysis task, density estimation has been used as a pre-processing step to perform clustering using other standard methods e.g. K-means. However the present work concerns with density estimation as an ingredient of clustering approach.

MARKET DATA SEGMENTATION WITH DCAIGMM

Dendritic Cell Algorithm (DCA): Danger Theory Based Clustering Method

To address to the issues related to clustering of multivariate customer purchase data, the proposed hybrid model applies the danger theory following strategy:

1. The danger theory based immune system model for recognition of incoming data and assigning them to one of the clusters or to create new cluster in case of anomalous data i.e. danger signal.
2. Incorporation of mixture of probability distribution functions to model (recognize) data in the current 'window' with respect to the mixture components (each represented by parameters vector).
   - **Function of Innate Immune Network:** As described above, the innate immune system viewed from artificial computational implementation, is a dual response system based on production of danger signals. Whenever an extraordinary anomaly arises, the innate system generates a danger signal. In turn the internal adaptive system consisting of the previously learnt antibody cells (DC) in an antigen recognition ball (ARB), generates immune response by producing corrective antibodies to handle further instances of such danger signals. However the aged antigens and danger signals die under a process called *apoptosis*. A heavily sized DC may get under stress and cause to split the event being called *necro-*

sis (Castro, & Von Zuben, 1999, 2000; Bentley, Greensmith, & Ujjin, 2005; Aickelin & Cayzer, 2002; Greensmith, Whitbrook, & Aickelin, 2010). Following can be viewed as motivation for employing the danger signal based for the task undertaken.

- **Danger model vis-à-vis task of Clustering:** The danger signals might be thought to resemble the outliers. Moreover memorizing the danger signal to find out similar antigen (input data) in future input and removal of an 'aged' danger signal would resemble de-memorizing unnecessary representative data elements. The dendritic cells (DCs) represent the clusters recognized in the processed data set (antigens).

- **Fault Tolerance and Robustness:** DCs in the ARB do not perform their function in isolation. Each member of the population can sample antigen and signals. This multiplicity of DCs is an important aspect of the natural system. Multiple DCs are required to present multiple copies of the same antigen type in order to invoke a response from the adaptive immune system. This is an error tolerant component of DC behavior as it implies that a misclassification by one cell is not enough to stimulate a false positive error from the immune system. Using a population of DCs also means that diversity can be generated within the population, such as assigning each DC its own threshold values, if desired. Such diversity may also add robustness to the resultant process (Aickelin & Cayzer, 2002; Yu & Dasgupta, 2008).

- **Infinite Gaussian Mixture Model (IGMM) Based Innate Immune Function:** Recognition of antigens by antibodies may be considered to be non-deterministic and the span of the recognition space being unequal. Thence, each antibody may be assumed to represent center of a probabilistic distribution function. Thus the complete set of immune elements i.e. antibodies may be mathematically modeled using mixture of distribution functions. The foundation for statistical clustering is a statistical model called *finite mixtures*. A *mixture* is a set of k probability distributions representing k clusters that govern the attribute values for members of that cluster (Witten & Frank, 2005). Here, the clustering problem translates into taking a set of instances and a prespecified number of clusters, and work out each cluster's mean and variance and the population distribution between the clusters. The mixture model combines several normal distributions, and its probability density function looks like a mountain range with a peak for each component. However, neither the parameters of the mixture model nor the distribution associated with a training instance may be assumed to be available a priori. Hence, typically the Expectation maximization (EM) algorithm given in Algorithm1 given below is applied to estimate the cluster belonging-ness of the instance (Fraley & Raftery, 2002; Porzak, 2008). However, the EM method has been observed to yield only local maximum, and needs trial over several alternative initial guesses to possibly give global maximum (Witten & Frank, 2005). Turning k to infinity by certain method to dynamically evolve clusters induces *infinite mixture*.

Algorithm 1: The Expectation Maximization Algorithm

1. Make an initial guess of the parameter vector: This involves randomly selecting k objects to represent the cluster means or centers as well as making guesses for the additional parameters e.g. std.dev in case of Gaussian.
2. Iteratively refine the parameters (or clusters) based on the following two steps:
   a. **Expectation Step:** Assign each object xi to cluster Ck with the probability given as in Equations 7, and 8 as:

$$P(x_i \in C_k) = p(C_k \mid x_i) = \frac{p(C_k)p(x_i \mid C_k)}{p(x_i)} \tag{7}$$

where

$$p(x_i \mid C_k) = N(m_k, E_k(x_i)) \tag{8}$$

follows the normal (i.e., Gaussian) distribution around mean, m_k mk, with expectation, E_k. In other words, this step calculates the probability of cluster membership of object x_i, for each of the clusters. These probabilities are the "expected" cluster memberships for object x_i.

   b. **Maximization Step:** Use the probability estimates from above to re-estimate (or refine) the model parameters. For example, means computed as in Equation 9 as:

$$m_k = \frac{1}{n} \sum_{i=1}^{n} \frac{x_i P(x_i \in C_k)}{\sum_j P(x_i \in C_j)} \tag{9}$$

Figure 4. Block diagram representation of the danger model and IGMM( ) based adaptive multivariate data clusterer

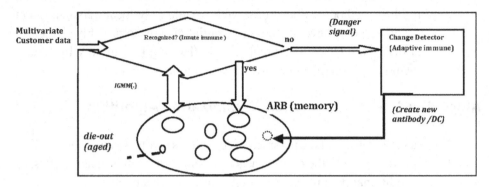

This step is the "maximization" of the likelihood of the distributions given the data. The likelihood computation is simply the multiplication of the sum of the probabilities for each of the instances defined as in Equation 10:

$$\text{Likelihood} = \prod_{i=1}^{n} \sum_{C} P(C_k) P(x_i \mid C_k) \tag{10}$$

As can be observed in the block diagram given in Figure 4, the danger signal based immune system model satisfies the requirements for being an *adaptive mul-tivariate data clusterer*. The Mutlivariate Customer data is input to the clusterer wherein its affinity to the existing cells in the ARB is estimated according to a matching function based on Gaussian mixture model marked *IGMM( )* in Figure 4. If the affinity is below a threshold, the antigen (data input) is considered unrecognized, hence a *danger signal* is produced, which activates the inner adaptive immune system to memorize the anomaly by creating another cell with the single element. The memory updation is an implicit function guided as in the Algorithm 2 given below.

Algorithm 2: DCAIGMM

Input: Unlabeled Multivariate Data
Output: Antigen Types and cumulative k values
Process:

%##initialize ARB (Antigen Recognition Ball)

1.   AG ← Input antigens (data set)

%##Initialize ARB with two DCs

2.   DCParam ← Randomly choose two data values (vectors in case of multidimensional data) to represent center(mean) of the first tow DC in the ARB
3.   ARB ← MVN(DCParam) %
     ## The DCs of ARB are implemented in form of the parameter vectors (DCParam), supported with corresponding vectors to store probabilistic affinity weights assigned to each data value in the input 'Data', as generated according to multivariate normal(MVN)pdf with the respective DCparam values, analogous to eq. A1.1 and eq.A1.2 of Algorithm1.

%## Process Further Antigens (Data values)

1.   for each Ag_i ϵ AG do steps 5-10
2.   find the affinity value with closest DC(in terms of probabilistic affinity weights for the Ag_i in existing DCs in the ARB)
3.   if affinity < τ %## Generate *'danger signal'*
4.   Create new DC in ARB (to memorize the danger signal), by assigning the new Ag_i as its center, std dev. Initialized to 1.
5.   Update all DCs' posterior affinity weights to include effects of addition of new cell, obeying eq. A1.3 of Algorithm1.
6.   else, if size of closest DC is bigger than a size threshold, split the DC.
7.   Update age of antigens and the danger signals
8.   if (age > maxantigen) remove the antigen(Set affinity with each DC to 0)
9.   Update cell parameters
10. Update DCs' affinity weights for each antigen using revised DC-parameters.
11. Compute likelihood value (Cluster quality) using eq. A1.4 of Algorithm 1.
12. Repeat through step4 to obtain maximum likelihood estimation of clusters.

All antigens and danger signal get aged with processing of each further antigen. After a certain age, they are forgotten i.e. removed from the ARB. The authors of (Pathak et al., 2011) modeled the danger signal based AIS phenomena using infinite Gaussian mixture model for the purpose of recognition of antigens by antibodies in a probabilistic way. An antibody would be taken as a parameter-set representing a distribution function; weight of each partition resembling stimulation level. Such a formalism blending AIS model with probabilistic distribution mixture model has been applied in INDIE by authors of Huertas & González (2008) for the task of density estimation, wherein they have tuned into the adaptive immune network metaphor of the AIS, and used the Gaussian kernels. A different approach for clustering through density estimation using AIS has been taken in ARIA (Bezerra, Barra, Castro & Von Zuben, 2005); their approach also utilizes the adaptive immune system metaphor. Adaptations of the AIS with Bayesian optimization and Gaussian mixture model for applications to multi-objective optimization and for continuous optimization have also been presented in (Castro & Von Zuben, 2008, 2009, 2010).

The adaptation of the statistical-probabilistic infinite Gaussian mixture model in DCAIGMM adapted from Pathak et. al. (2011) is entrusted to automatically yet non-deterministically learn the most-likely set of clusters. On the other hand, the danger signal based cluster formation avoids the overheads associated with the models based on adaptive immune system e.g. redundant clone formation steps involved in the 'Clonal Selection', a classical immune function principle applied for optimization in Castro & Von Zuben (2002). This combination, therefore, is entrusted to generate faster and more accurate results, and suits to the needs of segmentation of multivariate customer data.

SIMULATION RESULTS

To verify the effectiveness of the new algorithm, its performance for autonomous segmentation was tested over iris dataset for which natural clusters are known. As depicted in the silhouette diagrams corresponding to various test results as in results of Test1-Test5 in Figure 5, the program consistently produced three clusters, what is in coherence with the actual data characteristics, i.e. the three classes of objects represented by the FisherIris data set: *Iris-virginica*, *Iris-versicolor*, and *Iris-setosa*. With low data size of 150, the cluster sizes and number varied across different runs. This may be observed as the natural sensitivity of EM based algorithms to initialization of parameters. However, in all the runs the results were observed to generate very low misclassification percentage. It was presented in (Pathak et al., 2011) that the cluster concentrations had been similar to those of standard K-means algorithm with corresponding K-value's.

- **Description of Results and Comparison with Other Standard Method:** As the result of Test1 in Figure 5 and in respective columns of table given in Figure 6 show, the execution of the algorithm over small size of data, the classification error is 10%. However, the results of Test2-Test5 shown in Figure 5 and in Figure 6 show that for higher data sizes, the misclassification is tolerable, being around 0.02%. As presented in results of Test2-Test5 in Figure 5 and Figure 6, DCAIGMM consistently generated three clusters. The results of Test3-Test4 shown in Figure 5 and in Figure 6 represent the negli-

Figure 5. Clusters generated by DCAIGMM for IRIS data of various sizes

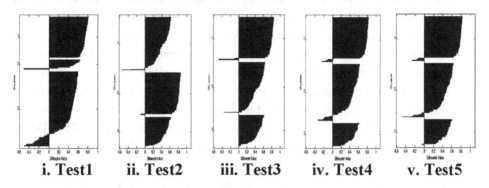

| i. Test1 | ii. Test2 | iii. Test3 | iv. Test4 | v. Test5 |

Figure 6. Output Parameters of the Clusters generated by DCAIGMM

	Test1	Test2	Test3	Test4	Test5
Data size	150	600	1050	2100	5250
No. of Clusters	3	3	3	3	3
Misclassified data	10%	0.003%	0.014%	0.02%	0.023%
Time Taken (sec.)	0.062	0.250	0.250	0.312	1.734

gible classification error generated when tested over other data sizes- 1050 and 2100 respectively. As admitted above, in results of the present algorithm, the minor misclassification error is also apparent there in form of the weight-lines in the negative direction. However, here the misclassification resulted in the two outcomes are comparable, estimated to be marginally lesser in that of presented algorithm.

- **Comparison of Performance:** The performance of the new algorithmic model was compared with existing algorithm Mclust, available in library "mclust" of R programming language (Fraley & Raftery, 2002; Fraley, Raftery, Murphy & Scrucca, 2012). The function Mclust() is intended to compute the segments in autonomous manner. It may be observed from the details of clusters generated by Mclust() as shown in Figure 7, Figure 8 and Figure 9 that the statistically optimal number of clusters is two for the iris dataset.

- **Verifying the Natural Clusters of the Reference Data Set:** As apparent from the projection of the iris dataset along its two major principal components in Figure 10-11, and the one by the K-means clusterer for k=2, given in Figure 12, the 2-segment segmentation performed by Mclust() as above is supported. However when the dataset was input to the K-means clusterer for k=3, the result presented in Figure 13 shows that two of the three clusters in fact overlap in the hyperplane. Thus it is observed that this overlap was not discovered in Mclust(). It is recalled here that the results of the DCAIGMM, presented in Figure 5, did discover three clusters in an autonomous manner.

The above observations thus establish applicability of the new model to the task of autonomous segment discovery in a multivariate data like customer-purchase history, to support market segmentation and strategic decision making.

Figure 7. Output of mclust() applied over Fisher iris dataset: Classification

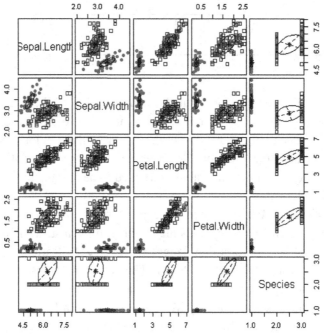

Figure 8. Output of mclust() applied over Fisher iris dataset: Density

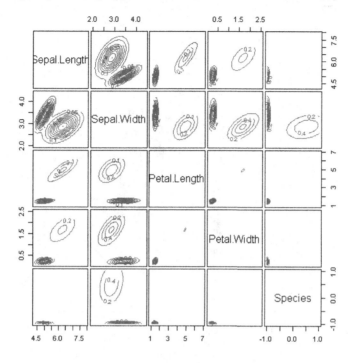

Figure 9. Output of mclust() applied over Fisher iris dataset: Uncertainty

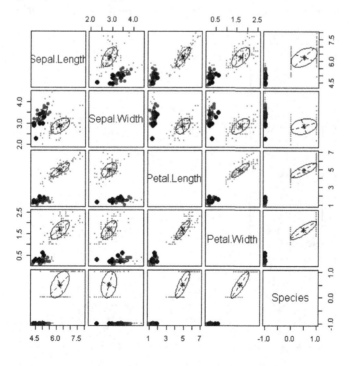

Figure 10. The principal components and data projection: i. Projection of iris along PC1, PC2

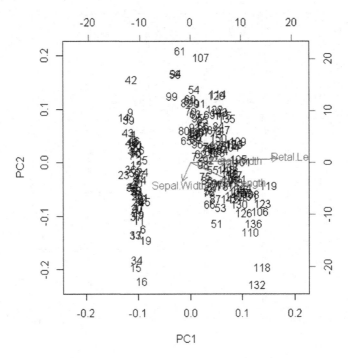

Figure 11. The principal components and data projection: Std. deviations of the PCs

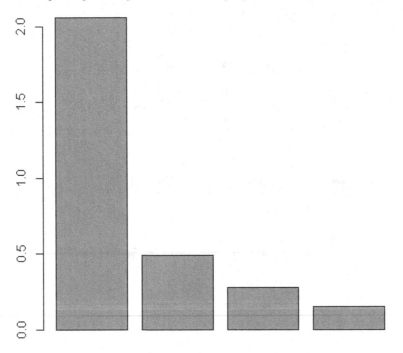

Figure 12. Results of K-Means: plot of clusters for kmeans(iris,2)

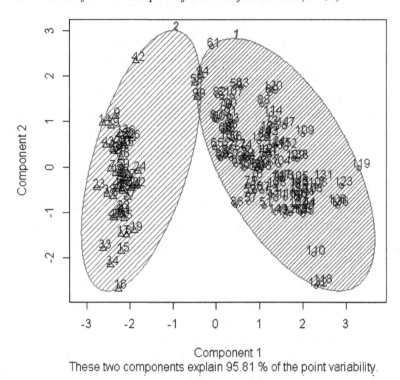

Component 1
These two components explain 95.81 % of the point variability.

Figure 13. Results of K-Means: plot of clusters for kmeans(iris,3)

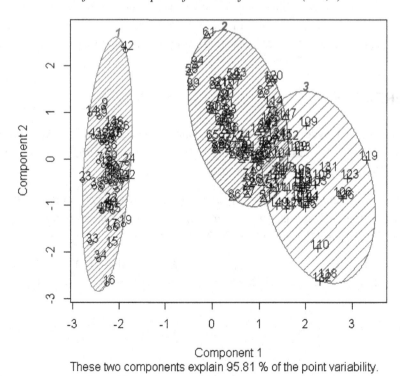

Component 1
These two components explain 95.81 % of the point variability.

CONCLUSION AND FUTURE DIRECTIONS

The results of experiment1 and several tests under experiment2 presented above verified the theoretically claimed strength of the model, namely dynamic evolution of clusters in autonomous fashion. Although due to characteristic sensitivity of the EM-based evaluation module, the number of clusters varied, however, as illustrated above in Figure 5, the classification error, although present, was negligible even in moderate sizes of data. Moreover the results had been consistent with those of standard K-means algorithm (Pathak et. al., 2011). From the knowledge of actual clusters of the dataset, and as shown in the verification of natural clusters existing in the reference dataset above, the correct number of segments is three only. This very fact establishes the employability of the proposed DCAIGMM model to any multivariate customer dataset in a way to discover hidden market segments.

Exponential growth in customer data continuously generated across different columns of business processes and rapid adoption of the data science techniques in enterprise data analysis and business intelligence unfold several challenges. A wide variety of data sources including structured as well as unstructured transaction records, complaints, replacement records, and customer feedbacks etc. are being generated. In the data analysis and mining community the issues of high volume, high dimensions, and noise present in the data always raise serious concerns. Next remarkable issue is of handling the data stream in the form of web clicks and audio and video feedbacks of customers. This simple observation opens up scope of rigorous analysis to design and implement effective models of data classification trying suitable blending of statistical and information theoretical pattern recognition techniques. The model discussed in the present chapter can be further adapted to meet the requirements of the various such data processing environments and issues.

REFERENCES

Aickelin, U., & Cayzer, S. (2002). The Danger Theory and itts Application to Artificial Immune Systems. *Proceedings of The First International Conference on Artificial Immune Systems (ICARIS 2002)*, 141–148.

Bentley, P. J., Greensmith, J., & Ujjin, S. (2005). Two Ways to Grow Tissue for Artificial Immune Systems. *Proceedings of the Fourth International Conference on Artificial Immune Systems (ICARIS 2005)*, 139-152.

Bezerra, G. B., Barra, T. V., de Castro, L. N., & Von Zuben, F. J. (2005). Adaptive Radius Immune Algorithm for Data Clustering. *LNCS, 3627*, 290–303.

Carol, M. C., & Prodeus, A. P. (1998). Linkages of Innate and Adaptive Immunity. *Current Opinion in Immunology, 10*(1), 36–40. doi:10.1016/S0952-7915(98)80028-9 PMID:9523108

Castro, L. N., & Von Zuben, F. J. (1999). Artificial Immune Systems: Part I – basic theory and applications. Technical Report No. DCA-RT 01/99. School of Computing and Electrical Engineering, State University of Campinas. Retrieved from ftp://ftp.dca.fee.unicamp.br/pub/docs/vonzuben/tr_dca/ trdca0199.pdf

Castro, L. N., & Von Zuben, F. J. (2002). Learning And Optimization Using The Clonal Selection Principle. *IEEE Transactions on Evolutionary Computation, 6*(3), 239–251. doi:10.1109/TEVC.2002.1011539

Castro, L. N., & Von Zuben, F. J. V. (2000). *Artificial Immune Systems: Part II – a survey of applications.* Retrieved from www.dca.fee.unicamp.br/~vonzuben/research/lnunes.../ rtdca0200.pdf

Castro, P. A. D., & Von Zuben, F. J. (2008). MOBAIS: A Bayesian Artificial Immune System For Multi-Objective Optimization. *LNCS, 5132*, 48–59.

Castro, P. A. D., & Von Zuben, F. J. (2009). BAIS: A Bayesian Artificial Immune System for the effective handling of building blocks. *Information Sciences, 179*(10), 1426–1440. doi:10.1016/j.ins.2008.11.040

Castro, P. A. D., & Von Zuben, F. J. (2010). GAIS: A Gaussian Artificial Immune System for Continuous Optimization. ICARIS 2010, LNCS 6209. Springer. doi:10.1007/978-3-642-14547-6_14

Chulis, K. (2012). Optimal segmentation approach and application- Clustering vs. classification trees. *IBM developerWorks*. Retrieved from http://www.ibm.com/developerworks/library/ba-optimal-segmentation/

Colaco, C. (1998). Acquired Wisdom in Innate Immunity. *Imm. Today, 19*(1).

Dinov, I. D. (2008). Expectation Maximization and Mixture Modeling Tutorial. *Statistics Online Computational Resource*. Retrieved from http://repositories.cdlib.org/socr/EM_MM

Fearon, D. T., & Locksley, R. M. (1996). The Instructive Role of Innate Immunity in the Acquired Immune Response. *Science, 272*(5258), 50–53. doi:10.1126/science.272.5258.50 PMID:8600536

Fraley, C., & Raftery, A. E. (2000). *Model-Based Clustering, Discriminant Analysis, and Density Estimation.* Technical Report no. 380, Dept. of Statistics, University of Washington.

Fraley, C., & Raftery, A. E. (2002). Model-based Clustering, Discriminant Analysis and Density Estimation. *Journal of the American Statistical Association*, *97*(458), 611–631. doi:10.1198/016214502760047131

Fraley, C., Raftery, A. E., Murphy, T. B., & Scrucca, L. (2012). *mclust Version 4 for R: Normal Mixture Modeling for Model-Based Clustering, Classification, and Density Estimation*. Technical Report No. 597. Department of Statistics, University of Washington. Retrieved from my.ilstu.edu/~mxu2/mat456/mcluster.pdf

Gonzalez, F. (2003). *A Study of Artificial Immune Systems Applied to Anomaly Detection* (Doctoral Thesis). University of Memphis. Retrieved from dis.unal.edu. co/~fgonza/papers/ gonzalez03study.pdf

Greensmith, J., Whitbrook, A., & Aickelin, U. (2010). Artificial Immune Systems. Handbook of Metaheuristics. Springer US.

Härdle, W., Müller, M., Sperlich, S., & Werwatz, A. (2004). *Nonparametric and Semiparametric Models: An Introduction*. Retrieved from http://sfb649.wiwi.hu-berlin.de/fedc_homepage/xplore/ebooks/html/spm/

Huertas, J. C. G., & González, F. A. (2008). INDIE: An Artificial Immune Network for online Density Estimation. *MICAI*, *2008*, 254–265.

Jain, A. K. (2009). Data Clustering: 50 Years Beyond K-Means. *Pattern Recognition*.

Janeway, C. A. Jr. (1992). The Immune System Evolved to Discriminate Infectious Nonself from Noninfectious Self. *Immunology Today*, *13*(1), 11–16. doi:10.1016/0167-5699(92)90198-G PMID:1739426

Janeway, C. A. Jr. (1993). How the Immune System recognizes Invaders. *Scientific American*, *269*(3), 72–79. doi:10.1038/scientificamerican0993-72 PMID:8211093

Janeway, C. A. Jr, & Travers, P. (1997). *Immunobiology The Immune System in Health and Disease* (2nd ed.). Artes Médicas. (in Portuguese)

Kim, J., Bentley, P., Aickelin, U., Greensmith, J., Tedesco, G., & Twycross, J. (2007). Immune System Approaches to Intrusion Detection - A Review. *Journal of Natural Computing, Springer*, *6*(4), 413–466. doi:10.1007/s11047-006-9026-4

Mattila, E. (2008). *Behavioral Segmentation of Telecommunication Customers* (Master of Science Thesis). TRITA-CSC-E 2008:075 ISRN-KTH/CSC/E--08/075--SE ISSN-1653-5715.

Matzinger, P. (2002). The danger model: A renewed sense of self. *Science*, *296*(5566), 301–305. doi:10.1126/science.1071059 PMID:11951032

Medzhitov, R., & Janeway, C. A., Jr. (1998). Innate Immune Recognition and Control of Adaptive Immune Responses. *Seminars in Imm., 10.*

Nasraoui, O., Cerwinske, J., Rojas, C., & Gonzalez, F. (2007). Performance of Recommendation Systems in Dynamic Streaming Environments. *Proceedings of the 2007 SIAM International Conference on Data Mining.* doi:10.1137/1.9781611972771.63

Nasraoui, O., Gonzalez, F., Cardona, C., Rojas, C., & Dasgupta, D. (2003). A scalable artificial immune system model for dynamic unsupervised learning. *Genetic and Evolutionary Computation—GECCO 2003,* 219-230.

Nasraoui, O., Gonzlez, F., Cardona, C., Rojas, C., & Dasgupta, D. (2003). A Scalable Artificial Immune System Model for Dynamic Unsupervised Learning. LNCS, 2723, 219–230.

Owens, N. D. L., Greensted, A., Timmis, J., & Tyrrell, A. (2009). T Cell Receptor Signalling Inspired Kernel Density Estimation and Anomaly Detection. *LNCS, 5666,* 122–135.

Parish, C. R., & ONeill, E. R. (1997). Dependence of the Adaptive Immune Response on Innate Immunity: Some Questions Answered but New Paradoxes Emerge. *Immunology and Cell Biology, 75*(6), 523–527. doi:10.1038/icb.1997.83 PMID:9492188

Pathak, V., Dhyani, P., & Mahanti, P. (2011). Data Clustering with Artificial Innate Immune System Adding Probabilistic Behaviour. *International Journal of Data Mining and Emerging Technologies, 1*(2), 77–84. doi:10.5958/j.2249-3212.1.2.5

Porzak, J. (2008). Using R for Customer Segmentation. *useR! 2008.* Retrieved from https://ds4ci.files.wordpress.com/.../user08_jimp_custseg_revnov08.pdf

Prabha, D., & Ilango, K. (2014). A Rough Set Approach for Customer Segmentation. *Arabian Journal for Science and Engineering, 39*(6), 4565–4576. doi:10.1007/s13369-014-1013-y

Rinaldo, A., & Wasserman, L. (2010). Generalized density clustering. *Annals of Statistics, 38*(5), 2678–2722. doi:10.1214/10-AOS797

Sembiring, R. W., & Zain, J. M. (2010). Cluster Evaluation of Density Based Subspace Clustering. *Journal of Computing, 2*(1).

Stein, B., & Busch, M. (2005). Density-based Cluster Algorithms in Low-dimensional and High-dimensional Applications. *Second International Workshop on Text-Based Information Retrieval (TIR 05), Fachberichte Informatik,* 45-56.

Stepney, S., Smith, R. E., Timmis, J., Tyrrell, A. M., Neal, M. J., & Hone, A. N. W. (2005). Conceptual Frameworks for Artificial Immune Systems. *Int. Journal of Unconventional Computing*, *1*, 315–338.

Stoica, P., & Moses, R. (2005). *Spectral Analysis of Signals*. Prentice Hall.

Taylor, D. (n.d.). *Behavioral Segmentation*. Fuzzy Logix White paper series, Fuzzy Logix, LLC. Retrieved from http://www.fuzzyl.com/wp-content/uploads/Behavioral-Segmentation-Paper.pdf

Timmis, J., Neal, M., & Hunt, J. (2000). An Artificial Immune System for Data Analysis. *Bio Systems*, *55*(1-3), 143–150. doi:10.1016/S0303-2647(99)00092-1 PMID:10745118

Tome, T., & de Felício, J. R. D. (1996). Probabilistic cellular automaton describing a biological immune system. *Physical Review E: Statistical Physics, Plasmas, Fluids, and Related Interdisciplinary Topics*, *53*(4), 3976–3981. doi:10.1103/PhysRevE.53.3976 PMID:9964709

Witten, I. H., & Frank, E. (2005). *Data Mining- Practical Machine Learning Tools and Techniques*. Morgan Coffman Publishers.

Yao, Z. (2013). Visual Customer Segmentation and Behavior Analysis A SOM-Based Approach. Retrieved from http://www.doria.fi/bitstream/handle/10024/92542/yao_zhiyuan.pdf

Yu, S., & Dasgupta, D. (2008). Conserved Self Pattern Recognition Algorithm. *Proceedings of the 7th International Conference in Artificial Immune System (ICARIS)*.

KEY TERMS AND DEFINITIONS

Adaptive Immune Function: A random process of generation of B-type and T-type of lymphocytes that match to the antigens not absorbed by innate immune function. The dynamics of this layer is described using the *Clonal Selection* principle.

Clonal Selection Principle: The antibody molecules formed by random adaptations of pieces of gene segments to make unique receptors in a way to enable the cell collectively recognize unseen infectious organisms. The matching cells then multiply to absorb similar *antigens*.

Customer Behavior Classification: Mining of customer data available in the forms of transaction records, feedback forms, online reviews, replacement record, complaints, surveys, etc. in a way to determine groups based on vast range of criteria like geographical, psychological, professional, economical, and occasional segments.

Danger Theory: A deviation from the earlier immune function principle of self-nonself recognition, which instead suggest eventual generation of a sequence of signaling termed *danger signals* as a result of distress caused by the unabsorbed foreign organisms. These signals stimulate the various immune systems cells to adapt and kill or absorb the antigens.

Dendritic Cell Algorithms: Simulation of the selective function of the *Dendritic Cells*, that, according to the danger theory, convey danger signals from the innate immune cells to stimulate the evolutionary adaptive immune function.

Innate Immune Function: Immune function wherein the pathogens bypassing the physical and physiological barriers are absorbed by the special blood proteins called *Complement*, and is therefore capable of identifying the foreign organisms as *self* and *non-self*.

Mixture Model: In statistics, a mixture model is a probabilistic model involving mixture distributions for representing the presence of subgroups within given dataset, each subgroup assumed to be associated with particular probability distribution.

Non-Parametric Model Estimation: Methods of unsupervised model estimation in absence of any guidance or constraint required as input, for example, the Expectation Maximization, Kernel Estimation, Nearest Neighbor Learning, Non-parametric Regression techniques, Self Organizing Maps etc.

Non-Parametric or Infinite Mixture Models: Mixture models in which the number of subgroups or categories is unbounded. The best known example is Dirichlet Process.

Chapter 7
Blue Ocean Strategy:
A Necessity Prescription for Companies

Akansha Bhargava
Institute of Management and Research Nagpur, India

ABSTRACT

The purpose of this conceptual paper is to introduce one of the controversial issues in the business world which is labeled blue ocean strategy, this study also highlight blue ocean`s barriers like imitation and emulation. Brief comparison between competitive environment (Red Oceans) strategy and blue ocean strategy and also importance of role of management in using blue ocean strategy to increase return for the firms are issues that explained. The review of the research contains role of innovation and its value for this strategy to help the firms survive in competitive market. First movers and second fast imitators also are the issues that in this study explain about their advantages and disadvantages in brief comparison.

1. INTRODUCTION

Issues like how the businesses transform their model is the completely new approach in driving value creation and push the firms to gain lucrative increase of sales activity, in this era role of management in increasing return for the firms, are subject that most of the firms are willing to figure out. Treating the whole company or firm to use purposeful guide for recruiting new strategy, with no doubt can protect the firm among competitive environment which is very popular these days. Provides a mostly

DOI: 10.4018/978-1-5225-2234-8.ch007

animated approach to assess how flourishing companies are able to create business model changes that underlie the creation of totally new value Offers in the market by recruiting new strategy (Kim, Mauborgne et al., 2008).Competitive strategy and the Blue Ocean Strategy Both draw attention to the importance of companies to avoid strong competition. Strong competition is that we called red oceans that are bloody due to this strong competitive environment. To avoid in the context of competitive strategy, as all know competitors have so many resource-based view of the firm, that have to implement some limitation for the resources to decrease simulation and creating sustainable competitive advantages and earnings increase. Of course, over time, it is always possible for other companies to provide a unique resource (Burke, Van Stel et al., 2009).

2. COMPETITIVE STRATEGY IN COMPARE OF BLUE OCEAN STRATEGY

During the past 25 years most of emphasizes were on competitive strategy and some part of this portion is because the main organizational strategies were very dependence on their roots which were protection strategy. In army science, strategy means to face and defense to a competitor which has a specific area and position, so the main current strategies also are based on this definition. The market would consider as a specific area where the firms are trying to achieve more customer to increase their returns and this action has nothing unless one firms would get a high return and other would face in disasters situation that face them to vanish from the market (Burke, Van Stel et al., 2009).

Although competitive aspects are very important for the firms but keeping more attention to this issue will make the firms become far away another attributes which is creating a new market that there is no competitor in that and makes competition meaningless, this is exact meaning of Blue Ocean strategy (Buisson and Silberzahn, 2010). Assume that global market is divided by two parts: Blue Ocean and Red Ocean. Red ocean defines the whole businesses that exist and they are known area of market. In the red ocean all the boundaries and limitations are obvious and also the play law which is using in the market is very clear. In red ocean firms try to perform the best to achieve much more return for their firms due to this fact that red ocean market is very crowded being lucrative is very hard, to make story short this competitive environment has made it so bloody and gain profit is very hard for firm to achieve (Parvinen, Aspara et al., 2011). To add more, in red ocean strategy there are some parameters that play significant role for existing in business like cost, competition and price, and competition should be suitable and good enough for expanding the companies' services and products.

Differentiation is another competitive advantage that makes a lot of cost because companies compete with the same practice rules (Chang, 2010).On the other hands Blue oceans are those industries which have not yet been defined, those which are not exit currently. Blue Ocean is a place with no competitor in it (Totally new market); therefore this environment is a place with high potential of getting lucrative and profitable return for those firms which create it. In addition we should consider that competitive environment does not exist in this market (Burke, Van Stel et al., 2009). Researchers believe that building Blue Ocean is not a static progress, it is dynamic. When a firm has competitive advantage, and its better performance shows all the things imitators show themselves in market. Studies prove that a good blue ocean strategy is the one that is hard to imitate. The factors which influence on cost structure and value proposition and value innovation are firm's action and strategy. It is obvious that the most powerful value innovation, will cause the least imitation, and also prevent imitators to enter market. Figure 1 illustrate that blue ocean strategy should raise the value and driving down costs, and there is win-win strategy for sellers and buyers. While a profit objective is reached value is accomplished. This approach shows that Functional and operational activities of firms are influenced by blue ocean strategy."Value innovation is something more than innovation" .It is something that is all about activities and strategies which companies try to achieve value and add value for their customers (Chang, 2010).

3. FIRST MOVERS AND THE SECOND FAST IMITATOR

First mover in the business and in the theory are those who have settle a business very fast and have brought innovation and extraordinary attributes which rarely have seen in the market, but in practice it means being first to do. In this case Gilbert/ Birnbaum-More (1996) have recommend to use early movers instead of that (Cleff and Rennings, 2011).These firms have three major advantage in compare of second movers that are: technological leadership, preemption of physical or spatial asset and buyer switching cost On the other hand those firms who called second mover or late mover typically are those which enter to the market after first mover. These firms are those who imitate and copy the innovation this attributes have three major advantages which are: simply to free ride on first mover investment, technological development or customers need and leapfrogging (Cleff and Rennings, 2011).

Being first in a new market and setting up a strong differentiation strategy make firm to show something special in compare of the other markets, firms can create lucrative and profitable return for that market shortly. It is creation of new demand in market to increase its profit by using that strategy which called Blue Ocean. Almost in the executive countryside, contends, on the contrary, that companies should

Figure 1. Value innovation: the cornerstone of blue ocean strategy (Chang 2010)

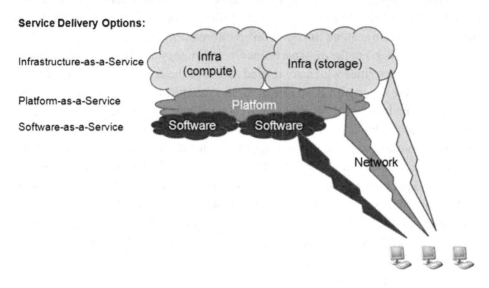

not try to become pioneer, but should rather objective the newly created market in second situation (Markides, 2010). An analysis on studies shows that until the mid of 1980 the most common think about the first movers was that those firms are the only market pioneers which can protect long live market share advantage (Cleff and Rennings, 2011).

4. IMPLEMENTING BLUE OCEAN AS A NEW BUSINESS MODEL IDEA

The perception of blue ocean strategy, base on Ansoff's generic market development strategy, even though, it brings in new perspective to by referring to market redefinition, as a substitute an alternative of simple traditional market-making. On the other hand this subject increasing the customer potential. In other words, "the difference between market-making and market redefinition is that the second movers are those who focused on novel value conception logics despite of the fact that change in customer statistics and also review the first movers` movement."Blue ocean strategy thus introduces the concepts of a) establishment and amusement of new business models, b) creating market space by redefinition and c) scientific improvement enabling new earnings logics to classical market progress in business strategy"(Parvinen, Aspara et al., 2011).

Fundamental altercations in any of these core processes may generate unexpected triumph in the marketplace relative to competition. Blue ocean strategy (Kim and Mauborgne, 2005b) can be linked to this reinforcement as an explanation of these radical approaches. For the most part Blue Ocean Strategy and business model uprising focuses on activities which are related to sale of the company. Additionally, we suggest that the successful Blue Ocean Strategy manifests as applications of overhaul prevailing logic by Vargo and Lusch (2004, 2006) and service business model prose generally. Blue ocean can be use as new model method to enhance the firm`s return due to the new environment that it create for itself. Marketing strategy for it offers a numberless of realistic remarks, but shortage of scientific data has always existed in this criteria. Using some tool like PDM, SCM and CRM are some suggestion that can use to exploit creating competitive advantage. Degree of recruiting and implementing blue ocean strategy is also important matter that cannot ignore, in business world. As a crystal cut example, level of the model that the firms are looking for, is a subject pricing model of ICT companies to represent the tactical core of value creation and economic logic in terms of revenue generation and to the managerial decision-making system that as shows face to some barriers in the way of implementing new strategy (blue ocean strategy) (Parvinen, Aspara et al., 2011).

The requirement of disturbance in business model change has also been verified in the contexts of vertical incorporation, diversification and new-product, new-market combinations. In these contexts, business model transformations are considered to take place in a networked context, by knowing the changing is the need of transforming structures. If the basic foundation of resemble business model prose, the conjectural basic concept of blue ocean idea could stanch from value creation theory in terms of business model changing (Moller, Rajala et al., 2005).

"Blue ocean strategy thus contributes through at least five central perspectives to business model thinking (Parvinen, Aspara et al., 2011);

- Process, evolution (vs. outcome-orientation)
- Radical recreation
- Managerial cognition
- Market space redefinition (different from market-making)
- Technological innovation"

5. BLUE OCEAN STRATEGY AND MANAGERIAL ROLE IN IMPLEMENTATION

Blue ocean strategy itself in sale shows as a method of increasing profitable growth of the firms by creating new demand that there is no competitor for that. Blue ocean strategy will face the managers to some problems such as how do these theoretical ideas come to real world and can enhance the returns? Or how should this new strategy implement through the business? Below are some answers about the most common question related to blue ocean strategy? Reinforcing the strategy is the main issue for the manager to think about. Potential innovation is the most vital factor that should the manager concern about. Sales question, staffs guide programs developing and cooperation is the next step of Blue ocean strategy implementation. Manager should think that whether they can be to recruit people and attract them to this new strategy. If their current service provider can respond to the market needs. During this implementation, changing management is also would occurs in most of the firms (Parvinen, Aspara et al., 2011). Put into operation this new strategy needs practical changing through its market. To some extend approaches through business such as technology innovation, market recession and also evolutions in markets links very suitable with sales management and some criteria's of business model. On the other hand managers should be aware of exercises and development which are related use and implement with blue ocean strategy. Implementing blue ocean strategy needs suitable tied staff with practical ability not knowledge, being deep in practical activities would help the firm in sudden change in strategy, change salesman positions and renegotiating point contracts due to downstream organic vertical integration can be mentioned as practical activities. Emphasizing on leadership and leading meetings, Instead of general attributes of management should be considered. Cognitive capacity is always limited by time shortage in managers view, recruiting blue ocean strategy with decision making process will enhance the quality of the firm much more (Parvinen, Aspara et al., 2011).

6. GLOBAL CURRENT TRENDS

In industries which are tending to grow, current pattern of competition is more focus on innovation. As we all see firms nowadays not only want to be more competitive but also being innovative is also noted in their future programs, beside tend to stability rather than change is also another subject for the firm that they may think about their firms` future and this may face them to some limitation(Cleff and Rennings, 2011). Although these constrain and so many conservatives' actions views that nowadays repeatedly was out by the news and reports, they seemed a little change of mode of developing is considering recently. However, several books on strategic perception have emerged that share an interest in the main factor for the firms is that to know and to understand how to innovate and distinguish the current situation to recruit innovation and entrepreneurship to make evolution in their business or company. As an illustration; airlines industries have done so many minor and major competitive option which passenger may want or desire or increase their facility during fly for them, but the only thing that may differ them among each other is certain factor which is innovation and creation.

7. BUILDING BLOCKS OF BLUE OCEAN STRATEGY

The building blocks of blue ocean strategy are

1. Value Innovation.
2. Tipping point innovation.
3. Fair process or 3E principles – engagement, explanation, clarity of expectations.

In blue oceans, demand is created rather than fought over. There is ample opportunity for growth that is both profitable and rapid. In blue oceans, competition is irrelevant because the rules of the game are waiting to be set. Blue ocean is an analogy to describe the wider, deeper potential of market space that is not yet explored.

So what's the status of Blue Ocean Strategy in India ? If we go through some cool startups which are life changing ones, we could see the strategy. I would like to share a few of them.

1. Naukri.com which was founded by Sanjeev Bikhchandani. Considering the platform and time of birth of Naukri, Mr. Sanjeev had many other options to do or start-up with and enters into the competition world. But Naukri was a way different stuff. Naukri.com was found on 1997 – days which internet wasn't that popular in India. Naukri.com entered the uncontested market space with a different business strategy of that time and we all know the status now!
2. *Subhiksha*, the rapidly grown retail chain in South India (may be India) founded by R Subramaniam. Subhiksha was founded during the days which it was difficult to find all the stuffs we require at a single place! With a different kind of thought and execution Subhiksha grew with 1600 outlets selling groceries, fruits, vegetables, medicines and mobile phones etc. Even though everything winded up in 2009, still Subhiksha is known for its startup and glory!
3. Varkeys Supermarket, from the God's own Country Kerala. The Varkeys Supermarket is the first and leading supermarket chain in Kerala. The stores and its concepts have played a vital role in revolutionizing the tastes & shopping patterns of the people of Kerala. Providing all the needs of a household under one roof, it has made its mark as a "single stop shop" for its customers.

8. CONCLUSION

The principles that drive the successful formulation and reconstruct market boundaries, focus on the big picture, not on numbers, reach beyond the existing demand, and get the strategic sequence right. It identifies the path by which you systematically create uncontested market space. It shows how to design a company's strategic planning process go beyond incremental improvements. It shows to maximize the size of the blue ocean and lays out the design of the strategy. With no doubt ability of the firm to compete to each other has been become entangled with entrepreneurship and belief that innovative ideas are the only way to sustain each firms or companies 'business in the market pushes them to work on this key success factor.

REFERENCES

Buisson, B., & Silberzahn, P. (2010). Blue Ocean Or Fast-Second Innovation? A Four-Breakthrough Model To Explain Successful Market Domination. *International Journal of Innovation Management, 14*(03), 359–378. doi:10.1142/S1363919610002684

Burke & Van Stel. (2009). *Blue Ocean versus Competitive Strategy: Theory and Evidence*. Academic Press.

Chang, S. C. (2010). Bandit cellphones: A blue ocean strategy. *Technology in Society, 32*(3), 219–223. doi:10.1016/j.techsoc.2010.07.005

Kim, W. C., & Mauborgne, R. (2008). *Blue ocean strategy: How to create uncontested market space and make the competition irrelevant*. Harvard Business School Press.

ADDITIONAL READING

Andersen, P. H., & Strandskov, J. (2008). The innovators dilemma: when new technologies cause great firms to fail/leading the revolution/blue ocean strategy: how to create uncontested market space and make the competition irrelevant. *Academy of Management Review, 33*(3), 790–794. doi:10.5465/AMR.2008.32465791

Chapter 8
Client–Centric Cloud Service Composition

Vivek Gaur
BIT Mesra Jaipur, India

Praveen Dhyani
Banasthali Univerisity Jaipur, India

Om Prakash Rishi
Kota Engineering College, India

ABSTRACT

Recent computing world has seen rapid growth of the number of middle and large scale enterprises that deploy business processes sharing variety of services available over cloud environment. Due to the advantage of reduced cost and increased availability, the cloud technology has been gaining unbound popularity. However, because of existence of multiple cloud service providers on one hand and varying user requirements on the other hand, the task of appropriate service composition becomes challenging. The conception of this chapter is to consider the fact that different quality parameters related to various services might bear varied importance for different user. This chapter introduces a framework for QoS-based Cloud service selection to satisfy the end user needs. A hybrid algorithm based on genetic algorithm (GA) and Tabu Search methods has been developed, and its efficacy is analysed. Finally, this chapter includes the experimental analysis to present the performance of the algorithm.

DOI: 10.4018/978-1-5225-2234-8.ch008

INTRODUCTION

Consumers of web based services continuously search for new and innovative approaches to increase service utility and gradually can minimize their costs. Technologies are required, which can maximize their profits using best available services at minimum expenses. Cloud computing has emerged among one of the potential solutions for delivery of on-demand services in a pay-as-you-go manner. Cloud computing provides customized service selection capability and customers pay only for what they use. Most of the companies are switching their services to cloud platforms. The merits of cloud computing include resource sharing, rapid elasticity, cost effectiveness and measured service. It also attracts more and more enterprises and service providers to provide their services through cloud computing models.

Cloud computing can be defined as an Internet-based computing, which usually offers the dynamically scalable and virtualized resources as their services. There are different definitions for clouds. As reviewed by (Mell and Grance, 2011), National Institute of Standards and Technology(NIST), Information Technology Laboratory defines it as a model which provides a convenient way for user to make on-demand access to a configurable pool of shared resources (e.g., computing, applications, storage, and services) and which can be easily provisioned and managed.

Cloud Computing has become an encouraging platform for delivery and consumption of scalable services in the area of service computing. Cloud services are designed to facilitate on demand services in a way to improve scalability, self-configurability, performance, robustness, and flexibility. According to the National

Figure 1. NIST Cloud Definitions

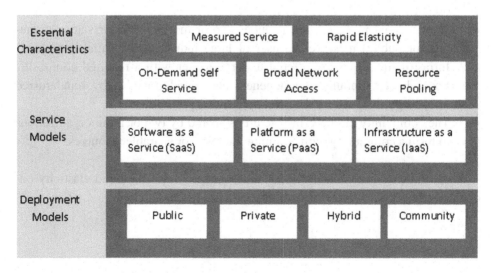

Institute of Standards and Technology clouds can be classified according to their service types, deployment models and essential characteristics as shown in Figure 1. There are three types of service models namely, Infrastructure as a Service (IaaS), Platform as a Service (PaaS) and Software as a Service (SaaS).

- Infrastructure as a Service (IaaS) includes the storage, processing, networks, and other resources. The user can deploy and execute software including operating systems and other application programs. This enables the user in easily managing on-demand access to scalable virtualized resources as a service. Microsoft's Azure, IBM, Amazon, are examples for IaaS.
- Platform as a Service (PaaS) covers resources through a platform which facilitates the user to create applications or deploy acquired applications onto the cloud, using different provider supported programming languages. Force.com, Google App Engine, Windows Azure, are the examples for PaaS.
- Software as a Service (SaaS) enables the user to run applications on the service provider's Cloud Infrastructure. Sales force, Google Docs, G-mail are examples for SaaS.

National Institute of Standards and Technology, Information Technology Laboratory offers four deployment models: private, public, community and hybrid. They are briefly explained as follows:

- Private cloud infrastructure is exclusively for an organization where all the services are operated and offered within an organization.
- Public cloud infrastructure can be used by any general user, enterprise, and organization in public and is managed and controlled by service providing organization.
- Hybrid cloud infrastructure includes two or more clouds (private, community, or public) to serve the user or large industries. The multiple clouds Infrastructure types are offered to serve a user with a required composite. Each cloud maintains its uniqueness but bounds together by standardized technology that achieve data and application portability.
- The community cloud infrastructure is shared by two or more organizations to form a community with common interests for sharable resources.

Essential characteristics of clouds are measured services, rapid elasticity on-demand self-services, broad network access, and resource pooling.

Figure 2. Cloud Service Coordination

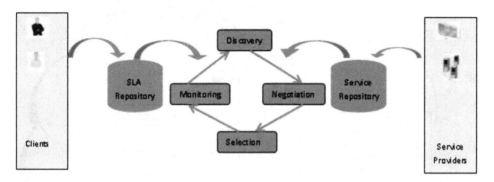

- Measured service is the metering facility of cloud systems that automatically control and coordinates to optimize resource use (e.g. bandwidth, storage, processing).
- Rapid elasticity means the capability of unlimited extendable services and can be requested at any time.
- On-demand self-service means that user can provision services as per requirement unilaterally.
- Broad network access means to encourage accessibility to the services and resources over the network by heterogeneous thin or thick client platforms.
- Resource pooling means to serve consumers with heterogeneous physical and virtual resources requirement by pooling the computing resources and reassigned dynamically according to the demand.

A cloud service- coordination model as shown in Figure 2 consists of four phases, namely discovery, Service Level Agreement (SLA) negotiation, selection, and SLA monitoring. In the service discovery phase, user requirements serve as an input for discovering the best-suited cloud services among various repositories of cloud providers. For SLA Negotiation, service providers and the user negotiate on the quality of services. An SLA contract comprises from a set of made agreements. Then, continuously monitors the acquired services in the SLA monitoring phase.

Most of the clients have their individual priorities for the different quality parameters such as reliability, response time etc. Therefore, the optimal service composition requirement is also different for every user. Such restrictions encourage building a framework that determines the composition of services matching best to the user objective.

As the Cloud Computing is gaining popularity, finding the optimal combination of services that are relevant to the user query becomes a necessity. The main reason behind it is that the need for a particular type of service is user dependent. The

Figure 3. Multiple Service Model

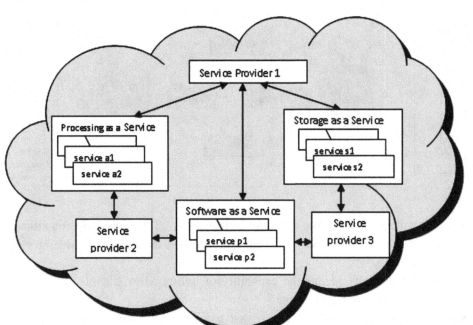

generic search engines like Google, AltaVista, and MSN etc) are available tools for searching URL's for generic user queries but they are not designed to reason about the relations among the different types of Cloud services and determining which service(s) would be the best or most appropriate service for meeting consumer's service requirements. The Figure 3 depicts the cloud environment where multiple functionally equivalent service providers exist to serve the client. A client requesting for storage service may be served either by service provider 1 or provider 3 each having different service values as a1, a2... s1, s2...p1, p2. In such case user need to distinguish and select services based on QoS parameters such as price, reliability, response time, throughput etc. Every user has different priorities so the different services can be used in conjunction to create a new QoS based service composition to fulfill client's requirement. Therefore, an efficient tool is needed for responding to the user cloud service requirement with QoS combination in a cost effective manner and with high relevance. The required QoS values are well recorded in a formal document called Service Level Agreement (SLA) as a contract between the service provider and end-user as defined by (Alrifai, Skoutas and Risse, 2010).

The QoS aware service combination selection aims to determine the best combination of cloud services candidates that satisfies a set of user constraints as per given SLA. The selected service composition is the one which maximizes the user related utility function. In case of multiple attribute type used for optimization the selection problem becomes a multidimensional optimization problem.

On the basis of the fact that the priority and weight-age for QoS attributes, such as price, response time etc. can vary with respect to end user demands, the task of prediction of optimal user-centric service combination has gained popularity. A number of service selection approaches have been proposed in their research by (Cardellini, Casalicchio, Grassi & Lo, 2007; Goscinski and Brock, 2010; Ardagna and Pernici, 2007; Hwang, Lim, Lee and Chan, 2008; Yu, Zhang and Lin, 2007; Alrifai and Risse, 2009, and Bhama, 2011). However, none of the approach fully responds to all the aspects of the user needs. The service selection system can be viewed as a collection of cloud services provided by different service providers, a collection of user requested service and method for determining the utility degree of services with respect to the user demands.

Most of the existing approaches emphasized more on the optimization of the selection methods to decrease the computation time and effective utility value of the service combination for the end user. QoS values for a service combination are usually determined by aggregated QoS values of the services provided by the various providers with different location and network. Based on the fact that the actual performance may vary dynamically thus end user must have a choice to accept or reject the service combination determined by the selection method. Further the sample space of service selection must be dynamic and the combination once not accepted by user must not participate in subsequent selection invocations for the user.

This work introduces a framework for QoS-based Cloud service selection to satisfy the end user needs. This chapter presents formulation of the problem as a QoS based service composition and presents the GA and Tabu search approaches for the problem. A hybrid algorithm based on genetic algorithm (GA) and Tabu Search methods has been developed, and its efficacy is analyzed. Finally, the chapter includes the experimental analysis to present the performance of the algorithm.

BACKGROUND

In the cloud computing environment, diversified services are delivered to the end user on pay-as-per use basis. A remarkable approach to address the service selection problem given by (Jaeyong, 2011) uses ontology- based matching and selects the services strictly according to the similarity reasoning. (Jaeyong, 2011) in his work "Towards Agents and Ontology for Cloud Service Discovery" used a cloud-based ontology to determine service utility. They suggested mainly three kinds of similarity reasoning methods: (1) concept similarity reasoning, (2) object property similarity reasoning, and (3) data type property, similarity reasoning. Similarly a service selection algorithm in view of cost and gains was proposed by (Wenying, 2009). Dastjerdi, Garg, Rana and Buyaa, 2014) proposed a framework called Cloud Pick to enable inter-cloud implementation mainly emphasizing on optimization of QoS model. A translator component for automatic semantic presentation of cloud services was proposed in their work resulting in better precision and recall of the discovered services, with advantage of multiple domain expressive QoS. They proposed two deployment optimization methods, one applying genetic algorithm (GA), and another applying Forward-Checking- Based Backtracking. The composition of virtual machine (VM's) was selected based on the QoS parameters such as latency, communication cost, and reliability among multiple clouds. Further, the deployment of VM's across the multiple cloud platforms and performance of the algorithms are evaluated based on the effects of factors such as latency between VM's, and reliability between appliances. The outcomes of the study presented the effect of data transfer rate between appliances on the efficiency of optimization algorithms. (Goscinski, 2010) proposed the attributes based provision of service discovery and selection which expresses the current status and characteristics of cloud services. (Ardagna and Pernici, 2007) introduced a new service composition selection approach based on optimization by loops peeling, QoS parameters negotiation and set of comprehensive constraints. Loop peeling involves removing of loop from the execution paths by rewriting the loop using branch conditions producing another execution path. The approach has limitation of generating redundant services with outsized search space as there is possibility of same service offered with different level of QoS by different providers. Hisham, (2015) considered the cloud service composition from consumer's point of view and addressed the problem using a GA based approach. The proposed approach is critically compared with other contemporary approaches such as Integer Linear Programming. (Yu, Zhang and Lin, 2007) proposed a heuristic solution which gives service composition with highest utility value among the random sample compositions, instead of searching for the best service composition exhaustively. Other similar approaches which proposed solution for selection of optimal service composition is the skyline service selection by (Alrifai, Skoutas and Risse, 2011), the dynamic service selection by (Alrifai and Risse, 2009) and heuristic service selection by (Jaeyong, 2011 and Silvana, 2012) presented a hybrid GA-Tabu approach. The basic Genetic Algorithm has restricted scope for further improvement because of its early maturity of the solution. The Standard GA is unable to maintain the diversity of population and local search ability of the conventional GA is not as effective. Therefore, population becomes premature and falls in local convergence early. The use of Tabu search approach is capable to get escape from trap of local optimality. As such, the Tabu search scheme memorizes and rejects inferior results in later runs of the optimization process. Tabu search is used to select the candidate service/ chromosome with the best fitness after the crossover and mutation operation by Genetic Algorithm. The approach increases the diversity of population and the span of the search space with further scope of optimized solution. In this chapter a heuristic service selection algorithm based on GA-Tabu search has been proposed. The presented approaches based on hybrid Genetic algorithm and Tabu search results in optimized service composition in general with no consideration for individual user's priorities for different QoS parameters.

Existing approaches also suffer from local optima problem which proves that the respective search algorithms are confined to a limited local sample space resulting in either the same or immediately followed results on every subsequent search. Moreover, these approaches lack the consideration of the clients' need for alternate service, based either on the personal or market experience in terms of reputation, service charges, service commissioning and other relates factors. Most of the approaches addressed the problem considering as providing the optimized service in general for the end user. The present work proposes a model that provides a user-centric service composition by allowing the user to assign the priorities in the form of weights for each QoS parameter related to each service.

CLOUD SERVICE DISCOVERY

QoS Based Optimization Criterion

Assuming the end-user considers the three service types S1, S2, S3 and four QoS attributes Price, Response Time, Reliability and Throughput with respect to the each service type. The optimization criterion is to maximize the reliability and throughput whereas to minimize the price and response time.

In the service composition, the candidate services (chromosomes) have different values of the QoS parameters. The fitness function F(C) in equation(2) used for finding the utility of the composition is similar to the work by (Yu, Zhang and Lins, 2007) where the minimum and maximum aggregated values of the ith QoS parameter of service composition C are computed as in equations (3) and (4).

$$F\left(C\right) = \sum_{i=1}^{n}\sum_{j=1}^{r}\frac{Q_j^{max} - W_{j,i}q_j\left(C_i\right)}{Q_j^{max} - Q_j^{min}} \tag{2}$$

$$Q_j^{max} = \sum_{i=1}^{n}Q_{i,j}^{max}F\left(C\right) = \sum_{j=1}^{r}\frac{Q_j^{max} - W_{j,i}q_j\left(C\right)}{Q_j^{max} - Q_j^{min}} \ , \ Q_{i,j}^{max} = \max_{\forall s_{ik}\in s_i} \ q_j\left(c_{ik}\right) \tag{3}$$

151

$$Q_j^{min} = \sum_{i=1}^{n} Q_{i,j}^{min}, \quad Q_{i,j}^{min} = \min_{\forall s_{ik} \in s_i} q_j\left(c_{ik}\right) \tag{4}$$

where, F(C) represents the overall utility of a composite service composition, i = 1 to n represents the service type (service1, service2, service3) and j = 1 to r represents the QoS parameters (price, response time, reliability and throughput) W_{ji} is the weight (0 to 1) assigned by the end user for j^{th} QoS of ith service. $Q_{i,j}^{max}$ are the maximum value of the jth parameter in all service candidates/ chromosomes of an ith service category, similarly $Q_{i,j}^{min}$ is the minimum value. Q_j^{max} is the maximum value of the jth parameter of a composite composition C and similarly Q_j^{min} is the minimum value. $q_j\left(c_{ik}\right)$ is the jth QoS parameter values for k^{th} candidate of ith service type. The values of the QoS parameters for a service composition are aggregated by the selected chromosomes / service candidates using the aggregation functions presented in Figure 4 as Table 1. In this work only sequential composition model is considered for aggregation similar to the work by (Wang, Zheng, Sun, Zou and Yang, 2011). The techniques presented by (Jang, Shin and Lee, 2008) can be used to transform the other models like parallel, conditional and loops to sequential model.QoS parameters can be partitioned into two types: constructive and destructive QoS parameters. Constructive parameters mean that the higher the parameter value is, the better the quality is (e.g., reliability, Throughput). Destructive parameters means higher the parameter value is, the inferior the quality is (e.g., price, response time). So the aim is to select the service composition which keeps the constructive parameters maximum and destructive parameters as minimum. There are other QoS parameters like availability and reputation also can be considered by (Wang, Zheng, Sun, Zou, and Yang, 2011) to form a part of service composition selection. The inclusion of the parameters (availability and reputation) needs the study of external factors like experience, previous performance history, SLA violation and market value of the service provider. In this work authors only consider the four attributes (price, throughput, reliability, response time) for the sake of simplicity.

User Interface and Algorithm Development

System Architecture

The Figure 5 depicts the proposed system architecture.

- **User Request:** End User request for a composition of cloud services.

Figure 4. QoS aggregation functions

QoS Attributes	Sequential Composition
Price	$q(c) = \sum_{i=1}^{n} q(c_i)$
Response Time	$q(c) = \sum_{i=1}^{n} q(c_i)$
Reliability	$q(c) = \frac{1}{n} \sum_{i=1}^{n} q(c_i)$
Throughput	$q(c) = \min_{i=1}^{n} q(c_i)$

Figure 5. General framework

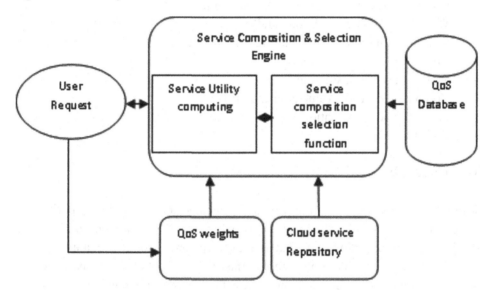

- **QoS Weights:** User specific priority values assigned for each QoS parameter.
- **Cloud Service Repository:** The Cloud service providers put all the functional and non-functional attributes of services in the repository.
- **Service Composition and Selection Engine:** Determines the utility of possible service compositions and selects the optimal one as per the weighted QoS requested by user.
- **QoS Database:** Contains the updated information for QoS parameters considered by the service providers.

Genetic Algorithm

Genetic algorithm is based on Darwin's theory of evolution and follows an evolutionary process. In Genetic Algorithm the chromosomes represent the candidate solutions and a set of solution is called as Population. New solutions (offsprings) are generated from the randomly produced population according to their fitness values. Better solutions are expected to be produced on every subsequent search with higher fitness value as suggested in work by (Bahdori, kafi, Zamani and Khayyambasi, 2009; Antonnio, Fernandez and Cartos, 2008 and Ahmed, 2014).

Steps required for BGA are as follows:

1. Randomly generate an initial population.
2. Compute the fitness of all selected solutions.
3. While terminating condition is false.
4. Select the solutions with higher fitness values to make new reproduction pool.
5. Crossover the selected solutions.
6. Mutate the chosen solutions.
7. Compute the fitness value after mutation.
8. Produce a new population.
9. End While.

Tabu Search

Tabu search is an improvisation of the basic local search method. The basic local search limitation is called the local optima which mean the search is confined to a local search space leading to degradation of the potential solution quality.

Tabu search makes a use of memory consisting of a list of recent search results that will not participate in selection process for next given N number of searches. This ensures that every time when function is called the searching will be done by exploring new search space as suggested in work by (Antonio, Fernandez and Cartos, 2008).

1. Quality of the solution depends on the fulfillment of the requirements and constraints according to the individual service preferences.
2. All the compulsory and optional constraint types are fetched to the method to evaluate the service quality.
3. Based on the individual's past experience of the related problem the method enables the dynamic tailoring to resolve and meet the specific constraints violations.

Client - Centric Service Composition Discovery Using GA-Tabu Based Algorithm

Service Composition Selection

Services with the identical functions and different QoS are escalating with the propagation of Service Oriented Architecture (SOA). It is required to identify and choose the best service composition from various schemas in order to meet the QoS requirement and optimize the satisfaction of users. The service composition is designed to compose the available services to generate a new value-added user centric service composition, which is one of the required features of web services.

This section presents the steps followed for selection of service composition with respect to user's QoS parameters and presents the overall design of the selection algorithm. It comprises of the reading of user input weight for each QoS parameter, definition of the GA_Tabu () function, call to the GA_Tabu () function, computes the fitness values of each candidate solution produced using GA_Tabu () function and then present the result to the end user.

Design of User-Centric Optimal Service Composition

The optimal service selection approach presented in our work uses genetic algorithm in conjunction with concept of Tabu-Search. The two important factors have been considered in designing the service composition selection algorithm. Firstly, since every individual user has different requirements and priorities for different quality issues therefore the each end-user is enabled to input the weight for different QOS parameters according to its own priorities. Secondly, the chance of getting caught in local -optima is handled using the concept of Tabu-Search.

The selection process ranks the alternative compositions on the basis of QoS parameters and user specified weight to each QoS parameter. The compositions form chromosomes for the GA. A Tabu-List is maintained to keep track of earlier compositions rejected by particular classes of customers. The flowchart and scheme of interaction for the proposed framework is depicted in Figures 6, 7 and 8 respectively.

Function GA_Tabu ()

```
        /*Input Service Candidates: (Options X 4): 4 relates to
the QoS parameters namely: 1. Price, 2. Response Time, 3. Repu-
tation and 4. Throughput, suppose there are 3 service-elements
namely: 1.Storage 2.Software 3.Processing and Suppose no. of
```

Figure 6. Flowchart for service composition selection function

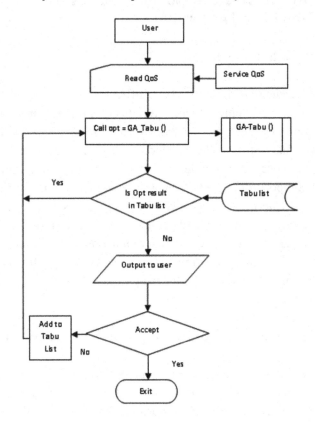

associates for each service element are: 1.Storage=10, 2. Software = 5 3.Processor: 4 */

/*TABU_LIST: List of compositions rejected ('Tabu') during Service Composition presentation to user; NULL on first execution.*/

/* Initialize GA*/

1.   Initialize 'Population' of size N_p- i.e. N_p number of chromosomes each represented as a vector of length N_s containing a combination of service vendor from each service category.

2.   W=Get User's weight for each QoS parameter to use in fitness computation.

3.   Repeat Steps (3-6) until specified no. GA iterations

4.   Compute Fitness of each chromosome using *(1)* to compute Utility.

5.   Determine the Best Rank chromosomes to fill the re-

Figure 7. Admin-sequence diagram

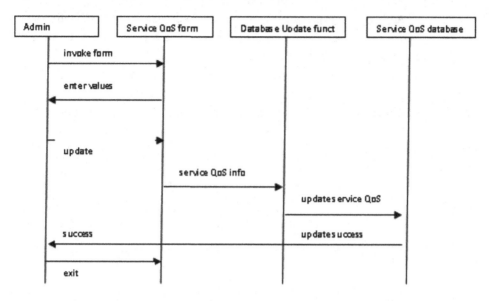

Figure 8. Composition Generation Sequence diagram

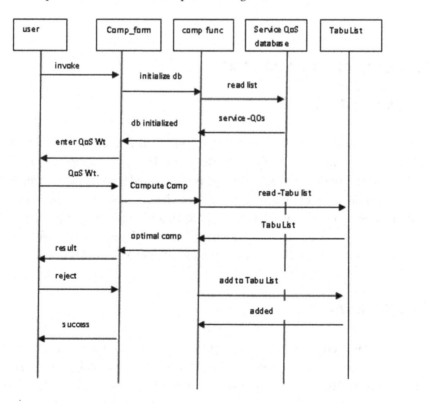

production pool of size ReprodPoolSize.

6.   Apply Single-random-point crossover over the chromo-somes in the reproduction pool and generate chromosome-population of size N_p for next iteration.

7.   Apply mutation operation over each chromosome in population checking as per given mutation probability.

8.   On completing the GA iterations BEST_COMP = Compute fitness of each chromosome using Equation (1) and get the Best Rank chromosome.

/* Now Apply Tabu*/

9.   If (Match_in(BEST_COMP, TABULIST))

10.   Goto step 1

11.   Else Present the BEST_COMP to user and ask for Se-lection/Rejection.

12.   If Rejected

13.   Enter BEST_COMP into TABULIST

14.   Goto Step 1

15.   Else

16.   Display Success and Exit.

SIMULATION AND ANALYSIS

Simulation Setup

In this experiment, authors use a randomly generated dataset that contains the values of four QoS parameters, namely Price, Response Time, Throughput, and Reliability.

The number of different service type is considered three (i.e. Storage, Software, Processing) and the number of service candidates per service type varies from 1 to 10 as shown in tables as Figure 9, Figure 10 and Figure 11. respectively. All the experiments are conducted on a computer system with Intel(R) core(TM) i7-3632QM CPU @ 2.20GHz, 8.0 GB of RAM, Windows 8 and Matlab 7.6.0.

RESULT ANALYSIS

The experiment conducted on the input QoS values for three services (service1: storage, service2: software, service3: processing) as shown in Figure 12 The output service composition 6, 4, 1 as shown in Figure 13 represents the composition of 6th

Figure 9. Storage service

Service\ QoS	Price (rupees)	Response Time (seconds)	Throughput (0-1)	Reliability (0-1)
S1	6594.5	0.3	0.7	0.5
S2	2549.4	1.6	0.1	0.1
S3	5093.5	2.0	0.4	0.7
S4	8642.4	4.4	0.1	0.9
S5	6520.0	4.1	0.9	0.0
S6	0908.3	4.8	0.5	0.7
S7	6196.0	2.3	0.1	0.2
S8	2225.2	1.3	0.0	0.3
S9	8724.8	3.3	0.0	0.5
S10	3487.4	3.7	0.5	0.5

Figure 10. Software service

Service\QoS	Price (rupees)	Response Time (seconds)	Throughput (0-1)	Reliability (0-1)
S1	2395.1	59	0.7	1.0
S2	1822.8	55	0.2	0.6
S3	2937.4	79	0.7	0.5
S4	3472.2	11	0.3	0.9
S5	0578.4	61	0.2	0.8

Figure 11. Processing service

Service\QoS	Price (rupees)	Response Time (seconds)	Throughput (0-1)	Reliability (0-1)
S1	0341.6	9.3	0.2	0.0
S2	1414.1	1.7	0.1	0.1
S3	1117.6	8.7	0.4	0.1
S4	1663.1	0.2	0.5	0.1

storage service, 4th software service and 1st processing service having the highest utility value with respect to the user input QoS values for different service types as depicted in Figure 14. In case the user rejects (Tabu) the output composition (e.g. 6, 4, 1) then the result is added to the Tabu-list and new composition is determined excluding the current result. The Figure 15 and Figure 16 shows the new service composition (8, 2, 4) and the respective utility-iteration plot.

The utility plot (Tabu2) shown in Figure 17 is generated by increasing the number of services from 3 to 10. The plot shows the utility value 3.99 (approx.) which is better than utility values 3.92 and 3.927 of the earlier generated compositions (6, 4, 1) and (8, 2, 4).

- The above results show that the most suitable service composition is determined efficiently incorporating the user-given-weights to the QoS parameters corresponding to each of the services.
- A QoS-based Cloud service composition selection incorporates user's priority of each individual QoS parameter e.g. response time, cost, throughput, reliability.
- The service composition is determined using a hybrid algorithm based on the genetic algorithm (GA) employing Tabu Search based local optimizer to determine a service composition that suits best to the user QoS requirements.
- The experimental results show that the model performs better in terms of determining user- centric QoS based service composition.

Figure 12. QoS input values

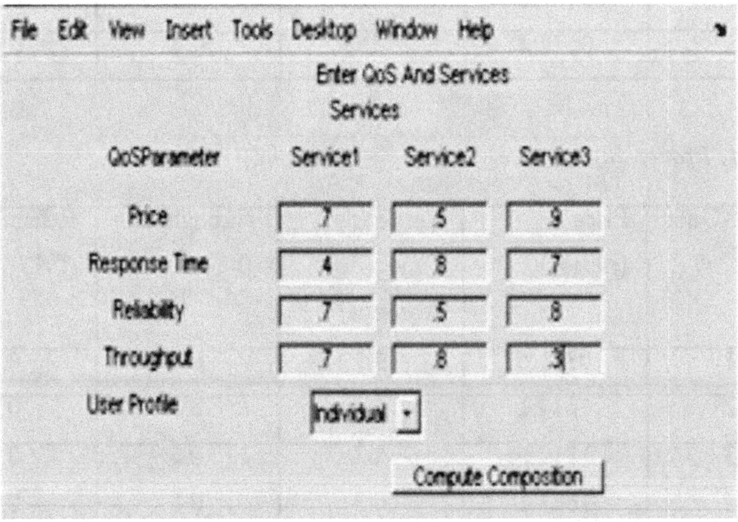

Figure 13. Output composition

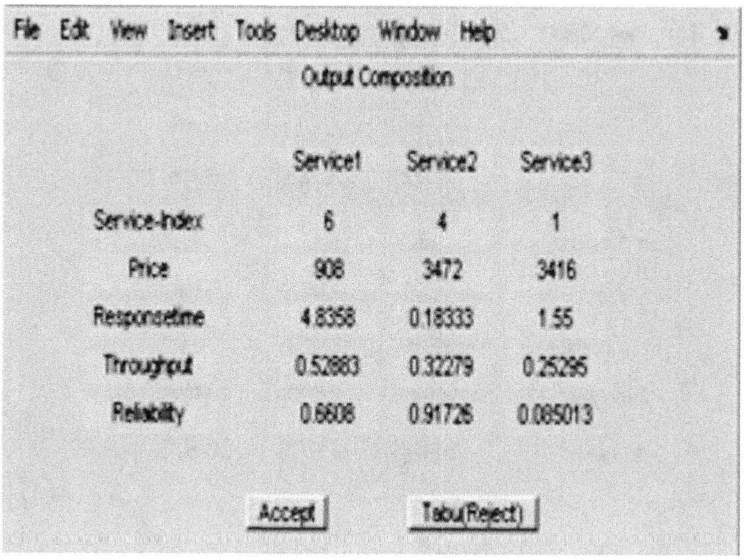

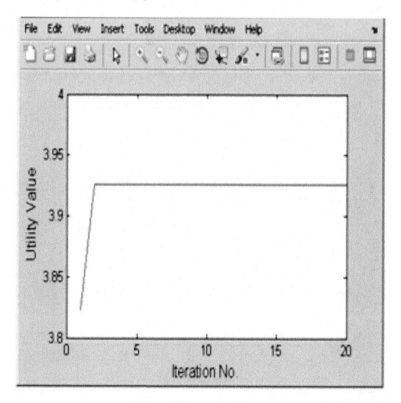

Figure 14. Composition utility plot

Figure 15. Composition on Tabu1

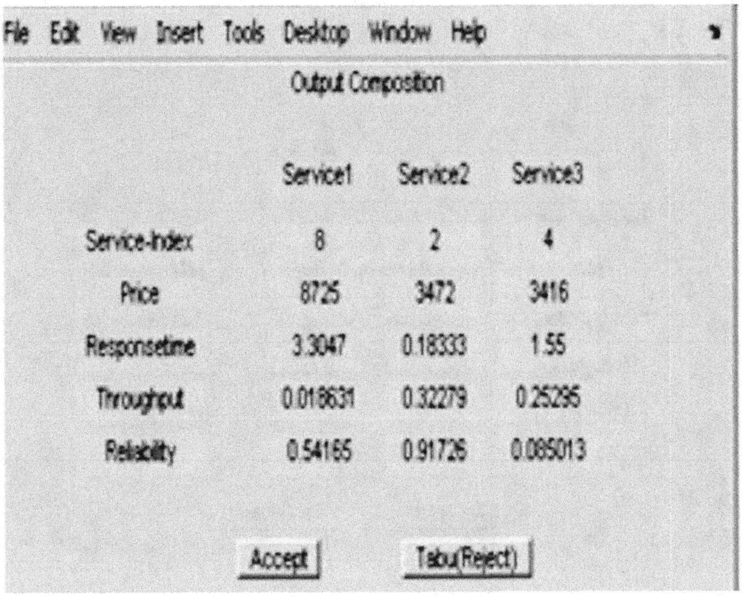

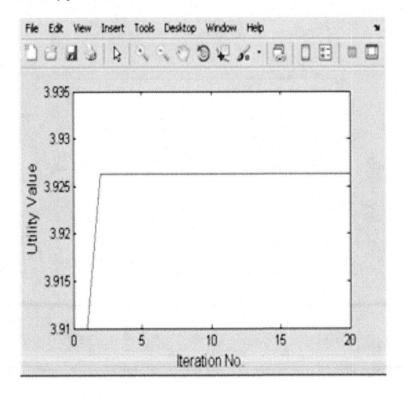

Figure 16 Utility plot (Tabu1)

Figure 17. Utility plot (Tabu 2)

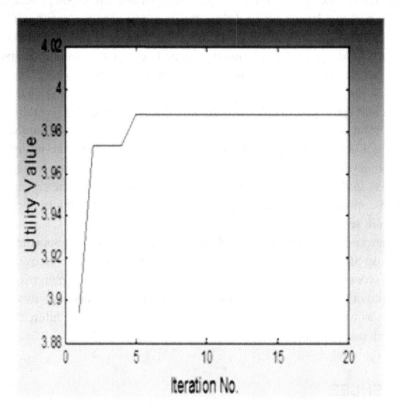

- The models also show the scalability property as it performance in terms of utility value increases with increase in the number of candidate services.

CONCLUSION AND FUTURE DIRECTIONS

Several industrial solutions for facilitation, specifically of software as a service (SaaS) over resource sharing environment of multi-cloud computing or internet of things do exist. The composition of services required to complete an intended business process is determined from among the available service providers form each component of the business process. A service level agreement (SLA) is established, which includes besides other specifications, the constraints in terms of certain quality of service (QoS) parameters for each service. However due to several reasons, eventually, one or more service components might violate the QoS-constraints. In such cases a suitable substitution of appropriate service component is required. The study presented a user-centric framework for QoS based Cloud service selection problem that considers the end-user's priority of each individual QoS parameter. The problem is addressed using a hybrid algorithm based on genetic algorithm (GA) and Tabu Search methods. The blending of genetic algorithm with a Tabu search as local optimizer is used to improve solution quality and determine a service composition that suits best to the user QoS requirements. GA's are observed to have a limitation of resulting only the best solution found in the final iteration, while intermediary iterations still could produce better outcome. This limitation can be addressed by applying Tabu-search based local optimal search strategy while performing repro-duction pool generation during the general steps of basic GA. The utility of this work is observed in the face of existence of industry level solutions competing to find market in the domain of cloud based service sharing, and the research level algorithmic model development approaches, as presented in the introduction and related work section.

It is also observed that such tool could also store the information about the services which cause SLA violation or those which gets rejected during service adaptation evolution process. This information may then be used to learn the patterns of viola-tion and provide prescriptive guidelines to the service providers, thus serving both the clients as well as the service providers. This work is seen as a future extension of the work presented in this chapter.

REFERENCES

Ali, A. F. (2014). *Genetic local search algorithm with self-adaptive population resizing for solving global optimization problems*. I.J. Information Engineering and Electronic Business.

Alrifai, M., & Risse, T. (2009). Combining global optimization with local selection for efficient QoS -aware service composition. *Proceedings of the 18th International conference on world wide web*, 881-890. doi:10.1145/1526709.1526828

Alrifai, M., Skoutas, D., & Risse, T. (2010). Selecting skyline services for QoS-based web services composition.*Proceedings of the 19th International conference on World Wide Web*, 11-20. doi:10.1145/1772690.1772693

Antonio, P.J., Fernandez, P., & Cortes, A.R. (2008). QoS-aware services composi-tion using Tabu search and hybrid genetic algorithms. *Actas de Tallers de Ingeniera del software y Bases de Datos*, 2(1), 55-66.

Ardagna, D., & Pernici, B. (2007). Adaptive service composition in flexible pro-cesses. *IEEE Transactions on Software Engineering*, *33*(6), 369–384. doi:10.1109/TSE.2007.1011

Bahdori, S., Kafi, S., Zamani, K., & Khayyambashi, M. R. (2009). Optimal web service composition using hybrid GA-TABU search. *Journal of Theoretical and Applied Information Technology*, *9*(1), 10–15.

Bhama, S. (2011). Realizing the need for similarity based reasoning of cloud service. *International Journal of Engineering Science and Technology*, *3*(12).

Cardellini, V., Casalicchio, E., Grassi, V., & Lo, F. (2007) Flow-Based Service Selection for Web Service Composition Supporting Multiple QoS Classes.*Proceedings of the 5th IEEE International Conference on Web Services (ICWS)*, 743-750. doi:10.1109/ICWS.2007.91

Dastjerdi, A. V., Garg, S., Rana, O. F., & Buyaa, R. (2014). Cloud Pick: A Framework for QoS -aware and ontology- based service deployment across Clouds. *Software, Practice & Experience*, *00*, 1–34.

Goscinski, A., & Brock, M. (2010). Toward dynamic and attribute based publication, discovery and selection for cloud computing. *Future Generation Computer Systems*, *26*(7), 947–970. doi:10.1016/j.future.2010.03.009

His ham, A.K. (2015). QoS Optimization for Cloud Service Composition Based on Economic Model. *Lecture Notes of the Institute for Computer Sciences, Social Informatics and Telecommunications Engineering, 150*, 355-366.

Hwang, S.Y., Lim, E.P., Lee, C.H., & Chen, C.H. (2008). Dynamic Web service selection for reliable web service composition. *IEEE Transactions on Services Computing*, *1*, 104-116.

Jaeyong, K. (2011). Towards Agents and Ontology for Cloud Service Discovery. *Proceedings of the International Conference on Cyber- Enabled Distributed Computing and Knowledge Discovery*. IEEE Computer Society.

Jang, J. H., Shin, D. H., & Lee, K. H. (2006). Fast quality driven selection of composite web services. *Proceedings of the 4th European Conference on Web Services*, 87-96. doi:10.1109/ECOWS.2006.21

Mell, P., and Grance, T. (2011). *The NIST definition of cloud computing (draft)*. NIST special publication, vol. 800, pp. 145.

Silvana, A., & Karim, D. (2012). A QoS Optimization Model for Service Composition. *The Fourth International Conference on Adaptive and Self-Adaptive Systems and Applications*, 24-29.

Wang, S., Zheng, Z., Sun, Q., Zou, H., & Yang, F. (2011). Cloud Model for Service Selection, Workshop on Cloud Computing. *IEEE INFOCOM*, 677 - 682.

Wenying, Z. (2009). *Cloud Service and Service Selection Algorithm Research. In GEC Summit* (pp. 1045–1048). ACM.

Yu, T., Zhang, Y., & Lin, K.J. (2007). Efficient algorithm for web service selection with end-to-end QoS constraints. *ACM Transactions on the Web, 1,* 1-26.

KEY TERMS AND DEFINITIONS

Composition: A service combination comprised of the user requested candidate service instances.

Genetic Algorithm: An evolutionary process to generate better solutions from the randomly produced population according to their fitness values.

Quality of Service (QoS): Parameters such as response time, throughput, reliability and price of the user requested service, defines the quality of service.

Repository: A database of the available service published by service providers.

Service Level Agreement (SLA): A contract between the consumer and service provider comprised of the agreed service details signed by both the parties.

Tabu Search: Maintain the diversity of population and is capable to get escape from trap of local optimality.

Utility: Defines the fitness value of the composition as per the user QoS requirements.

Violation: The breach of the agreed service quality parameters by service providers results in violation.

Virtual Machine: Interface provides masking over the heterogeneous service environment.

Chapter 9
Internet Finance

Marta Vidal
Complutense University of Madrid, Spain

Javier Vidal-García
University of Valladolid, Spain

Stelios Bekiros
European University Institute, Italy

ABSTRACT

New developments in the Information and Communications Technology industry have substantially increased the importance of the internet over the last decade. As a result, the finance sector has developed its technological capability to be able to compete in an online marketplace with other financial services providers and to be able to serve their customer. This chapter examines the use of technology in the financial industry and the various factors associated with it, as well as introducing the reader to the main types of project initiators-contributor business relations in online crowdfunding.

INTRODUCTION

E-Banking also written as electronic banking refers to the usage of computers in carrying out bank transactions. Examples of such transactions include withdrawal of money through cash dispensers or engaging in funds transfer through a point of sale. Electronic banking is also known as internet banking or online banking (Ainin, Lim & Wee, 2005). Therefore, this illustrates the complex nature of the concept of

DOI: 10.4018/978-1-5225-2234-8.ch009

financial services as there is not a universal definition of E-banking. However, it is significant to note that internet or E-banking refers to the use of various electronic services that allow a financial account holder with a particular bank to access all his or her information through a computer. Therefore, in the context of this discussion E-banking will be defined as a self-service activity that permits bank account holder to get access to their accounts, as well as their updated general information on a financial institution's products and services. In addition, these users have the liberty of conducting financial transactions without time or geographical limitation by accessing the bank's website (Kallstrom, 2000, p. 20).

The technological advancement and the use of the Internet have raised a new platform for fundraising known as crowdfunding. Crowdfunding involves three parties: the project initiator or owner who needs funding, the contributor who is willing to give their money and the moderating organization that facilitates the engagement between the contributor and the initiator (Young, 2013, p. 33). Moderation can also be done through technology by the project initiator himself, using Web 2.0 and outside of platforms. The platform involves entrepreneurs or potential business owners asking for funding for their projects from the "crowd" or users from all over the world who may be interested in supporting their cause or business. Crowdfunding allow individuals the possibility to develop into their business ideas, even if it is only with a small amount of money. Governments encourage crowdfunding due to its positive impact on the economy as a whole, as it creates new jobs and fosters the economic growth of countries.

This chapter seeks to introduce the reader to e-banking services, online investments, and the main types of project initiators-contributor business relations in online crowdfunding.

BACKGROUND

In the late 1970's home banking was the only way of offering financial products without the customer being present at the banking hall (Xu, Wikes, & Shah., 2006, p. 19). Financial institutions call this service home banking; however banks offer this service through phones.

Banking customers were able to transfer money, pay their invoices or check their account credit through touch-tone telephone while they were at home. New software was created that permitted connecting customer to the bank through a dial-up connection. Although in the late 1980s this service was not very popular for several reasons. First, home banking was only allowed for some services agreed by the bank. Second, this new service needed an important investment in technology, and only few financial institutions could afford this cost.

The use of computers was not common at the time in many households (Lao-podis, 2013, p. 26). Among the financial institutions that offered home banking services are the leading banks like Citibank, Manufacturers Hanover and Chase Manhattan. All of them had its origin in America, thus showing the contribution of the United States to the e-banking industry. In the mid-1990's banks were starting to realize the need to move their financial services into the virtual realm. Apparently, e-banking was becoming an attractive concept as it helped banks diminish transaction costs; it was helpful in promoting easy integration of services as well as introduced interactive marketing capabilities. Additionally, online banking was instrumental towards boosting the bank's customer lists and profit margin faced by the businesses. Furthermore, internet banking allowed institutions to bundle their services into single packages; thus, attracting more customers at minimal overheads. The period of late 1990s saw the advent of the clicks and bricks euphoria; as a result, many banks realized that e-banking was a strategic and imperative innovation (Lassar, Woodford, & Moschovitis, 2005, p. 15). More so, during this period there were a lot of mergers and acquisitions within the financial industry that resulted in expanding customer base Therefore, financial firms viewed the World Wide Web as the only channel that would help in maintaining customers, as well as build loyalty. However, in the wake of the banks realizing the potential of e-banking a lot of customers across the globe remained hesitant to conduct their financial transaction over the internet. For example, there was the Y2K scare that was a disambiguation about a world crisis by the year 2000. In this connection, many customers feared online transactions because of the fear that all computers would fail. Therefore, to avoid this problem a number of financial consumers were reluctant to move into the virtual world of financial service provision. Companies such as America Online, eBay and Amazon.com invested in marketing purchase of items through online platforms. For example, Bank of America took about 10 years to reach 2 million e-banking clients. In 2009 as per a report by Gartner Group, at least 47 percent of American adults were banking online.

Computational investing is another topic that provides insights on investing and stocks. It includes a collection of theories that have effectively been used as strategies for investing. For instance, John Bogle's passive investment approach recommends that entrepreneurs should allocate resources to assets that have minimum trading expenses. The reason for that is that active involvement in market-stock trade cannot match the returns of the market (Laopodis, 2013, p. 32). In other words, Bogle advocates for a long-term view approach to investing – one should pay attention to taxes and costs. Therefore, according to him, a well-diversified portfolio is an assortment of low-cost assets that have been in the market for a considerable number of years. That is, investors should adopt a buy-and-hold strategy.

Another theory of computation investing is value investing. According to Warren Buffet, who developed the idea, investors should exercise discipline, intelligence, and patience in relation to buying stock (Laopodis, 2013, p. 32). In other words, the entrepreneurs should purchase shares of reputable companies only.

MAIN FOCUS OF THE CHAPTER

1. E-Banking

Internet banking allows access to financial information through accessing internet over a computer or by use of mobile phone that has Internet connection. Mobile banking is the latest revolution in virtual banking, it involves conducting financial transactions via a mobile device; for example, a mobile phone or tablet. The introduction of mobile banking led to new methods of payments by using a mobile phone to pay for commodities or services remotely. The first form of mobile banking was referred to as SMS banking. However, the invention of smart phones has overtaken SMS banking and now users of the internet-enabled mobile phones can use various applications based on the operating system to carry out financial transactions. There has been a remarkable growth in the number of households using virtual banking services. Population born between 1970 and 1990 also referred to as the generation Y embrace technology very fast once it comes to the market. Generation Y account for the highest number of users of online billing services to settle their account on student loans, credit cards and expenditures aimed at improving their lifestyle for example shopping online. Noteworthy, e-banking is highly entangled in every individual way of life without discriminating against age or those with disabilities (see Friedman (2000)).

Internet banking offers various services depending on the bank of choice for each customer:

Account Opening and Access Information

Banks that provide e-banking services allow their clients to open new accounts by accessing the bank's website. In order to complete this service, an individual logs in into the bank's website, fill an application online and submit the application. Afterwards, an account holder with online banking services enjoys the opportunity of accessing financial information wherever they are with an Internet connection. Such information may include closing or opening accounts, checking updates as well as make inquiries captured in the account or even making payments.

Electronic Check Conversion and Transfer of Funds

Electronic check conversion allows customers to convert their paper check to a new electronic payment. Essentially, the benefit of electronic payment is that the account holder with a bank can withdraw money from their account and wait until the other party receives the check. This service is faster as the normal check takes longer duration to process. Customers can also transfer funds across personal accounts and to different users as a way of covering the shortage in some accounts or make payments.

Download Online Bank Statement

Clients can go through this document because it allows one to check even the previous year transactions so as to make sure accounts are in order (Lassar et al., 2005, p. 24). In the event of complaint, users can save their bank statement either as word or as PDF on their computer, tablets or smartphone for future evidence.

Buy Financial Products

E-banking allows clients of the bank to buy financial products online. Examples of such products may include deposits, stocks, mutual funds and mortgages. The bank products vary across different financial institutions.

Buy Good Online

Users of online banking benefit from the ability to login into their accounts and to buy goods online or make payment to their credit card. Nowadays, it is easy to buy goods online safely and quickly or simply make enquiries; therefore, saving on travel costs and time.

Order for a Check Book

This is a booklet of blank checks that facilitates bank account holders to draw money from their account or deposit funds for the purpose of settling other company accounts or payment of bills (Lassar et al., 2005, p. 30). These checkbooks can be ordered online by e-banking service users, they receive the booklet through their mail.

Make IRD Payments

IRD refers to the income that an individual is not entitled to receive during his or her lifetime. Such payments include IRA or other retirement schemes that an account holder cannot receive before death. The amount of IRD payments is not part of the final income tax return. This service is now available through internet banking, and it is easy to process all information an individual may need pertaining to IRD payments electronically.

Tax Information and Documents

Financial institutions assist their customers to complete several tasks such as offering tax documents online. Additionally, the banks help their clients to fill and submit the forms online. Overall, a financial firm helps in resolving tax related issues and usually this service is available to the customers free of charge.

Alerts

An account holder with the access of internet banking can subscribe to receive alerts of every processed transaction by the financial institution. Consequently, the service will inform the customer about the existing bank account balance, and introduction of new products and transactions completed.

The Importance of E-Banking

The main important characteristic of internet banking is significant time management, elimination of queues due to the automation of most financial services and availability of easy maintenance tools for managing one's money. E-banking offers cheaper costs of attaining banking services and increased comfort. With regard to the latter, customers are able to make financial transactions any time of the day, and without physical interactions with the bank.

Another characteristic of e-banking is rapid and uninterrupted access to information. For example, business firms can enjoy easier access to information by checking on multiple accounts at the tick of a button. In addition, internet banking allows for better management of cash by speeding up cash cycles and increasing efficiency of business transactions since numerous cash management tools are available on the World Wide Web. For instance, it is possible to manage a firm's short-term cash through internet banks in money market funds, in commercial papers, in over-night deposits, or in bonds and equities (Appei, 2009, p.7).

Furthermore, e-banking allows a customer to enjoy the convenience of carrying out financial transactions from the comfort of his or her office or home. The fact that e-banking allows a rapid response enables customers to wait until the end of a financial transaction without any fuss about it. Finally, internet banking allows for effective management of funds. Customers are allowed to download their account history and fund analyses on their computers or mobile phones before carrying out any actual transaction.

2. Benefits and Challenges of E-Banking

E-banking has transformed the provision of financial services around the world (Liao, Yuan, & Chen, 1999, p. 66). Financial institutions as well as customers obtain certain benefits from using e-banking as compared to the conventional method of banking.

Online banking allows account users to make payments across accounts to just about anyone. For example, client of the bank can choose anybody or any company whom he or she wants to make payments to and the bill pay service will facilitate this transaction.

Internet banking gives the account holder the liberty to control almost every aspect of his or her account. Besides this control over personal or business bank accounts, the customer can access other services within the financial industry (Liao et al., 1999). For example, buy or sell interest-earning assets, keep an update on stock market and money market. It is imperative to mention that accessing internet banking services on the bank's website is free, the only requirement is being an account holder with the entity and have access to the internet.

Customers enjoy the benefit of comparing best deals across banks and get access to the best special offers. Often individuals operate more than one bank account; therefore, it is easy using e-banking services to compare products offered by different banks. E-banking service allows bank account holders to access the financial institution on a 24 hours basis (Krantz, 2013, p. 19). Automated teller machines, and access to their bank account through the internet is convenient to the clients. Virtual banking is beneficial to customers because this system helps bank account holders to avoid queues common in banking facilities. Many of the customers who use online banking feel that this system saves time unlike when they spend time queuing in banks.

Internet banking contributes to a reduction of operational costs in the financial Institutions. In the long run commercial banks save on resources that would be paid to the tellers to manage the growing customer base in the bank. Therefore, it is relatively cheap to conduct financial services over the internet for the banks. Virtual banking has allowed banks to acquire a greater customer base through reaching new target markets (Liao et al., 1999). Precisely, the use of internet surmounts any geographical boundaries that would be difficult and expensive to break when using traditional banking systems. Interestingly, the banks use internet to reach the well-off households as internet penetrates highly in households that have a sustainable income. E- Banking reduces the costs affiliated to marketing especially with the introduction of internet marketing, helping to create a similar playing field for small and big banks. Therefore, the upcoming financial institutions can fight for survival through competing for customer base in the same market with the successful banks (Liao et al., 1999). Otherwise, it would be impossible for the small financial firms to compete with the leading companies through the traditional systems of marketing because of capital and market power challenges enjoyed by the big banks.

There has been a significant change in the level of efficiency in commercial banks after the introduction of e-banking. Use of internet in banking facilities allows the firms to operate in a paperless environment. For example, it is easy to keep records within a single file for a huge number of clients. The level of customer service and satisfaction continues to improve remarkably with e-banking systems. Principally, this improvement is attributed by the levels of efficiency in banks. In addition, internet banking offers the customers services that would be difficult to access through bank's branches (Liao et al., 1999). Online banking contributes to a reduction of the number of people visiting the facilities daily; therefore, improving on customer service both online and offline. Using e-banking services helps a financial entity to improve its public image by giving a good impression to existing and prospective customers. Noteworthy, an account holder may not be willing to use e-banking system, but by providing such services a bank helps in promoting a good reputation to the prospective and current customers.

Internet banking is beneficial to the stakeholders in the financial industry. Banks and customers enjoy extensive benefits by using this modern way of accessing financial information and products (Sarlak, & Astiani, 2011, p. 29). However, there are certain concerns or challenges that arise in the use of internet banking. Firstly, with the introduction of this new technology by the commercial banks there is a need to create a customer service support system that will provide support to the clients. Commercial banks face the challenge of maintaining a fast and reliable customer support system in a bid to protect their reputation as well as image in the market. Establishing such systems is costly but it is important towards getting the customers to trust internet banking as a way of undertaking financial transactions. Secondly, laws governing different countries present an interesting challenge to e-banking. Internet banking cannot be limited within a geographical location or borders (Lassar et al., 2005, p. 45). However, each country or state has different laws that are distinct and are not applicable in territories beyond where the laws are enacted. Therefore, there is a need to harmonize some laws pertaining to electronic banking worldwide so as to ensure access to financial information and products is not restricted. Thirdly, the issue of security over the internet is another challenge that continues to affect online banking. In fact, this is one of the challenges for banks as customers inquire know the level of security or protection that virtual technology offers to them before they proceed to open online banking accounts. Internet technology attracts online cyber-crimes, and often bank customers become victims of fraud or theft especially with the use of ATM's (Lassar et al., 2005, p. 45). Hacking and phishing of financial information is an emerging trend and a challenge that banks deal with every financial year. Fourthly, internet banking creates regulatory challenges because of globalization of the financial industry. Internet allows provision of services from any location in the world posing a danger in regulation of financial intermediaries by the central bank. Inherently, commercial banks will find ways to avoid any supervision or regulation by the relevant authorities. For example, it is mandatory for every business to acquire a license from the government; similarly, financial institutions have to establish a licensed branch before they are granted permission to venture into virtual banking (Marina, 2009, p. 4). Fifthly, internet banking has led to increased activities of money laundering Anonymity is one of the features evident with electronic banking. A client opens an account in a bank, but it is difficult for the financial entity to identify the type of business the nominal account holder is undertaking or even the location of the transactions. Presently, many governments have put up guidelines to combat money laundering. For example, it is mandatory for every individual opening a bank account to verify their identity and notify the bank of their residential address (Marina, 2009, p. 6). Finally, online banking poses serious macroeconomic challenges to the country's economy. For instance, the technological revolution in the finance industry particularly the advancement of banking practices makes it difficult for central bank to implement monetary policy. Consequently, it is always a challenge for the central bank trying to control economic activities and inflation especially with the globalization of financial services. In essence, expansion of electronic banking leads to a significant decline in financial transaction costs. Consequently, this leads to cheap credit in the economy hence eroding the effectiveness of monetary policy. Tobin tax is an example of a tool used by many governments towards controlling availability of credit in the economy especially it helps to increase costs of accessing financial products from the banks by the borrowers.

3. Investing Online

Some of the concepts discussed in Modern Investment Theory and computational investing are useful to stock brokers, especially when opening an online account. A stock broker is an individual or company that trades in shares on behalf of a client. If the interaction between the client and the broker is through a website, the broker is referred to as an online broker. The online service allows the investor to allocate some funds to the brokerage firm for the purchase and sell of stock. Normally, the transactions occur on order basis, that is, the client must request the broker to buy or sell profitable shares. Apart from trading in shares, a significant number of online brokers also provide other support services such as tax reporting, creation of financial statements, and so on. Optionally, an investor may decide to do the online trading independently. That means the entrepreneur will need to open an online stock brokerage account. To succeed in such a venture, the entrepreneur must consider several factors.

Firstly, the investor needs to acquire a portfolio tracking tool, which is a set of online tools that provide information on the trading of stock. Hence, the tool allows investors to keep a close eye on the performance of their stock while shopping for additional profitable investments. The portfolio tracking tool can be treated as an additional expense to the cost of opening an online brokerage. However, an effective method would be to treat portfolio tracking as a support service provided by an online broker (Hart, 2005, p. 36).

Secondly, transaction costs are incurred in operating the online brokerage account. Normally, the online broker that hosts the independent stockbrokerage account charges a specific amount for each transaction executed. In other words, an online broker may provide the portfolio tracking tool at a low cost, but charge the investor highly per transaction (Hart, 2005, p. 42).

Apart from that, some hosts charge for stop-sell order requests. Therefore, investors should take time to compare the charges of different hosts to ensure that they get value for their money.

Thirdly, the type of account matters. Often, investors have the option of opening either an individual retirement account (IRA) or retail account. Before opening an IRA, the entrepreneur should consult a tax advisor because some of the transactions done through the account are taxable. For instance, if a transfer of funds is done from the investor's IRA to an online broker's IRA, there are no tax penalties or consequences. However, taxes apply if the investor withdraws money from an online brokerage IRA. Conversely, transferring funds to a retail account has no tax implications. Similarly, the purchase of stock through the use of funds in the retail account has no tax implications. However, the income from the stocks sold through the account is taxable (Hart, 2005, p. 50).

Additionally, investors expect returns in form of dividends from companies in which they own shares. The dividends may be scrip dividends or dividend reinvestment plans (DRIP). For the investors that subscribe to the scrip-dividend policy, the expected cash returns are automatically converted to new shares. Conversely, for those in DRIP, the cash dividends are first sent to a scheme administrator who then may use the funds to acquire the company's shares through the stock market or send the money to the stakeholders. Therefore, before opening an online account, the investor should consider the reinvestment service offered by the host (Hobson, 2012, p. 15).

Also, the investors need to determine the means through which they will fund their online brokerage accounts. Firstly, capital may be sourced from savings. In this case, keeping money in bank accounts yields low annual interest. Depositing the money into an online brokerage account will result in better cash benefits. Secondly, the IRA is also a source of funding. In this case, the funds can be transferred from an existing IRA to the online brokerage IRA mentioned earlier. Thirdly, the investors can opt to make direct deposits. In this regard, the cash-in-hand that they possess should be greater than or equal to the bare minimum required to open the online brokerage account. Given that the option will force the entrepreneurs to develop a working plan on how to make regular deposits into the account, discipline is required (Hart, 2005, p. 55). The investors can obtain additional hard cash from gifts, financial assets converted to money, extra income, refunds, and so on.

Therefore, before opening an online brokerage an account, one must consider several things. These include the type of account to be opened, transaction costs involved, and customer service. The investor should also take into account how the online brokerage shall be funded, the cost of the portfolio tracking tool, and the dividend re-investment policy provided. Once these queries have been addressed, the next step is to open an online brokerage account (Hart, 2005, p. 57). In reference to that, it is worth noting that managing a profitable stock investment portfolio requires thorough knowledge of ways of investing.

4. Trading Stocks and Options Online

Online stock trading is another important subtopic of investing and stocks. This type of trade is to some extent similar to regular transactions that involve one walking into a shop, picking the required items, paying for them, and leaving. That is, the online traders select the shares they prefer and electronically transfer the sum required for the purchase. Once the money is received, the sale is reflected. However, online trading has some complications because the prices of stocks are set in real time (Krantz, 2013, p. 129). Thus, the online investors have to use the following options in trading through the internet.

Firstly, customers can trade their stocks online through market orders. In this case, they have to instruct their stock brokers to sell their stock. Normally, the brokers are requested to sell the shares at the highest price that a willing customer is ready to pay. As a result, such orders are quickly executed (Krantz, 2013, p. 129). Given that it is easy to find such willing buyers, the online investors pay a small commission for the brokers' services.

Secondly, stocks can be traded online through limit orders. In this case, the online investors are allowed to set the prices at which they are willing to purchase or accept the sale of stock (Schwartz, 2010, p. 156). For instance, consider an entrepreneur who owns 40 shares, each valued at $100. Suppose the price of the stocks is declining and hence the investor estimates that soon the value of a share will plunge to $70. In this case, the online investor can sell the shares in two ways. The first option is through the market order, which was discussed above. However, that may not give the best returns since the buyers may momentarily offer lower prices than the projected minimum. Optionally, the online investor could set the lowest selling price at $85 to minimize losses. Thus, so long as the decline proceeds as expected, the limit order is the preferable alternative. When the shares' price falls to $85 per unit, the broker will sell all stocks if possible. Limit orders are not based on price alone. Some investors give a deadline within which to sell the stocks (Krantz, 2013, p. 129).

Sometimes, one may not obtain the returns expected after the sale of shares through the limit orders. This is because the shares' price may decline so rapidly that the seller is unable to place the stocks on sale at the agreed price. In this case, the broker may only sell a restricted number of stocks. The rest of the shares are kept in the investor's portfolio. Thus, the limit orders provide a false sense of security.

Online investors can also use stop market orders to trade online. This type of order is similar to a limit order in that a minimum buying or selling price is set. However, for the stop market orders, when shares' price reaches the designated value, the orders are converted into market orders (Krantz, 2013, p. 130). For instance, using the previous example, the broker may be instructed to execute a stop market order when the stocks' price reaches $85. In this case, if the value of shares suddenly plunges to $80 per unit, the online broker would still have to sell the shares at that price.

Fourthly, the shares can be traded through a stop limit order. This option is similar to a stop market order. However, once the defined price is exceeded, the stop limit order is converted into a limit order (Krantz, 2013, p. 130). Thus, the stop limit order prevents the sale of shares if the value of the stocks falls beneath the limit price. To elaborate further, still using the same example, suppose the activation price for selling stocks is $85 and the limit value is $75. When the shares' value falls below $85 per unit, the order becomes a limit order. Hence, when the price reaches $75, the broker is supposed to sell every available stock at that price (Krantz, 2013, p. 130). However, a further decline in price would result in no sale at all. That is, the remainder of stock is kept in the online investor's portfolio.

Lastly, the online stocks can be traded through a trailing stop. This type of order basically follows the market. For a favorable market, rising stock prices, the online investor instructs the broker to retain the shares until the value of the securities reaches a predetermined value. This order is referred to as a trailing sell stop. For a bearish market, the broker is expected to sell the shares as the stocks' price approaches a set minimum value (Pardo, 2008, p. 85). This order is known as an exit trailing stop. Thus, the online investors continuously search for positive yields during the stocks' transaction life.

Apart from stocks, options can also be traded online. An option is a financial instrument that gives one the right to sell or purchase a precise quantity of underlying stock at a prearranged price within a defined time period. The option seller is not legally obliged to carry out all the tasks stipulated in the contract when the financial instrument is handed over to a buyer. The online trading of options is done through screen-based or electronic methods. In the United States of America, there are several institutions – exchange companies – that specialize on options trading. They include the International Securities Exchange (ISE), Boston Options Exchange (BOX), and NASDAQ. The online trading of options has advantages as well as prerequisites that are worth discussing in details (Fontanills & Cawood, 2009, p.43). The online trading of options yields more benefits to the online investor than full-service or traditional brokerage. For example, for this type of trade, commission expenses are lower. That is, the traditional broker may charge $100 for a round turn, whereas an online brokerage charges only several dollars (Fontanills & Cawood, 2009, p. 45). In this case, a round turn refers to each deal or sale. Normally, a commission cost is charged on all orders. The charge applied varies depending on the service being offered. Also, the commission expenses decrease as the services offered to the investors increase. Another advantage of the online trading of options is that the online investors receive considerable support in terms of information as opposed to what happens in traditional brokerage.

5. Online Crowdfunding

A new startup needs some amount of funds in order to get the business started. In order to transform the entrepreneurial project into a reality, then it is necessary to have adequate cash to execute all such plans. Moreover, the fundraising will help the entrepreneur to develop the business model for the growth of the project and a successful business marketing plan (Damos, 2014, p. 32).

The technological advancement and the use of the Internet have raised a new platform for fundraising known as crowdfunding. Crowdfunding involves three parties: the project initiator or owner who needs funding, the contributor who is willing to give their money and the moderating organization that facilitates the engagement between the contributor and the initiator (Young, 2013, p. 33). Moderation can also be done through technology by the project initiator himself, using Web 2.0 and outside of platforms. The platform involves entrepreneurs or potential business owners asking for funding for their projects from the "crowd" or users from all over the world who may be interested in supporting their cause or business. Crowdfunding allow individuals the possibility to develop into their business ideas, even if it is only with a small amount of money. Governments encourage crowdfunding due to its positive impact on the economy as a whole, as it creates new jobs and fosters the economic growth of countries.

This chapter seeks to explain the main types of project initiators-contributor business relations in online crowdfunding.

The term crowdfunding is a relatively new concept to the market, however its origin comes from the construction of the Statue of Liberty's Pedestal. John Pulitzer, who was a popular publisher at the time, employed his newspaper to collect money for the construction of the pedestal. The initiative raised 100.000 dollars in only six months. Pullitzer promised to print the name of each donor, regardless of the amount of money donated. In August 1885, Pulitzer announced that he had collected the amount to $100.000 for the statue's pedestal. The Statue of Liberty, that had arrived from France packed in crates, was erected the next year. (See Young, (2013)). Nowadays, Crowdfunding is becoming is already very popular around the world and the Internet platforms are leading the rasing of funds.

In 2013, Crowdfunding raised over 5.1 billion dollars to help people in various projects all over the world and the figure is projected to increase in the future with the new platforms becoming more popular (See Crowdfunding Industry Report from Research firm Massolution). The new law of the Jumpstart Our Business Startups (JOBS) by President Obama in 2012 introduced a regulatory framework. Most of it still has to be translated into active regulatory elements to this date, protecting donors to crowdfunding projects and enabling businesses to use crowdfunding as a real source of funding. The Act enhanced the credibility of the platforms for crowdfunding while at the same time ensuring that the project owners or entrepreneurs had a viable and a good source of funding for their projects. Kickstarter and Indiegogo are some of the most popular platforms boasting of members in millions of all parts of the world, these websites have enough people to pool huge amounts of resources for the funding of their businesses.

There are different types of relations between project initiators and contributor in online crowdfunding:

Reward-Based Crowdfunding

The reward-based form of crowdfunding is the most popular type with most contributors and initiators preferring this method due to the security of their funds under this method (See Crowdfunding Industry Report from Research firm Massolution, 2014). In reward-based crowdfunding, the target amount has to be established first for the completion of the project (Steinberg, 2012, p. 97). Then, the person or organization sets up donation amounts with an attached incentive that is proportional to the amount donated for the project. This method is hugely popular for artists, movie directors and other projects that have an aesthetic or prestigious value to the donor. For instance, if an artist was looking for a donation to help with a tour of Europe, he may offer signing autographs to people that will contribute $500 and backstage preparation with the cost to people contributing $1.000. These incentives ensure that the enthusiasts and the music lovers are motivated to donate to the cause (Young, 2013, p. 79). One of the unique characteristics with this method is that if the set platform allows for the project owner to get the amount only after the targeted amount is reached, he/she cannot be awarded the amount collected in case the donors do not raise all amounts. The donors can therefore get their money back and they have the confidence of recovery of the raised amount as a result (Agrawal, Catalini, & Goldfard (2015)).

One of the major benefits of reward-based crowdfunding is that it has low risks for the promoter or the company that is behind the campaign to raise funds or donated amounts. Once a company has raised the required amount for the project and they may have had the donations only with a special clause for the specific project they are able to avoid dealing with debts, credit implications or interest that is attached to the loans or government grants (Bruntje, & Gajda, 2016, p. 45). The reward-based crowdfunding method offers the chance to completely avoid all these problems and start their business or project without any possibility of future shortcomings due to any changes in the plans or the success of the project. The reward-based method also runs on low cost with the project owners being offered a chance to showcase their projects for only a small fee of their total collection and there are no high costs of managing the platform. As opposed to raising money through other conventional methods, where a person could end-up incurring a lot of costs for setting up the funds, crowdfunding sets this up at only a small fee and the project is viewed and supported by millions from all over the world (Roebuck, 2011, p. 104). The reward-based method also offers the donors a chance to gain a personal connection with the project they have donated towards and the people they have funded.

Equity-Based Crowdfunding

Equity-based crowdfunding is a form of crowdfunding where the contributors become part-owners of the company raising funds. Equity-based is not a popular form of crowdfunding since the majority of the projects are not huge companies that donors and people funding the projects can get a stake and own part of (Douw, 2012, p. 60). Most of the projects are by entrepreneurs who do not have shares that the investors can invest in. However, since the enactment of the Act in 2012 this form of crowdfunding has gained popularity with most people seeing it as an investment opportunity for the interested investors in lucrative projects that the investors deem to pick up and be beneficial in a near future. This is offered at very low rates as compared to the market rate since the project owners will need to make their proposal and project attractive to the potential investors through their competitive prices and growth potential in the future (Douw, 2012, p. 60).

Equity-based form of crowdfunding is slowly catching up with the other methods of crowdfunding. It is, however, a safe and viable method to raise money for the company and beneficial for the donor if the company makes profits in the future and they gain from the dividends or distribution. Equity-based crowdfunding can also be used to create a venture finance market. Equity crowdfunding does not only involve the shares as the only forms of securities, but also debt notes, convertible notes, and hybrid forms of equity and debt (see Freedman & Nutting, 2015, p. 5). In addition, there are some forms of partnerships that qualify as securities in equity-based crowdfunding. One of the main attributes of equity-based crowdfunding in creating venture-based market is its ability to connect startup business and the medium businesses to the larger investor community. Equity-based crowdfunding offers a platform to reach out to the companies through a single advertisement on the web. It ensures that the information reaches out to interested potential buyers and sells the business to the investors (Mollick, 2014). The venture space is therefore in ensuring that the investors and the business people meet. In addition, the venture space ensures that people with similar businesses and ideas can interact and advise each other on the best practices and the best ways to improve the businesses. The venture space is not only useful in raising the funds, but also ideas and plans on the best ways to improve the business given that there are other members of the crowd with the same ideas. It can also lead to mergers and amalgamation of two or more different venture businesses since the equity-based crowdfunding targets the business people who are interested in increasing their venture capital either through shares or other securities. The equity-based finance structure has a pool of professional small and large businesses that need a regular appraisal either through funding or through further investments (Steinberg, 2012, p. 113). Economic growth is also a factor that is hugely influenced by the success of the equity-based crowdfunding, since the growth of business companies contribute to the economic growth of the country. Most governments all over the world are taking up the new platforms and legislations have already been passed to ensure that crowdfunding for businesses and individual projects help the larger financial community that is the whole country. The venture finance marketplace has therefore transformed the equity-based crowdfunding concept to rally the support of the government and security legislations since it has been viewed as a milestone and a new trend in the financial sector.

Reward-Based Crowdfunding

Credit-based crowdfunding is a method where the donors to a specific project loan out money to the person in the hope of future repayment of the amount owed. This is the safest method of crowdfunding for the donors since in case the project owner defaults in payment of the advanced loans the platform is liable for the payment of the loan to the donor (Tomczak & Brem, 2013, p. 341). Under this method the borrowers submit an amount that they wish to be loaned and the donors interested in the specific project advance the borrower the amount with a promise of repayment at a future date. The platform acts as the intermediary and or surety for the borrower and the donor to ensure that the donor gets the amount back and facilitate the pooling of funds for the borrower. The borrowers find crowdfunding attractive since it has very low or no interest rates for the borrowers and they only have to incur a fee to process the funds by the platform and agree on a flexible payment plan to refund the amount forwarded. In the event that there is any interest to be charged on the amount of money borrowed the borrower sets the interest to be charged that they are comfortable and can guarantee a refund within the stipulated time period (Mollick, 2014). This makes the method attractive for the borrowers since they are not required to pay a minimum or set interest rate that is predetermined and as a result they can guarantee payment. The lenders on the other hand have to evaluate the project for its risks or benefits and potential and establish if they are willing to lend money at the interest rate set by the borrower. The arrangement is similar to that of a bank loans with the main difference being the predetermined interest rates. Whereas in credit-based crowdfunding the borrower sets the interest rates, inviting donors to fund the project in a bank loan the borrower must agree to the terms set by the bank or the authorities involved (Althoff & Leskovec (2015)).

One of the main advantages is that the borrower does not have to give any form of collateral to the lender and they transact only in terms of good faith from the borrower and the donor of the project. The donor funds the borrower in the hope that they will repay the money not because they have a history of repaying or they have presented evidence to suggest that they are capable of repaying the money but only on faith they have on their project. This ensures that the platform eradicates many processes of loan funding and borrowing that would slow the timeline of acquiring a loan. Background checks run by the banks and also the examination of the presented information are a large part of the processing process making it tedious and time consuming. The process also rules out borrowing from poor and new business people that are looking for money to kick start their business and have no collateral or no history to guarantee payment of the amount that they have borrowed. Crowdfunding offers such people a chance to borrow even huge amounts of money without any form of guarantees and guarantors. Credit-based crowdfunding has been immense in eliminating the factors that hinder borrowing and lending since there are none in crowdfunding. The project and presentation of the ideas are the most important aspects of a project if one aims to be funded for a project accordingly. It is therefore advisable for one to lend both their time and resources in the presentation of the project to as many people as possible.

Donation-Based Crowdfunding

Donation-based crowdfunding is the last method available for funding new initiatives. In this method, funds are raised for an initiative of public interest, although there is no economic benefit to the community financing the initiative. One of the greatest challenges of social entrepreneurs today is accessing startup capital, that´s why donation-based crowdfunding makes this method an interesting financing solution. One example of donation-based crowdfunding is the 2008 election campaign of President Obama, the campaign team collected more than $137 million by this method.

One of the risks in a crowdfunding initiative is targeting and unrealistic financing initiative, as crowdfunding platforms charge a larger percentage fee if the target is not met, failing to deliver on the project's promise will negatively affect the project's reputation. Thus, it is very important to engage the potential community into the project and design the project according to their interests. That´s why advertising the campaign is an important part of the crowdfunding process, always keeping costs in mind, it is important to advertise the campaign through several channels and reaching the largest possible potential supporters. Most donations-based crowdfunding initiatives reward donors with something in exchange for their contribution. Typically this is some kind of perk, this is usually the most expensive part of the crowdfunding campaign. The most challenging part of the crowdfunding process is moving from the zero donation phase, as potential donors usually imitate what other supporters did, then a potential donor might be not willing to give funding to a project when no money has been raised yet. Encouraging close friends and contacts to contribute in the initial stages of the campaign will be helpful. The Regional Studies Association (RSA) explains that the most critical zone is when the 10%-50% of the initiative has been funded, as most unsuccessful campaigns fail somewhere in this range. Thus, in order to take the initiative to reality it is essential to push the campaign after the launch with advertising and showing previous donations. In initiatives involving social entrepreneurship like the ones involving this type of crowdfunding it is more important to have the certainty that it is a feasible project, as a poor crowdfunding campaign could harm the reputation of the company and affect future initiatives to get funding. Another important issue to consider is that the amount raised can be affected by declined funds later on coming from credit cards, wrong donations, or fraud.

6. Security in E-Banking and Finance

Some factors affect the safety of internet banking and online financial services. These include regulatory body supervisions, customer awareness, and internet infrastructure. On the other hand, according to Chavan (2013), increased use of the internet and mobile services as a new channel for distribution of banking services requires more thought towards security against sham activities. However, this responsibility should not be left to banks alone; Lee (2012) explains that customers and regulatory bodies also have a role in e-banking security. Furthermore, banks do not have any influence regarding the electronic devices and channels used by their customers to perform transactions.

The bank should create a procedure to increase security. Firstly, it is supposed to formulate a secure online banking infrastructure. Then it should ensure the implementation of an appropriate information security policy. Thirdly, the bank should provide a robust monitoring system for fraudulent activities and notify its account holders of any high-risk transactions through SMS. Fourthly, the bank is supposed to offer a two-factor authentication (TFA) protocol for its account holders. The first factor is something like a PIN number, which the customer knows, whereas the second factor is something that the customer will own such as a smart card with a chip authentication (Lee, 2012, p. 8). On the other hand, the customers' responsibility is to ensure that they have enough knowledge regarding the safety tips required in e-banking. For instance, a customer should always stay alert in safeguarding his or her identity as well as limiting public access to personal computers. According to Lee (2012), there are numerous tips for safely logging on and off to a computer (Lee, 2012, p. 10). For example, a customer should never use a public computer to access his or her internet banking website. Customers should also close any open tabs and windows in a browser before logging on into e-banking. Moreover, after using the online service, the customer should always remember to log off. In safeguarding their identity, customers should use unique passwords that are difficult to guess. According to Lee (2012), a strong password should have at least six characters with a combination of numbers and letters. Furthermore, it is good for customers to often change their passwords and disable the 'Autocomplete' function in their browsers so that it does not remember previously input data.

Lee (2012) also advises that customers should never leave their TFA devices unattended (Lee, 2012, p.14). Other tips include disconnecting internet connections when not in use, backing up critical data on removable hard drives or Compact Discs, and installing internet security software for real-time detection of intrusions on a customer's computer. The roles of regulatory bodies in e-banking security are also several. According to Lee, regulatory bodies should develop adequate policies that promote customer protection and international cooperation among partners (Lee, 2012, p. 19).

CONCLUSION

The e-banking revolution has quickly changed the global business of banking. As a result, banks all over the world have reoriented their business strategies in order to encompass the new opportunities offered by online banking. In other words, the banking sector has led global electronic trade in recent years. Internet banking has enabled banks to change strategic behavior, scale borders, and create new possibilities as a result. Furthermore, internet banking has changed banking services towards the neoclassical economic theories of market functioning. Due to this, the market has become transparent and clients can easily compare banking services from different banks. For example, while using the internet, the customer is only one-click away from competitors. Thus, if a client is not satisfied with the products or services offered by one bank, he or she is able to change to a preferred banking partner faster and more easily.

Online investing has tremendously reduced the physical costs of operations. As Williamson (2006) stated, technological advancements in information technology have reduced the costs of processing financial information, whereas use of the internet facilitates transmission of financial information. In fact, this is why online financial services have gained popularity in recent years. In the future, this will ensure that banking rates are friendly as well as encouraging to more innovations regarding the current products and services being offered by banking institutions. In addition, electronic delivery of financial services has enabled banks to meet their clients' expectations and create close customer relationships (Williamson, 2006). Hence, as discussed by Chavan (2013), online banking will eventually triumph over traditional banking in the coming years as more developing nations are now building their economies with specific focus on e-learning, e-commerce, and e-banking.

Online crowdfunding has funded many new companies and initiatives in their initial stages and is substituting the funding of organizations with more online platforms being created. The examination of the risk from both sides, the borrower and the donor, is essential before making an investment or borrowing to make sure that the business is finally successful. The legislation of the Act has enabled the platforms to conduct business better and have a larger crowd since the donors have the backing of the government and the law while engaging in the business.

Online Crowdfunding has introduced new funding new funding mechanism and rules for news businesses. Most of crowdfunding funds are collected through reward-based platforms, however equity crowdfunding is becoming more popular. It is expected that online crowdfunding will grow in popularity as many new crowdfunding opportunities become available. A new business that seeks funds through the online crowdfunding process comes out stronger as for the questions that has to answer and the scrutiny that it is put under, compared to convince a single angel investor. It is worth mentioning that because a startup does not obtain online crowdfunding does not necessarily mean that the business is not viable. It might be that investors may not be on that platform or perhaps is not the right time. One of the biggest challenges ahead will be communicating efficiently and engaging with investors after successful funding. Investors will possibly be interested in the big numbers and updates instead of the news from daily operations. Investors will be more likely to reinvest if they are kept engaged and the company is looking after them. Creating a mutual interest might foster that investors act as ongoing mentors in the business.

The importance of e-banking and online financial services can be summarized as significant time management, elimination of queues, cheaper costs. Customers are able to make financial transactions any time of the day, and without physical interactions with the bank. Another characteristic of e-banking is rapid and uninterrupted access to information. Furthermore, e-banking allows a customer to enjoy the convenience of carrying out financial transactions from the comfort of his or her office or home.

Security is an important issue in e-banking and finance. Banks have to create the organizational procedure for security. A secure online banking infrastructure is necessary, as well as the implementation of an appropriate information security policy, the bank should provide a robust monitoring system for fraudulent activities. Finally, the bank is supposed to offer a two-factor authentication (TFA) protocol for its account holders.

REFERENCES

Agrawal, A., Catalini, C., & Goldfarb, A. (2015). Crowdfunding: Geografy, social networks, and the timing of investment decisions. *Journal of Economics & Management Strategy*, *24*(2), 253–274. doi:10.1111/jems.12093

Ainin, S., Lim, C. H., & Wee, A. (2005). Prospects and challenges of E-Banking in Malaysia. *Electronic Journal of Information Systems in Developing Countries*, *22*, 1–110.

Althoff, T., & Leskovec, J. (2015). Donor retention in online crowdfunding communities: A case study of donorschoose.org.*Proceedings of the 24th International Conference on World Wide Web*, 34-44. doi:10.1145/2736277.2741120

Appei, M. (2009). *Investing with exchange trade funds made easy: A start to finish plan to reduce costs and achieve higher returns* (2nd ed.). Upper Saddle River, NJ: Pearson Education Inc.

Benklifa, M., & Olmstead, W. (2013). *Learn how to trade options (Collection)*. Upper Saddle River, NJ: Pearson Education.

Bruntje, D., & Gajda, O. (2016). *Crowdfunding in Europe. State of the art in theory and practice*. Berlin, Germany: Springer. doi:10.1007/978-3-319-18017-5

Chavan, J. (2013). Internet banking - Benefits and challenges in an emerging economy. *International Journal of Research in Business Management, 1*, 19–26.

Damos, M. (2014). *Online crowdfunding platforms*. Frankfurt, Germany: Epubli.

Douw, S. (2012). *Crowdfunding*. Haarlem, Netherlands: SBP Editorial.

Fontanills, G., & Cawood, R. (2009). *Trade options online*. Hoboken, NJ: Wiley.

Freedman, D. M., & Nutting, M. R. (2015). *The foundations of online crowdfunding, in equity crowdfunding for investors: A guide to risks, returns, regulations, funding portals, due diligence, and deal terms*. Hoboken, NJ: Wiley. doi:10.1002/9781118864876

Friedman, B. M. (2000). Decoupling at the margin: The threat to monetary policy from the electronic revolution in banking. *International Finance, 3*(2), 261–272. doi:10.1111/1468-2362.00051

Hart, C. M. (2005). *I want to make money in the stock market: Learn to begin investing without losing your life savings*. Denver, CO: Outskirts Press.

Hobson, R. (2012). *The dividend investor: A practical guide to building a share portfolio designed to maximise income*. Hampshire, UK: Harriman House Ltd.

Krantz, M. (2013). *Investing online for dummies*. Hoboken, NJ: Wiley.

Laopodis, N. (2013). *Understanding investments: Theories and strategies*. New York, NY: Routledge.

Lassar, P., Lambert, L., Woodford, C., & Moschovitis, C. J. P. (2005). *The internet: A historical encyclopedia*. Santa Barbara, CA: ABC-CLIO.

Liao, S., Pu, S., Yuan, W. H., & Chen, A. (1999). The adoption of virtual banking: An empirical study. *PERGAMON International Journal of Information Management, 19*(1), 63–74. doi:10.1016/S0268-4012(98)00047-4

Marina, K. (2009). *Reference in the e-banking.* Cairo, Egypt: The Publisher of the Universities.

Massolution. (2014). *Crowdfunding industry report.* Author.

Mollick, E. (2014). The dynamics of crowdfunding: An exploratory study. *Journal of Business Venturing, 29*(1), 1–16. doi:10.1016/j.jbusvent.2013.06.005

Northcott, A. (2009). *The mutual funds book: How to invest in mutual funds and earn high rates of returns safely.* Ocala, FL: Atlantic Publishing *Group.*

Pardo, R. (2008). *The evaluation and optimization of trading strategies.* Hoboken, NJ: Wiley.

Roebuck, K. (2011). *Crowdfunding: High impact strategies what you need to know.* Amsterdam, Netherlands: Tebbo Publisher.

Sarlak, M. A., & Astiani, A. A. (2011). *E-banking and emerging multidisciplinary processes: Social, economical, and organizational models.* Hershey, PA: IGI Global. doi:10.4018/978-1-61520-635-3

Schwartz, R. A. (2010). *Micro markets: A market structure approach to microeconomic analysis.* Hoboken, NJ: Wiley. doi:10.1002/9781118268131

Steinberg, D. (2012). *The Kickstarter handbook: real-life crowdfunding success stories.* Philadelphia, PA: Quirk Books.

Tomczak, A., & Brem, A. (2013). A conceptualized investment model of crowdfunding. *Venture Capital, 15*(4), 335–359. doi:10.1080/13691066.2013.847614

Williamson, D. G. (2006). Enhanced authentication in online banking. *Journal of Economic Crime Management, 4,* 1–42.

Xu, M. X., Wikes, S., & Shah, M. H. (2006). *E-Banking application and issues in Abbey National PLC. E-Technologies. In Encyclopedia of E-Commerce, E-Government, and Mobile Commerce.* Hershey, PA: IGI Global.

Young, T. E. (2013). *The everything guide to crowdfunding: learn how to use social media for small-business funding: understand crowd psychology: gain an online presence: create a successful crowdfunding campaign: promote your campaign to reach hidden funding sources.*Avon, MA: Adams Media.

ADDITIONAL READING

Kallstrom, O. (2000). *Business solution for mobile e-commerce*. Ericsson Review 2000-03-27.

Lee, S. (2012). *E-banking security*. Information Security (InfoSec) Government of Hong Kong Working Paper.

KEY TERMS AND DEFINITIONS

Angel Investor: An investor who provides funding for small startups or entrepreneurs.

Crowdfunding Platform: Internet platforms which enable companies to advertise over the internet and obtain investments from registered users in return.

E-Banking: The performance of banking business through the internet. It is also known as "Internet banking" or "Online banking".

Electronic Commerce: A business model that enables to conduct business over the internet.

Financial Institutions: An institution that provides financial services to potential clients.

Information Technology: It is the use of any computers, storage, networking and other processes to create, store and exchange electronic data.

Online Security: Computer security related to the internet involving browsing and network security. It is designed to establish measures to use against attacks through internet.

Online Trading: Individual investors buy and sell stocks over an electronic network through a brokerage company.

Chapter 10
Marketing and Social Media

Reshu Goyal
Banasthali Vidhyapeeth, India

Praveen Dhyani
Banasthali Vidhyapeeth, India

Om Prakash Rishi
University of Kota, India

ABSTRACT

Time has changed and so does the world. Today everything has become as a matter of one click. With this effort we are trying to explore the new opportunities features and capabilities of the new compeers of Internet applicability known as Social Media or Web 2.0. The effort has been put in to use the internet, social media or web 2.0 as the tool for marketing issues or the strategic business decision making. The main aim is to seek social media, web 2.0 internet applications as the tool for marketing.

INTRODUCTION

Internet and its applications have enabled the firms to adapt and implement innovative form of interactions and compositions with real end users or rightly called as consumers (Ainscough & Luckett, 1996). To facilitate the study and have a close look as to the hindrances and the opportunities for the empirical implementation of the social media in the marketing strategies, Portugal data of 2000 firms was studied

DOI: 10.4018/978-1-5225-2234-8.ch010

which revealed that firms are under both internal and external pressure to adopt digitalization of social content (Bayo-Moriones & Lera-López, 2007) Relationship-based interaction should go hand in hand with the customers, merging the traditional mode with the new technologies.

JOLT AND JERK FOR THE COMPANIES AND THE SOCIAL MEDIA

Customers at large are using the internet based social mode of communication at large which forces the majority of the concerns to charter with it as well. Initial mode of communications were e-mails, direct marketing, telemarketing, informational websites, television, radio, and other interactive modes to share knowledge related to the company and the articles (Berthon, Pitt, Plangger & Shapiro, 2012), (Budden, Anthony, Budden, & Jones, 2011).Though initial means of communication served as the data or the information reaching larger number of people in short time but didn't promote the direct communication or interaction between the buyer and the seller. To track down the abiding collaborative and delightful friendship, substitute have to be sorted of? To effectuate it, word of mouth communication (facilitating the use of social networking sites) seemed to be of usage (Agarwal, 2009), (Ellison, Steinfield & Lampe, 2007), (Budden, Anthony, Budden, & Jones, 2011). Present technologies have become more customers oriented.

Figure 1. Depicts the plan to be followed by the business personal for marketing in integration with social media
Source: Budden, Anthony, Budden, & Jones (2011)

Step-1-Listen	Step-2 Plan	Step-3 Strategy	Step-4 Tools
• Locate consumers • Assess their social activities • Look for small focused audience	• Define business objectives • How can your brands strengths be extended online?	• How and where will you do it? • How will the relationship with the consumers change? • Who will be leading this effort?	• Decide what social tools you will use • How will you monitor activities and measure success?

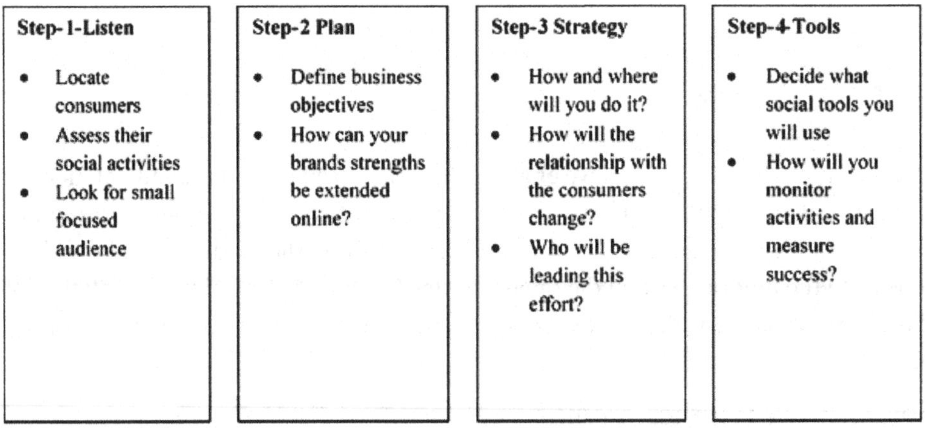

Figure 2. Shows the various sources of Social Media Marketing
Source: (http://www.zenithoptimedia.com/zenith/zenithoptimedia-releases-september-2012-advertis-ing-expenditure-forecasts/)

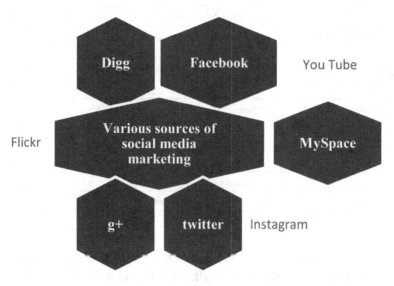

Actually, the initial boom or the first tide of the Internet application was not taken seriously by large, but rapid changing scenarios the situations have also changed and so does the application of the Internet. Even the companies with low capital and manpower strength go in for this form of media and communication sources maximum of the employees have sorted to have the blogs (Weinberg, Pehlivan, 2011, Barnard, 2012). Other side of the coin also says the same thing i.e. from the consumer front, also are readily accepting the mode of purchasing. Participation has increased with reduction in the price of the broadband and increase in concurrence by the consumers in the form of messaging, blogs, experience sharing etc. (Fisher, 2009) (See Figure 1 for the business plan in integration with the social media marketing).

EXPLAINING THE TERM WEB 2.0/SOCIAL MEDIA MARKETING

See Figure 2, showing various sources of social media from the pool of mediums. Web 2.0 is termed as the internet based application/s which is the collective formation of online portals, web interactions, open ended data/discussions which smoothens the communications, synergy of the customers and result in formation of business, marketing and strategic decisions if required. Web 2.0 also supports formation of congenial peer groups, free-flow of idea or knowledge and thus coming out with some important results or just the casual relationship building (Pitt, Berthon, Wat-

Table 1. Shows various applications of the social media in marketing, its social effects and the enabling technologies (Union, 2009)

Web 2.0 Dimensions		
Applications Types	**Social Effects**	**Enabling Technologies**
Blogs	Empowerment	Open Source
Social Networks (Content)	Participation	RSS
Communities Forums/Bulletin Boards	Openness	Wikis
Content Aggregators	Networking	Mashups
	Conversation	AJAX
	Community	
	Democratization/User Control	

son, & Zinkhan, 2002), (Union, 2009) (Study table 1 which showcases various applications of the social media in marketing, its social effects and the enabling technologies).

WEB 2.0, SOCIAL MEDIA AND MARKETING STRATEGIES

The way companies run their business, the way the people buy the products have changed with time. Thinking of the people and so the scenarios have modified to such an extent that being the part of this social fraternity have become the need of an hour. It has become an essence for the marketers and the business personals to understand what comes in with social media, or how to operate in sync with this form of businesses (Kondopoulos, 2011), (Rizzotti & Burkhart, 2010). It is not that application of social media in marketing would generate results; it is rather the correct usability of the medium to generate adequate results. Inabilities of the business personal to correctly use it still make it a trial and error medium of application into the business.

Figure 3. Shows reasons for the business decisions firm takes when investing in social media and using it as a source for marketing
Source: Berthon, Pitt, Plangger and Shapiro (2012)

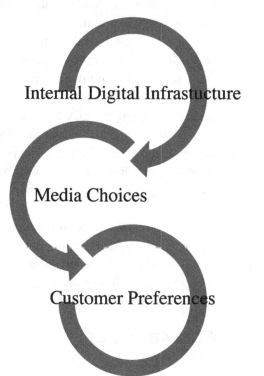

SPOTTING THE OUTLAY FOR THE SOCIAL MEDIA IMPLEMENTATION OR DIGITALIZATION

There is no canonical formula for decision making, as to how much a firm should spend on digital social media. It depends upon every firm and the peculiarity they possess which enclose (Figure 3).

Figure 3 depicts the reasons business uses in investing in social media and using it as a tool of marketing. Faster the benefits of the social media are growing, doubly it is being used by the firms to fill up their lockers. Dotingly the marketing director of a reputed firma said "investment in digital media is worthless, claiming that the most important factor for the involvement of companies in digital media is the very low investment required when compared with traditional media." (Ellison, Steinfield & Lampe, 2007), (Hoffman, & Fodor, 2010), (Mangold & Faulds, 2009). Notwithstanding the declarations and the statements made firms have still increased their investments in digital media up to 18%. With increasing importance and changing scenario studies and researchers believe that number would increase considerably (Kumar, Novak, & Tomkins, 2010). Statistics state that more than 81% of the participants plan to go in for this mode of marketing strategies. Records claim that where are the increase in the investment in traditional mode of the marketing is 4% which is far behind the increase in digital mode which ranges up to 14% by 2013(Hutchings, 2012), (Bayo-Moriones & Lera-López, 2007). Figures may reflect major changes with advent of mobile computing and app based technologies in 2015.

For any organization to succeed employees play a major role because they are the key stake holders in forming firms strategies. Firms are also focusing on such employees who are digitally equipped and the number is supposedly to increase to 45% ANACOM, 2012). (Berthon, Pitt, Plangger, & Shapiro, 2012).

After effects of the survey were two inevitable conclusions:

1. Digital media or social networking play grave role in business marketing and its relevance and utility is increasing with changing scenarios.
2. It has become critically important for the organizations to implement the digitization or the internet based mode of communications.

ASCERTAINING THE CAPABILITY OF SOCIAL MEDIA MARKETING

There are different views about measuring the return on investment of digital marketing. Some of the digital calculators have been proposed to measure return on investment like the model suggested by (Fisher, 2009), (Weinberg & Pehlivan, 2011), (Hoffman & Fodor, 2010) suggested different models to measure the income generated by digital marketing like measuring the competitors' actions, return on investment, brand awareness etc.

Overall the studies reveal that the kind of model to be adopted depends upon the firm's strategic decision making and the objectives which are core importance for the success of the firm.

NEED OF AN HOUR-SOCIAL MEDIA

Web or the Internet Applications have become the essence in right from conceptualization, movement and the establishment of the business activities. It has become the need of the hour and to gain the maximum competitive advantage the firms should instrument this mode of interaction and relationship building. To take full advantage of Internet, organizations have to adopt Internet to fullest that is from people communication to customer interaction, stakeholder's connections and finally make profit and sales. As the need and the usage of Internet and its applications is increasing with time so as its need is being felt by the customers (Berthon, Pitt & Watson, 1996), (Budden, Anthony, Budden, & Jones, 2011) and integration into marketing practices have been done.

Sinking with internet or creating the tech enabled firms does not appear overnight it needs whole lot of resource management, planning, management and administration with time. Lot of energy and efforts have to be put in to move from the traditional marketing methods to digital prone world but nothing is impossible.

REFERENCES

Agarwal, A. (2009). *Web 3.0 concepts explained in plain English*. Retrieved June 12,fromhttp://www.labnol.org/internet/web-3-concepts-explained/8908/

Ainscough, T., & Luckett, M. (1996). The Internet for the rest of us: Marketing on the World Wide Web. *Journal of Consumer Marketing*, *13*(2), 36–47. doi:10.1108/07363769610115393

ANACOM. (2012). InformaçãoEstatística do Serviço de Acesso à Internet: Vol. 3. *Trimestre de 2012*. Lisboa: ANACOM.

Barnard, J. (2012). *ZenithOptimedia releases September 2012 advertising expenditure forecast*. Retrieved January 4, 2013, from http://www.zenithoptimedia.com/zenith/zenithoptimedia-releases-september-2012-advertising-expenditure-forecasts/

Bayo-Moriones, A., & Lera-López, F. (2007). A firm-level analysis of determinants of ICT adoption in Spain. *Technovation*, *27*(6-7), 352–366. doi:10.1016/j.technovation.2007.01.003

Berthon, P., Pitt, L. F., & Watson, R. T. (1996). The World Wide Web as an advertising medium. *Journal of Advertising Research*, *36*(1), 43–54.

Berthon, P. R., Pitt, L. F., Plangger, K., & Shapiro, D. (2012). Marketing meets Web 2.0, social media, and creative consumers: Implications for international marketing strategy. *Business Horizons*, *55*(3), 261–271. doi:10.1016/j.bushor.2012.01.007

Brown, J., Broderick, A. J., & Lee, N. (2007). Word of mouth communication within online communities: Conceptualizing the online social network. *Journal of Interactive Marketing*, *21*(3), 2–20. doi:10.1002/dir.20082

Budden, C. B., Anthony, J. F., Budden, M. C., & Jones, M. A. (2011). Managing the evolution of a revolution: Marketing implications of Internet media usage among college students. *College Teaching Methods & Styles Journal, 3*(3), 5–10. doi:10.19030/ctms.v3i3.5283

Eid, R., & El-Gohary, H. (2011). The impact of E-marketing use on small business enterprises marketing success. *Service Industries Journal, 33*(1), 31–50. doi:10.1 080/02642069.2011.594878

Ellison, N. B., Steinfield, C., & Lampe, C. (2007). The benefits of Facebook friends: Social capital and college students use of online social network sites. *Journal of Computer-Mediated Communication, 12*(4), 1143–1168. doi:10.1111/j.1083-6101.2007.00367.x

Fisher, T. (2009). ROI in social media: A look at the arguments. *Journal of Database Marketing & Customer Strategy Management, 16*(3), 189–195. doi:10.1057/dbm.2009.16

Hoffman, D. L., & Fodor, M. (2010). Can you measure the ROI of your social media marketing? *MIT Sloan Management Review, 52*(1), 41–49.

Hutchings, C. (2012). Commercial use of Facebook and Twitter–risks and rewards. *Computer Fraud & Security, 2012*(6), 19–20. doi:10.1016/S1361-3723(12)70065-9

Kaplan, A. M., & Haenlein, M. (2010). Users of the world, unite! The challenges and opportunities of social media. *Business Horizons, 53*(1), 59–68. doi:10.1016/j.bushor.2009.09.003

Kondopoulos, D. (2011). Internet marketing advanced techniques for increased market share. *ChimicaOggi-Chemistry Today, 29*(3), 9–12.

Kumar, R., Novak, J., & Tomkins, A. (2010). Structure and evolution of online social networks. In P. S. Yu, J. Han, & C. Faloutsos (Eds.), *Link mining: Models, algorithms, and applications* (pp. 337–357). New York: Springer. doi:10.1007/978-1-4419-6515-8_13

Lampe, C. A. C., Ellison, N., & Steinfield, C. (2007). A familiar face(book): Profile elements as signals in an online social network.*Proceedings of the SIGCHI Conference on Human Factors in Computing Systems*. doi:10.1145/1240624.1240695

Mangold, W. G., & Faulds, D. J. (2009). Social media: The new hybrid element of the promotion mix. *Business Horizons, 52*(4), 357–365. doi:10.1016/j.bushor.2009.03.002

Pitt, L., Berthon, P., Watson, R., & Zinkhan, G. (2002). The Internet and the birth of real consumer power. *Business Horizons*, *45*(4), 7–14. doi:10.1016/S0007-6813(02)00220-3

Rizzotti, S., & Burkhart, H. (2010). useKit: a step towards the executable web s3.0.*Proceedings of the 19th International Conference on Worldwide Web*. doi:10.1145/1772690.1772861

Rodríguez-Ardura, I., Ryan, G., & Gretzel, U. (2012). Special issue on qualitative approaches to E-marketing and online consumer behaviour: Guest editors' introduction. *Journal of Theoretical and Applied Electronic Commerce Research*, (August), 2012.

Seybert, H. (2012). *Internet use in households and by individuals 2012*. Retrieved January 25, 2013, from http://epp.eurostat.ec.europa.eu/cache/ITY_OFFPUB/KS-SF-12-050/EN/KS-SF12-050-EN.PDF

Silva, J. M., MahfujurRahman, A. S. M., & El Saddik, A. (2008). Web 3.0: a vision for bridging the gap between real and virtual. *Proceeding of the 1st ACM International Workshop on Communicability Design and Evaluation in Cultural and Ecological Multimedia Systems*.

Union, I. T. (2009). *Media statistics: Mobile phone subscribers (most recent) by country*. Retrieved December 6, from http://www.NationMaster.com/graph/med_mob_pho-media-mobile-phones 17

Van Belleghem, S., Thijs, D., & De Ruyck, T. (2012). *Social Media around the World 2012*. Retrieved November 3, from http://www.slideshare.net/InSitesConsulting/social-media-around-the-world-2012-by-insites-consulting

Weinberg, B. D., & Pehlivan, E. (2011). Social spending: Managing the social media mix. *Business Horizons*, *54*(3), 275–282.

Whitla, P. (2009). Crowdsourcing and its application in marketing activities. *Contemporary Management Research*, *5*(1), 15–28.

Chapter 11
Strategic Planning of Cold Supply Chain Towards Good Manufacturing Practices:
Issues and Challenges in Indian Market

Supriyo Roy
Birla Institute of Technology, India

Kaushik Kumar
Birla Institute of Technology, India

ABSTRACT

Cold Chain addresses subset of supply chain involving production, storage and distribution of products that require 'level of temperature control' to retain 'key characteristics and associated value' in terms of life expectancy and perishability. Successful cold chain management is essential for pharmaceutical companies, transportation providers and health care practitioners. With growing population and their demand; especially in retail and pharmaceutical sectors drives Indian cold chain market and it has huge potential to grow in the near future. India's greatest need is for an effective and economically viable cold chain solution that will integrate the supply chains for all commodities from the production centers to the consumption centers; thereby reducing physical waste and loss of value of perishable commodities. This article highlights the importance of cold chain concepts with Indian business scenario. Strategic planning of cold supply chain and their real value towards good manufacturing practices are critically highlighted.

DOI: 10.4018/978-1-5225-2234-8.ch011

INTRODUCTION

A Cold Chain is a 'temperature controlled' supply chain linked to the material, equipment and procedures used to maintain specific shipments within the appropriate temperature range (Carla Reed, 2005; Bishara, 2006). An unbroken cold chain is an uninterrupted series of storage and distribution activities which maintain a given temperature range. It is used to help extend and ensure the shelf life of products; namely fresh agricultural produce, seafood, frozen food, photographic film, chemicals and pharmaceutical drugs, etc. Such products, during transport and when in transient storage, are called cool cargo. Unlike other goods or merchandise, cold chain goods are perishable and always en route towards end use or destination, even when held temporarily in cold stores and hence commonly referred to as cargo during its entire logistics cycle (Ali and Kumar, 2011; Fearne et al., 2006).

Cold Chain originates from the terminology of *'chain of custody'* in production, packaging, distribution and control of temperature sensitive product (Blanchard, 2007). This includes traditional areas of supply chain, raw material acquisition, transformation and manufacturing process, packaging and product protection, storage and distribution. The cold chain market was valued at nearly 90 Billion and is expected to grow at a Compound Annual Growth Rate (CAGR) of 28.75%. Government backing will help boost the capacity creation for cold storages while new players are gradually venturing into the more profitable refrigerated transport services. There are a large numbers of small players present in the Indian cold chain industry; some of the well-known organized companies are Snowman, RK Foodland Pvt. Ltd., MJ Logistic Services Ltd., Brahmanand Himghar Ltd. etc. It is anticipated that cold chain market in India will get more organized with the entry of large private players in this arena.

One of the most critical constraints in the growth of food processing industry in India is the lack of integrated cold chain facilities (Cunningham, 2001). According to warehouse report 2013, India has approximately 5,400 cold storage facilities of which 4,875 are in the private sector, 400 in the cooperative sector and 125 in the public sector. The combined capacity of cold storage facilities is 23.66 million metric tons; still India can store less than 11% of what is produced. Most of the infrastructure used in cold chain sector is outdated technology and is single commodity based. India's controlled atmosphere storage facilities and other cold storage facilities with the technology for storing and handling different types of fruits and vegetables at variant temperatures would have a very good potential market in India (Khan, 2005).

With the growth on domestic manufacturing and retail segments, demand for efficient warehouse management service has improved. Despite growing demand, warehousing continues to see little investment. Current spending on organized warehousing in India constitutes 9 percent of total logistics spending, as against

25 percent in the US. According to World Bank's 2014 Logistics Performance Indicator, India is ranked 54th and is behind countries like Japan, United States, Germany, China etc. Logistics costs account for around 6-10 percent of average retail prices in India as against the global average of 4-5 percent. Therefore, there is a clear scope to improve margins by 3-5 percent by improving efficiency of supply chain and logistics processes (Kumar, 2008). Developing an 'integrated supply chain including cold chain' can save up to 300 billion annually with the reduction of wastage of perishable horticulture produce. It is worth noting that the price of vegetables, fruits, milks and eggs, meat and fish have been rising faster in spite of the fact that India is the 2nd highest producer of fruits and vegetables. This is led by inadequate supply chain and logistics infrastructure and management (Maheshwar and Chanakwa, 2006).

Agriculture in India is witnessing a major shift from traditional farming to horticulture to dairy products to perishable one (Joshi et al., 2009). Demand for fresh and processed fruits and vegetables are increasing with the rise of urban populations and their change of habits. Due to this increase in demand, 'diversification' with 'value addition' is the mantra of todays' Indian agriculture. Changes along with emergence of an organized retail food sector spurred by changes to Foreign Direct Investment laws are creating opportunities in domestic food industry; including sector like cold chain (Tulsian and Saini, 2014). With Govt. of India's new focus on food preservation, cold storage sector is undergoing a major metamorphosis. Government has introduced various incentives and policy changes in order to curtail production wastage and control inflation; increase public private participation. They also laid out elaborate plans and incentives to support large scale investments essential for developing an effective and integrated cold chain infrastructure throughout India (Viswanadham, 2006).

Issues, Controversies, Problems

Designing a cold chain is not easy; requires multiple factors to be considered (Carla, 2005; Hann, et al., 2004). These include:

- **Temperature Tracking:** Even in refrigerated units, temperatures can vary. Temperature tracking is important to confirm appropriate temperature throughout.
- **Selection of Containers:** Container selection influences temperature variation within the unit.
- **Transportation Provider's Ability:** While, the availability of temperature-controlled transportation is increasing, it is still necessary to look at experience and what processes the transportation company has in place.

- **Distribution Route:** Certain transportation routes experience greater temperature variation or higher average temperatures than others. A more stable external temperature influences the internal stability.
- **Contingency Plans:** Decisions about route, provider, container and tracking can help in the development of contingency plans, but it is important to think about backup should equipment not work, or transportation take longer than expected.

Cold chain involves transportation of temperature sensitive products along with supply chain through thermal and refrigerated packaging methods to protect the integrity of these shipments (Fearne and Hughes, 2000). There are several means in which cold chain products can be transported, including refrigerated trucks and railcars, refrigerated cargo ships as well as by air cargo. India's integrated cold chain industry - a combination of surface storage and refrigerated transport - has been growing at a CAGR of 20 percent for the last three years. The cold chain market in India is projected / anticipated to reach 624 Billion by 2017.

Current statistics show that, India has still only 6,300 cold storage facilities unevenly spread across; with an installed capacity of 30.11 million metric tonnes. They can store less than 11percent of the country's total product. Out of these, organized players contribute only 8% -10% of the cold chain industry market and 36% these cold storages in India have capacity below 1,000 MT. 65% of India's cold chain storage capacity is contributed by the states of Uttar Pradesh and West Bengal.

Cold chain infrastructure includes infrastructure on cold storage, transport and point of production also (Dunne, 2008). Refrigerated transport or cold chain distribution is still in its nascent stage in India and is way behind if compared to world standards for cargo movement. Presently reefer transport business in India is estimated at 10-12 billion which includes reefer transportation demand for both exports and domestic. Various industries covered under cold chain are agriculture, horticulture and floriculture, dairy, confectionery, pharmaceuticals, chemicals, poultry, etc. Out of 105MT of perishable produce is transported across India annually, only 4mn MT is transported via reefers.

India is bestowed with varied agro climatic conditions which are highly favorable for growing a large number of horticulture crops like vegetables, fruits, aromatic plants, herbs and spices, dairy products etc. (Salin et al., 2003; Jackson et al., 2007). However, despite the rise, India is way behind the similar neighboring country China in per-hectare yield and processing of horticulture products. India can store only 2 percent of its horticulture products in temperature-controlled conditions, while China stores 15 percent and Europe and North America stores 85 percent. Adequate cold storage facilities are available for just about 10 percent of India's horticulture production. Of the total annual production, 35-40 percent is wasted before consumption. During the peak production period, the gap between the demand and supply of cold storage capacity is approximately 25 million tons (Blanco et al., 2005; Bourlakis and Bourlakis, 2005).

Although cold storage capacity of over 30 million tonnes has been created in the country, the concept of cold-chain is still in its infancy in India. Considering the fact that India is producing about 270 million tonnes of horticulture produce every year, the development of cold-chain networks assumes high priority. Owing to the tremendous pressure on improving supply chain and reducing losses during produce handling and movement, the need for creation of a cold chain network is crucial for perishable food commodities (Bogataj et al., 2005; Collins et al., 1999). Regionally, the existing cold storage capacity is concentrated in terms of both number and capacity in the northern region. Pharmaceutical companies are increasingly relying, and spending; on cold-chain storage as temperature sensitive drugs are becoming more prevalent. The demand for generic drug in emerging markets such as India, China and Brazil are expected to increase the need for low temperature handling and transportation facilities (Yu and Nagurney, 2013). Cold chain for pharmaceuticals needs to be temperature controlled as the shelf life of the products needs to be maintained. A well-organized cold chain system has the capability of reducing the deterioration of drugs as well as retaining the quality of the product. The cold chain segment is of critical importance as the pharmaceutical compounds being exported have the likelihood of getting damaged with excessive heat or freezing during shipment, resulting in reduced efficacy.

Demand from the Pharmaceutical Sector

India is among the top five emerging pharma markets and has grown at an estimated compound annual growth rate of 13 percent during the period 2009-'13. The Indian pharmaceutical market is poised to grow to 3300 billion by 2020 from the 2009 levels of 756 billion. The ever-growing pharmaceutical industry is acutely temperature and time sensitive. Cold supply chain acts like a backbone for pharma industry. It is a big responsibility to have a regulatory supervision and to maintain the efficacy of the drug throughout the supply chain in order to main the quality of drugs and comply with statutory requirements.

In an increasingly global market the demand for temperature controlled food and nonfood is increasing in many markets across the globe (Chopra and Meindl, 2007). One important factor is the movement of manufacturers and retailers to emerging markets in Asia and Latin America, as well as the changing tastes of consumers in more mature markets. This has resulted in high levels of investments by logistics companies and their associate suppliers as they have acquired or partnered local players in order to access these markets and to open temperature controlled operations in these regions to serve the growth in prosperity of local populations (Global Cold Chain Logistics Report, 2009). Temperature monitoring and control are essential mechanisms in cold chain management, because they are necessary for maintaining food safety and quality.

According to Salin and Nayga (2003) multinational restaurant companies like McDonalds, KFC and Burger King etc. manage technical challenges in target markets with tight specifications and exclusive supply chains, while smaller firms use extensive networks to supply imported frozen potatoes. Cold chain distribution process is, thus, considered as an extension of Good Manufacturing Practices (GMP) which ensures that all drugs and biological products are required to adhere to and enforced by various health regulatory bodies. GMP guidelines provide guidance for manufacturing, testing and quality assurance in order to ensure that a food or drug is safe for human. Countries like USA, UK, China etc. have legislated that any pharmaceutical / medical device manufacturers create their own GMP guidelines and follow standard GMP procedures. As such, the distribution process must be validated to ensure that there is no negative impact to safety, efficacy or quality of the drug substance. GMP environment requires that all processes that might impact the safety, efficacy or quality of the drug substance must be validated, including storage and distribution. GMP guidelines are not prescriptive instructions on how to manufacture products. They are a series of general principles that must be observed from strategic sourcing to manufacturing to distribution. Company related to cold chain when setting up its quality program and manufacturing process, set the GMP requirements / guidelines.

Quality is essentially a guide to cold chain system. Quality should be analyzed, measured, controlled, documented and finally validated. The overall approach to validation of a distribution process is by building more and more qualifications on top of each other to get to a validated state (Donk et al., 2008). This is done by executing a component qualification on the packaging components, an operational qualification to demonstrate that the process performs at the operational extremes and finally a performance qualification that demonstrates that what happens in the real world is within the limits of what was demonstrated in the operational qualification limits (Folinus et al., 2006; Jahre and Hatteland, 2004).

During the distribution process one should monitor that process until one builds a sufficient data set that clearly demonstrates the process is in compliance and in a state of control. Each time the process does not conform to the process, the event should be properly documented, investigated and corrected so that the temperature excursion does not occur on future shipments. Any anomaly is thus considered to be a Non Conformance and should be assigned as a tractable event. The event must be reported immediately when it is identified and it is the expectation of the Food and Drug Administration (FDA) that all adverse events to documented and investigated.

The investigation should be completed in a timely manner and must come to some form of a 'root cause' and also some form of 'corrective action'.

- Carriers and logistics providers can assist shippers. These providers have the technical ability to link with airlines for real time status, generate web-based export documentation and provide electronic tracking.
- The use of refrigerator trucks, refrigerator cars, reefer ships, reefer containers, and refrigerated warehouses is common.
- Shipment in insulated shipping containers or other specialized packaging.
- Temperature data loggers and Radio-Frequency Identification tags help monitor the temperature history of the truck, warehouse, etc. and the temperature history of the product being shipped. They also can help determine the remaining shelf life.
- Documentation is critical. Each step of the custody chain needs to follow established protocols and to maintain proper records. Customs delays occur due to inaccurate or incomplete customs paperwork, so basic guidelines for creating a commercial invoice should be followed to ensure the proper verbiage, number of copies, and other details.

COLD CHAIN TECHNOLOGY

Several technologies are closely interacting in a sequential manner to support a cold chain (Montanari, 2008; Ali and Kumar, 2011):

- **Monitoring:** Usually refers to devices and systems able to monitor the condition of the cold chain, such as temperature and humidity, throughout all the involved stages, namely in the reefer and at the warehouse. These technologies provide an account of the integrity of the chain and help identify potential weaknesses. For instance, the ISO 10368 standard (1992) was established to provide a series of guidelines in order to monitor the temperature of reefers.
- **Fabrication:** Cold chain products such as food or pharmaceutical products are fabricated in specialized facilities, requiring specific equipment and methods. For instance, blast freezers are able to quickly freeze meat, preventing the formation of damaging ice crystals. Once a product is ready to be shipped, various forms of packing technologies (e.g. crates, perforated boxes) are available to help maintain its temperature integrity as well as protect it from damage. Vacuum packing is often used to efficiently pack meat and extends its shelf life.

- **Storage:** Like any other good, cold chain products can rarely be made immediately available for final consumption and must thus be stored in cold storage facilities. Large refrigerated warehouses are used to store cold chain products until an order has been filled. Further, specialized distribution centers have been designed to support the efficient and timely storage of grocery goods before being brought to the store. Among key technological issues for storage is a better energy efficiency of the facility, while being able to maintain a range of temperatures.

- **Terminal:** Since a growing quantity of cold chain goods are shipped internationally, transport terminals such as ports and airports are dedicating areas to cold chain logistics. A container port terminal commonly has dedicated space available to store refrigerated containers.

- **Transport:** A range of transport technologies are available and have been improved to transport cold chain goods. Reefer vehicles (e.g. trucks) and containers (maritime containersand unit load devices) are among the most common technologies being used. They usually rely on attached refrigeration plants, requiring a power generator.

ISSUES AND COSTS IN COLD CHAIN IMPLEMENTATION

Although cold supply chain practices has introduced a lot of benefits and advantages to the related industries supply chain efficiency and competitiveness, this advantages come at price, below are a few issues to be addressed when considering a cold supply chain design and implementation (Blanchard, 2007) The use of non-environmental gas compounds All cold chain equipments must contain at least one type of "organic gas compounds", these gas components are called CFC gases, and it was recently discovered that these components can cause a serious environmental damage if released to the atmosphere, therefore, a new generation of cold chain equipment was introduced in 1996 to replace those using CFC gases, The new equipment is considered as CFC-free which comes for a higher price of course. The symbol shown below is used on refrigerators, air conditioners and drug carriers to highlight that the equipment has been made using CFC-free gazes and hence; has no harmful environmental effect (Handfield et al., 2014; Blanchard, 2007).

Frosting Ice can slowly build up on the freezing surface of the refrigerator during its operation; this frost layer must be continuously removed as it lowers the cooling efficiency of the cold chain equipment, that's why regular defrosting is important which have to be added to the equipment maintenance total cost. Safety concerns Since all of the cold supply chain equipments are powered by electricity, a qualified electricity technician has to be used to confirm the proper installation and deployment of all connections, plugs and switches, safety kits and circuit breakers has to be considered to protect the personnel and the equipment in case of any failure (Donselaar, 2006; Blanchard, 2007).

Continuous Control and monitoring of temperatures maintaining correct temperatures during storage and transportation is a very important task for the cold supply chain cycle (Boyd et al., 2003; Stank et al., 1999); temperature readings must be continuously taken in order to:

- Ensure that the vaccines are stored at the correct temperature condition.
- Ensure that the cold chain equipment is operating successfully.

Continuous monitoring of temperatures should be a regular task, and should be performed at the start and end of each day, although there are a lot of monitoring devices and equipments to help measuring, controlling, and recording the cold chain equipment temperature, it still needs extra man power overhead than the regular non temperature controlled supply chain logistics (Taylor, 2006; Tulsian and Saini, 2014). To develop a world-class cold chain infrastructure, government and industry bodies need to work in collaboration to encourage the adoption of better and more efficient refrigeration technologies that can prolong the shelf life of food products and bring commensurate economic returns to the farmers (Revilla and Seenz, 2014).

Challenges Foreseen by Cold Chain Industry

- **High Energy Costs:** Operating costs for the cold storage business in India are approximately 80-90 per cubic ft. per year as compared to 40 per cubic ft. per year in the West. Energy expenses alone make up about 30 percent of the total expenses for the cold storage industry in India compared to 10 percent in the West. These factors pose as a high entry barriers to potential players in the business. Rising Real Estate Costs: With the rising real estate price, the cost of setting up a cold storage units is also rising. It constitutes approximately 10-12 percent of the project cost. Also, as these units are not mobile, so choosing the right location becomes a critical factor. Being a capital-intensive project, it requires heavy investment in fixed assets like plant and machinery, building, insulation and panels. Depending on the size of the project and design of the infrastructure, the Capex is derived. Typically, a traditional cold storage of multi-tier walk in with a capacity of 6,000 tons would cost 5 crore, excluding land. Uneven Distribution of Capacity: A majority of investment in setting up cold storages in India has been in states like Uttar Pradesh, Maharashtra, Gujarat, Punjab and West Bengal. Further on analyzing the commodity wise storage capacity it is found that major cold storages have been set up to cater single commodities and this creates bottleneck for other perishable commodities.

COLD SUPPLY CHAIN AND LOGISTICS MODEL

Cold Chain Management can be defined as the network of facilities and distribution options that performs the usual functions of a standard supply chain cycle but with temperature and humidity control throughout the supply chain stages and entities. Each enterprise needs technology that helps them manage their activities-their contribution to the process-from farm to fork. By adhering to data standards, these solutions can work together to enable cross-enterprises sharing of the required information. Solving the Cold Chain challenge will take integration-within the enterprise and across the chain. Cold chain supply chain is the network of facilities and distribution options that performs the usual functions of a standard supply chain cycle but with temperature and humidity control throughout the supply chain stages and entities. Some of the managerial implications identified from this study are: Cold supply chain has major benefits on the industries that use it like valuable extension to the product shelf life, gives the ability to access overseas markets and gives the ability to meet the huge local demand. Cold supply chain implementation has some costs and concerns like: the use of non-environmental gas compounds, frosting, safety concerns, continuous control and monitoring of temperatures. Figure 1, model of 3Pe's is depicted; starting with enterprise level, managerial level and finally execution level (Figure 1). As per their performance management in related to cold chain, combination of enhanced Policy, Process, Performance and Enablers provides the key to success.

3Pe (stands for Performance, Policy, Process, and Enablers), is ChainLink's framework for enabling supply chain excellence (Figure 2). It is an effective and flexible model for analyzing a supply chain and developing a roadmap across much different industry.

Notations stands for:

- **Policy:** Stands for Ensuring Alignment across the Cold Chain,
- **Processes:** It's all About Managing the Links,
- **Performance:** Ultimate goal is to move from current to best practice, ensuring that each of the Cold Chain components is operating at optimal performance, and
- **Enablers:** Stands for making the Business Case for Cold Chain Technologies.

Figure 1. General vision of system support engineering framework (multi-level 3PE)
Source: Alsaidi, Md. S. and Mo, J. P. T., (2014)

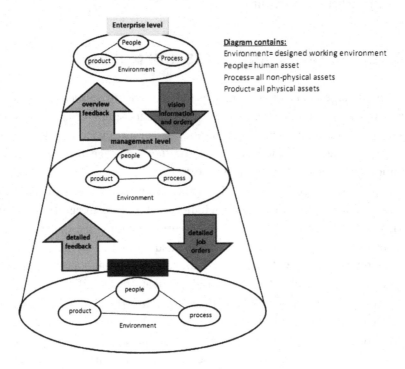

In processes, a clear understanding of the links and node level activities that take place through the cold chain process- starting from sourcing to ultimate consumption will enable all players to work collaboratively and ensure an optimal satisfaction model.

The transition from 'better to best practices', adopted by all players in the cold chain, and adoption of state of the art technologies will ensure that cold chain products are distributed with the same level of care as the manufacturing processes that ensure quality and consistency.

As an emerging market with an economy which is developing at an exuberant and attractive growth rate, India faces a piquant situation in a strategically important sphere of its rapidly developing economy - the slow and poor development of the cold chain supply and logistics system in the country. Cold chains or what in effect is the cold supply chain, has often been scarcely understood or worse, misinterpreted, leading to parlous conditions in the economy which could stymie its growth. A burgeoning economy with global aspirations can hardly afford to be sidetracked by reasons which span the entire gamut from not having understood the cold supply chain system to callous neglect.

Figure 2. Flow Diagram: Cold Chain Practices: Future direction towards Best Practices
Source: Carla Reed (2005, ChainLink Research), Modified as per Indian cold chain perspective by Authors

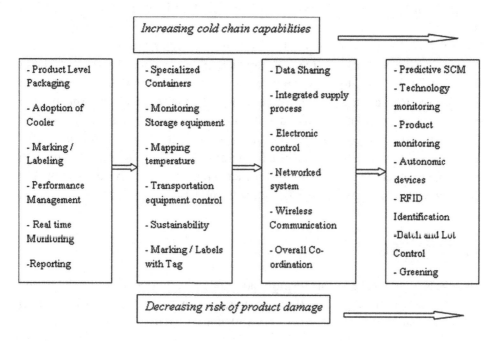

CONCLUSION

Cold supply chain has become more and more important within the changing global economy today due to the huge increasing demand on the products of temperature controlled industries, especially fresh agricultural products, manufactured food, chemicals, military services, and medical vaccines. Recent studies have shown a critical absence of a strong and dependable cold chain in developing economies. Cold chains are essential for extending shelf life, period of marketing, avoiding over capacity, reducing transport bottlenecks during peak period of production and maintenance of quality of produce. The development of cold chain industry has an important role to play in reducing the wastages of the perishable commodities and thus providing remunerative prices to the growers. Cold chain is, therefore, considered as an 'integral part of the supply chain of perishable items'.

Cold chain industry is emerging as a fast-growing business sector in India, with developments in the food processing sector, organized retail and government initiatives driving growth. For good manufacturing practices, technology of construction from warehouses to fleets to distribution centers has undergone a phenomenal change. Conventional brick wall construction has transform to sandwich insulated panel and reinforced concrete structures to pre-engineered buildings steel structures. Energy-efficient practices like energy recovery systems, energy-efficient designs of refrigeration equipment and automation are some of the innovative features. Efforts need to be made in order to introduce the latest concepts like 'green technology', 'sustainability' and 'use of renewable energy' for this sector. Special emphasis needs to be laid on development of 'reefer infrastructure' in view of India's exports thrust and potential. Besides, to boost the investments, financial institutions should play a major role to encourage the investment in cold chain industry in terms of loan sanctioning, nominal interest rates and disbursement without their support growth cannot happen. State government also take some step towards subsidizing electrical tariffs, encouraging use of renewable energies, etc. with keeping harmony with central government in order to boost 'long term planning and development of cold chain infrastructure' towards good manufacturing practices.

REFERENCES

Ali, J., & Kumar, S. (2011). Information and communication technologies (ICTs) and farmers decision-making across the agricultural supply chain. *International Journal of Information Management, 31*(2), 149–159. doi:10.1016/j.ijinfomgt.2010.07.008

Alsaidi, M., & Mo, J. P. T. (2014). System Support Engineering Framework: A Tool to Achieve Strategy Transformation. *Technology and Investment, 5*(1), 32–44. doi:10.4236/ti.2014.51005

Bishara, R. H. (2006). *Cold chain management-an essential component of the global pharmaceutical supply chain.* American Pharmaceutical Review.

Blanchard, D. (2007). *Supply chain management best practices.* John Wiley & sons, Inc.

Blanco, A. M., Masini, G., Petracci, N., & Bandoni, J. A. (2005). Operations management of a packaging plant in the fruit industry. *Journal of Food Engineering, 70*(3), 299–307. doi:10.1016/j.jfoodeng.2004.05.075

Bogataj, M., Bogataj, L., & Vodopivec, R. (2005). Stability of perishable goods in cold logistic chains. *International Journal of Production Economics, 93*(8), 345–356. doi:10.1016/j.ijpe.2004.06.032

Bourlakis, C., & Bourlakis, M. (2005). Information technology safeguards, logistics asset specificity and fourth-party logistics network creation in the food retail chain. *Journal of Business and Industrial Marketing*, *20*(2), 88–98. doi:10.1108/08858620510583687

Boyd, S. L., Hobbs, J. E., & Kerr, W. A. (2003). The impact of customs procedures on business to consumer e-commerce in food products. *Supply Chain Management: An International Journal*, *8*(3), 195–200. doi:10.1108/13598540310484591

Chopra, S., & Meindl, P. (2007). *Supply Chain Management: Strategy, Planning and Operation* (3rd ed.). Upper Saddle River, NJ: Prentice Hall.

Collins, A., Henchion, M., & OReilly, P. (1999). The impact of couple deconsolidation: Experiences from the Irish food industry. *Supply Chain Management: An International Journal*, *4*(2), 102–111. doi:10.1108/13598549910264789

Cunningham, D. C. (2001). The distribution and extent of agri-food chain management research in the public domain. *Supply Chain Management: An International Journal*, *6*(5), 212–218. doi:10.1108/EUM0000000006040

Donk, D. P. V., Akkerman, R., & Vaart, T. V. (2008). Opportunities and realities of supply chain integration: The case of food manufacturers. *British Food Journal*, *110*(2), 218–235. doi:10.1108/00070700810849925

Donselaar, K., Woensel, T., Broekmeulen, R., & Fransoo, J. (2006). Inventory control of perishables in supermarkets. *International Journal of Production Economics*, *104*(2), 462–472. doi:10.1016/j.ijpe.2004.10.019

Dunne, A. J. (2008). The impact of an organizations collaborative capacity on its ability to engage its supply chain partners. *British Food Journal*, *110*(4/5), 361–375. doi:10.1108/00070700810868906

Dzever, S., Merdji, M., & Saives, A.-L. (2001). Purchase decision making and buyer-seller relationship development in the French food processing industry. *Supply Chain Management: An International Journal*, *6*(5), 216–229. doi:10.1108/13598540110407769

Fearne, A., Barrow, S., & Schulenberg, D. (2006). Implanting the benefits of buyer-supplier collaboration in the soft fruit sector. *Supply Chain Management: An International Journal*, *11*(1), 3–5. doi:10.1108/13598540610642402

Fearne, A., & Hughes, D. (2000). Success factors in the fresh produce supply chain: Insights from the UK. *British Food Journal*, *102*(10), 760–772.

Folinas, D., Manikas, L., & Manos, B. (2006). Traceability data management for food chains. *British Food Journal, 108*(8), 622–633. doi:10.1108/00070700610682319

Hahn, K. H., Hwant, H., & Shinn, S. W. (2004). A returns policy for distribution channel coordination of perishable items. *European Journal of Operational Research, 152*(3), 770–780. doi:10.1016/S0377-2217(02)00753-1

Handfield, R. B., Monczka, R. M., Giunipero, L. G., & Patterson, J. L. (2014). *Sourcing and Supply Chain Management* (5th ed.). Cengage Learning.

Jackson, V., Blair, I. S., McDowell, D. A., Kennedy, J., & Bolton, D. J. (2007). The incidence of significant foodborne pathogens in domestic refrigerators. *Food Control, 18*(4), 346–351. doi:10.1016/j.foodcont.2005.10.018

Jahre, M., & Hatteland, C. J. (2004). Packages and physical distribution: Implications for integration and standardization. *International Journal of Physical Distribution & Logistics Management, 34*(2), 123–139. doi:10.1108/09600030410526923

Joshi, R., Banwet, D. K., & Shankar, R. (2009). Indian cold chain: Modeling the inhibitors. *British Food Journal. Emerald Publishing, 111*(11), 1260–1283.

Khan, A. U. (2005). *The domestic food market: Is India ready for food processing?* Conference on SPS towards Global Competitiveness in the Food Processing Sector, Pune, India.

Kumar, S. (2008). A study of the supermarket industry and its growing logistics capabilities. *International Journal of Retail & Distribution Management, 36*(3), 192–211.

Maheshwar, C., & Chanakwa, T. S. (2006). Post-harvest losses due to gaps in cold chain in India-a solution. *ISHS Acta Horticulturae 712: IV International Conference on Managing Quality in Chains - The Integrated View on Fruits and Vegetables Quality.*

Montanari, R. (2008). Cold chain tracking: A managerial perspective. *Trends in Food Science & Technology, 19*(8), 425–431. doi:10.1016/j.tifs.2008.03.009

Reed. (2005). Cold Chains are Hot! - Mastering the Challenges of Temperature-Sensitive Distribution in Supply Chains. *Chain Link Research.*

Revilla, E., & Seenz, M. J. (2014). Supply chain disruption management: Global convergence vs national specificity. *Journal of Business Research, 67*(6), 1123–1135. doi:10.1016/j.jbusres.2013.05.021

Salin, V., & Nayga, R. M. Jr. (2003). A cold chain network for food exports to developing countries. *International Journal of Physical Distribution & Logistics Management, 33*(10), 918–933. doi:10.1108/09600030310508717

Stank, T., Crum, M., & Arango, M. (1999). Benefits of inter-firm coordination in food industry supply chains. *Journal of Business Logistics, 20*(2), 21–41.

Taylor, D. (2006). *Global Cases in logistics and Supply Chain Management.* Thompson, South Western.

Tulsian, M., & Saini, N. (2014). Market-driven innovations in rural marketing in India. *International Journal of Scientific & Engineering Research, 5*(5), 1439–1445.

Viswanadham, N. (2006). *Can India be the food basket for the world?* Available at: www.isb.edu/faculty/Working_Papers_pdfs/Can_India_be_the_Food_Basket_for_the_World.pdf

Yu, M., & Nagurney, A. (2013). Competitive food supply chain networks with application to fresh produce. *European Journal of Operational Research, 224*(2), 273–283. doi:10.1016/j.ejor.2012.07.033

Chapter 12
Simulation for Distributed Assembly Line Manufacturing Processes:
A Framework on Petri. Net Simulator 2.0

Shwetank Parihar
ISM Dhanbad, India

Chandan Bhar
ISM Dhanbad, India

ABSTRACT

In the given study we have undertaken a comprehensive analysis on the simulation of different products emerging out from the assembly line. The study starts from collection of point of view of different authors from various studies. Then it has been found that the system of distributed manufacturing can be used to prepare a model that can be simultaneously simulated. The introduction of systems under a bigger system is introduced for accommodating the complete supply chain in a single diagram. The system is then implemented with the help of Petri NET software and the operational parameters are analysed by the output. The case study undertaken is of a cable manufacturing firm in which the methodology suggested is implemented and it is validated that such a methodology can help on controlling the different systems from a single point of control.

DOI: 10.4018/978-1-5225-2234-8.ch012

INTRODUCTION

The use of technology is always helpful in the management of operational processes. In the case of multi node manufacturing processes it becomes even more necessary to optimize the process with the help of simulation. In the case of a distributed assembly line the raw material is converted into finished goods with the help of many sub processes. These processes are helpful in designing the value addition of the product in a smooth fashion.

In this study we are mainly concentrating on those aspects which are more related to the manufacturing processes which have a long manufacturing process, which can be under the control of different suppliers present at the different geographical locations. This can be very well understood that in case of certain high end and technically sensitive products like air bus manufacturing assembly lines, the single product is manufactured at different sites around the globe and requires a huge amount of monetary inputs at stake. In such a system it becomes very necessary to maintain the processes in a simulated condition and this can be done very efficient by the use of simulation in different channels prevalent in the assembly lines. The risks or fluctuations associated with these production systems or projects are given by many authors like Castro et al. (1995), Dey (2001), Baccarini et al. (2001), Thevendran and Mawdesley (2004), Wyk et al. (2007), Fan et al (2008), Iyer et al. (2010), Chen et al. (2011), Aloini et al. (2012) and Fang et al. (2012). The various costs associated and fluctuations or problems that may arise are studied at first in order to create a system which is capable of handling these problems. Exhaustive literature survey for analyzing the pool of fluctuations or risks is being done for making the system practical in its approach and accurate in its analysis.

Distributed assembly lines are a reality of modern production systems. Most of the products which we use ranging from daily use products to technically sensitive products are now being manufactured at different sites. The coordination and central control for such manufacturing types is the need of the hour. Technical sensitivity in the product is increasing and along with that the outsourcing of services and manufacturing is being done. In this scenario the concepts like Just-in-time, Kanban etc. are very difficult to apply for complete and distributed assembly lines. The main risk factors that emerge in this condition are market related risks and abrupt fluctuations in the productivity and production process. This problem is being solved in this study. The manufacturing systems are shown in an integrated fashion in this study by developing a central system in which there many sub systems as a result of production process. This technique proved very efficient for controlling the distributed production scenario. The steps and elaborate methodology used for this new application in explained in the next sections of this study.

RESEARCH METHODOLOGY

In this framework we have suggested the division of system into various sub systems and then development of output parameters can be done for each unit which can be combined to give the overall scenario. The role of simulator can be very encouraging in these aspects since the effect of maintenance charges, quality costs, supplier upliftment can be simulated with the help of these parameters since all these parameters define production scenario which in turn greatly affects the maintenance charges, quality costs, supplier upliftment.

In this study the assembly lines are divided into sub processes and these processes can be magnified for each section clutched on the basis of other parameters. The job break down structure advocated in this study is in particularly helpful in management of those suppliers which are manufacturing crucial parts or sub assemblies of these systems but they do not have the privilege to use state of art automation and simulation techniques. In this case this system can be infused by the main or central manufacturing unit and it will be transferred to the suppliers without much hassle. The cost required for developing and installing such a system will be very less as compared to conventional simulated processes. The central processes are basically those processes which are being built in these manufacturing units but they are sub assembled by other small supplier. Like in the example of "Air Bus" we can see that the fabrication etc non core activities are performed by mid level manufacturers so managing quality in this aspect is a very difficult thing, so instead of developing simulated state of the art facilities in the supplier end we are developing a central server that will cater the need of very unit.

The main studies on handling uncertainties are done by authors like Favari (2012), Ismail et al. (2012), Dawei and Xuefeng (2012), Singh (2014), Rolfe (2013), Shariff et al. (2013), Bouras et al. (2013), Kähkönen et al. (2013) and Alketbi and Gardiner (2014). Along with these risks needs to be monitored and these operational difficulties for analysis are collected from recent studies of authors like Pinto and Dominguez (2012), Abdullah and Rahman (2012), Abdullah and Rahman (2012), Alias et al. (2012), López and Salmeron (2012), Tohidi and Jabbari (2012), Favari (2012), Yanwen (2012), Alias et al. (2012), Purnus and Bodea (2013), Sheykh et al. (2013), Lindkvist et al. (2013), Marques et al. (2013), Maravas and Pantouvakis (2013), Pinheiro et al. (2013), Marques et al. (2013), Lindkvist et al. (2013), Nahod et al. (2013), Kuchta (2014), Sato (2014), Singh (2014), Sidawi and Al-Sudairi (2014), Hussein and Klakegg (2014), Tenera and Pinto (2014), Papadaki et al. (2014), Binder et al. (2014), Stare (2014), Smitha (2014) and Christoph and Konrad (2014). On the contrary while considering the supplier perspective The quality changes in one of the remote supplier can be simultaneously simulated for its effect on the whole system. In order to implement this discussed framework we are analyzing it with the help of simple and cost effective simulation tool Petri.NET Simulator 2.0 and the framework is explained in the next section.

PETRI.NET SIMULATOR 2.0 FRAMEWORK

The Petri NET simulator works on development of a system in which the central control can be practiced for a distributed system of manufacturing. The framework consists of developing an input and output based system. This system consists of different units at manufacturing and supplier stations. In the next step this system is further investigated on the basis of workshop breakdown structure. In this manner the complete assembly line is represented in the form of different systems and this allows for a central control system for the whole of the distributed assembly line. This is shown in the form of an explanatory process diagram in Figure 1. The complete process is described as an interconnected system. The logistics and other transportation functions along the whole chain mainly depend upon many different factors. The logistics and other compatible sources of transportation can be managed more efficiently in order to manage the whole system. In the later part of the study we have analyzed the various aspects like flexibility and coordination in order to make the transportation easier. In the case considered it is being found that the overall production process involves a great deal of transaction delays of materials or work in process inventory. This particular fact is analyzed in this study after seeing the performance parameters and hence special care is being given to these transportation delays shown in the production process.

Figure 1. Showing the framework developed for centralized simulation of distributed manufacturing

The framework explained in the Figure 1 can be understood from the fact that the series of suppliers shown in the figure as Supplier I, II and III are centrally aligned in the system and the manufacturing units like Manufacturer I, II and III are all based on the fact that they are all aligned to the central simulation hub and in the next unit which is represented for logistics providers, it is advocated that most of the supply chain related activities are being taken over by this central simulation itself. In the same manner two sub systems are explained in the central system developed in this study.

In the next section of this study it is being explained with the help of a case study on a manufacturing company, which is a cable manufacturing firm. It includes the conversion of scrap into stranded wirer and then the PVC (Ply Vinyl Chloride) coating is done. The manufacturing is done in different locations and then the PVC coating is provided in different locations and finally it is send for ISI mark certifications and then distributed through different retailers. The simulation is started with the help of designing a Petri NET based simulation hub for this entire system.

Petri NET Based System's Analogy

The given system mainly works on reduction of risks present in various aspects of production line. In order to analyze these risks before studying the production system comprehensive literature research is being done in order to have a complete list of riks that rae needed to be analyzed before starting the system development on Petri NET. The main authors considered are Boute et al. (2004), Herroelen and Leus (2004), Aurich and Barbian (2004), Savci and Kayis (2006), Canbolat et al. (2008), Blackstone et al. (2009), Weerakkody and Irani (2010), Lockamy and Mc-Cormack (2010), Kolisch (2010), Alawamleh and Popplewell (2011), Diabat et al. (2012), Lee et al. (2013), Chen et al. (2013), Samvedi et al. (2013), Wagner et al. (2014), Micheli et al. (2014), Rajesh and Venkata Rao (2015) and Carvalho and Rabechini (2015). The works of all these authors have been very profound in listing of various problems which are included in our study.

The operational aspects are also needed to be sort after before designing the system. In order to design a complete system a detailed literature survey is being done to understand the system. The various studies helpful in this aspect are by authors like Black (2007), Akyuz and Erkan (2010), Vanichchinchai and Igel (2011), Harik et al. (2015), Lin and Ying (2015), Yu et al. (2015), Liu and Liang (2015), Ng et al. (2015), Chen et al. (2015) and Mehrjoo and Pasek (2015). These authors have pointed towards various operational difficulties like job flows, productivity etc in the operational activities. Special care has been given in the designing of system for these parameters. Now we are explaining the real system developed after analyzing these concepts.

Figure 2. Showing the central simulation model developed for the manufacturing firm

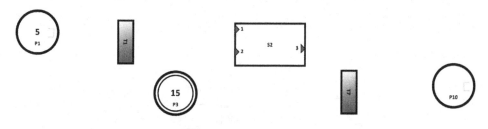

In the given system we have analyzed the distributed production system. First of all the scrap is collected from the suppliers which is denoted by P1 and it goes directly to the bundling machine at another site. This system where bundled conductors are kept is called S2. In S2 the bundled conductors are stranded in the system S2 where input is the wires going for the stranding machine and coming out as stranded conductors.

The stranded conducted then move back to the second unit where it goes to the output in the form of P4 and then after series of transportations from one machine to another it goes for the next resource P6 which is PVC then once again it is continuously fed to the final operation P9 which is the continuous coating of PVC on the stranded and bundled conductors, this marks the completion of the wire manufacturing at Out3. The transportation from one unit to another is cause of delays shown by the transition T4, T7, T5, T1, T3 and T2.

Figure 3 shows the implication of this system of Petri NET based simulation tool. It is shown in Figure 4. The suppliers are P1 which are contributing for manufacturing in the system S2 which contains the central and auxiliary manufacturing units. The system S2 is further explained in Figure 4 and it explains various components in these sections.

The system shown in Figure 2 is the overall system and this system is further broken into sub systems shown as S2. This model is implicated with desired parameters as shown in Figure 3 in Petri Net. The screen short of this system in ready to run condition is shown below in Figure 3. The associated parameters are shown in the left hand side of Figure 3 and this is done to provide a clear understanding for the reader. In Figure 2 we have P1, P3, and P10 which are Input ports, Control ports and Output ports respectively. The symbolic representation is shown in Figure 3 the transition delays are shown in the form of rectangular blocks T1 and T7.

Figure 3. Showing the complete system framed on Petri NET

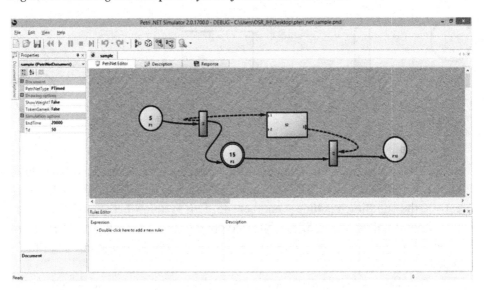

Framework for System S2

The system S2 contains further sub systems which are explained in the Figure 4, which contains a manufacturing unit by the name of S1 and is shown in Figure 5. The inputs In1 and In2 are fed directly to the system S1 and the output P4 is achieved by transition delays T2 and T3. The output is fed directly to the resource P6 through T4 and finally the semi processed materials went on to the Operation P9 and the transition Delay T5 is experienced through passing with S1.the output Out3 is finally received after passing though operation P9.

Figure 5 is the last segment of our case it is a manufacturing job shop in the system S2 which is simulated in the form of a different sector but is actually contained in the main system.

In this way the framework is explaining the simulation with the help of a cable manufacturing unit, in which the system is developed in Figure 2 and 3 and further sub manufacturing units are which are a sub part of system explained in Figure 2 are also simulated as a part and parcel of complete central system.

CONCLUSION

The system is simulated after designing the parameters. In our case six important parameters are decided. They are P1, P2, P3, P4, P5 and P6. In the description win-

Figure 4. The system (S1) simulation

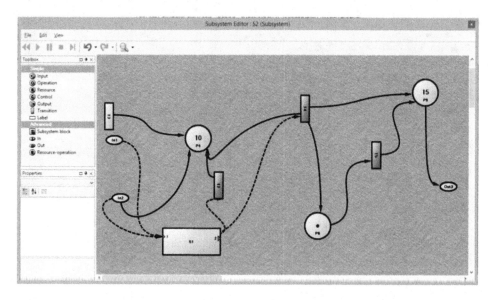

Figure 5. Sub system S1 simulated as a part of system S2

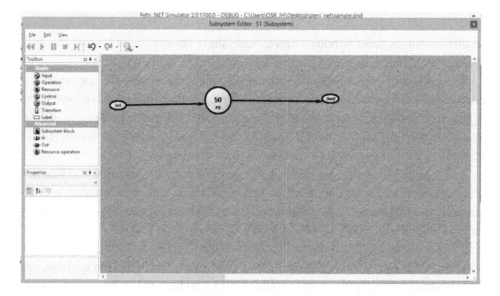

dow these parameters can also be shown with the help of matrices. The output after simulation can be seen in the different windows like Spreadsheet, Oscillogram and statistics. All these are present only under the response sheet of the software. The

Figure 6. P6 operation percentage (%) utilization shown in the output screen

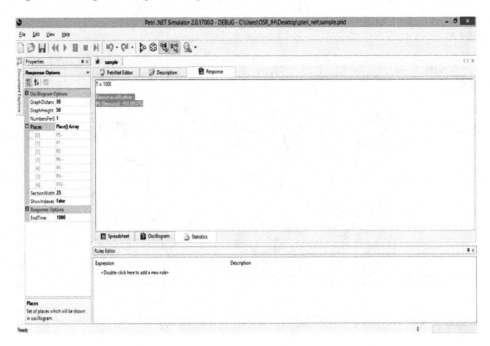

results shown on these windows for our case study are explained below. The snap shots of the simulated results are also shown in Figure 6 and Figure 7.

The utilization of the system parameters can also be shown in the response window under statistics section, like for example P6 operation utilization is shown in the Figure 6. It is shown in the highlighted portion and it shows the percentage utilization as 95 percent. This particular function can be used to determine the maximum utilization level of parameter as per the desired simulated attributes.

The logistics division also shows a low level of optimal condition and due to a lot of transactional waits and losses in between there is a need to focus upon coordination and flexibility as two important aspects. These aspects are dealt by many authors like Vasiliauskas (2002), Liedtke & Schepperle (2004), Lummus et al. (2005), Chan et al. (2006), Tang and Tomlin (2008), Choy et al. (2008), Gong (2008), Jayaram and Tan (2010), Naim et al. (2010), Gosling et al. (2010), Denant-Boèmont and Hammiche (2010), Naim and Gosling (2011), Ishfaq (2012), Ivanov and Sokolov (2013), Purvis et al. (2014), Wang et al. (2014) and Spiegler and Naim (2014). All these mentioned authors have mainly stressed on the need of flexibility as a whole in the supply chain. Different studies are done on different supply chains and the need of flexibility is shown in most of them and this is the reason why in order to create the less transportation and transition waits in the process it is necessary to include flexibility among the transportation means so that the product is transported without delay and through multiple options present. The problems of lead time etc are also reduced when flexibility is present for the transportation. In the same manner is being found that coordination among various transport means reduces the cost associated, improves the frequency of transportation system used in the firm itself. Several transport means or firms are combined to give a supply to different firms, while dealing with single or multiple types of products. This coordination is advocated by many authors like Bergqvist and Pruth (2006), Nof et al. (2006), Clifton et al. (2008), Schwind et al. (2009), Cantor et al. (2010), Audy et al. (2012), Meixell and Norbis (2012), Richey et al. (2012), Souza et al. (2014), Šalkovska (2014) and Choudhary (2014). All of these authors have provided insights on the various aspects of coordination among various types of products. Hence coordination and flexibility are the two main measures suggested in this study in order to have a reduced number of transaction delays in the system considered. This particular fact proves how much easier it is for the system to improve itself by using our methodology.

The final output is shown in Figure 7 in the form of an oscillation graph which tells us the level of each parameter during simulation. This particular figure explains the values of various parameters. In this figure all the six parameters P1 – P6 are shown. The end time for simulation can be adjusted like in our case for convenience and understanding we have changed the end time to 50. Although 1000 response time is considered to be more than sufficient for most of the response sheets or in general distributed assembly lines simulation. The section width can be adjusted from these set of panels only. We can also add any new rules by just double clicking the expression window. The section of graph can be selected by just moving the curser at that point and finally clicking on that selected point. The graph can be copied to a particular clip board or it can be opened in any picture formatting software like paint etc. for any further editing.

The role of such a simulation is very huge in assembly line based systems and the most striking fact is that the resources can be continuously tracked. The application of this software does not need a very huge amount of resources. The analysis has been done basically on a conventional assembly line. The results showed that simultaneous reports are generated in order to have a complete control over the production system. The analysis is hence forth updated by the inclusion of simulation. The flexibility is maintained by changing the models and the overall assumption is that reports built can be centrally located to most of the research and development division. The changes can be very well efficiently reflected by the research team. The small level industries can use this system in a very efficient manner since the requirement is much more and the resources needed for using such a system is very less. The analysis is very helpful since in our case study we have not introduced

Figure 7. Output characteristics on Oscillator Graph for T = 50

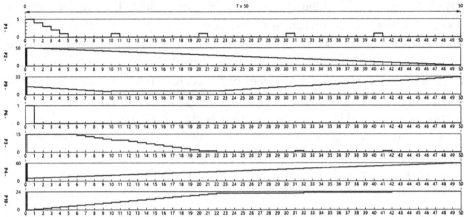

any changes in the system itself but only the formatting needs to be done on the model and the effect of change can be very well monitored.

The findings were very applicable in nature like most of the quality related issues are coming out only due to the faulty PVC coating on the wires and most of these systems can be rectified when we see the parameters in the Sub system 2. It can be seen here that the model containing the manufacturer assembly line replication, is the most important one and the complexity is also greater. In the output parameter window it can be seen that the process of transferring stranded conductors to the PVC coating machine can be one of the most daunting task since the wires are needed to be transferred and a lot of repetitive steps are present in such a system. The overall proficiency in such a system can be increased when a single machine can do the job for the complete analysis. This a flaw can be very well analyzed from the fact that the parameters in this sub system of manufacturer assembly line can be having a very complete control over the whole of the efficiency. The parameter does not show a very high level of optima. This clearly shows that this repetition in the sets of processes needs to be eliminated. The fact that needs to be analyzed here is that the policy issues can be very well managed. In our case the solution for this low level of efficiency can be solved in any manners and this efficiency can be increased, like one of the solutions can be related to the combining of these processes by a new machine which can change the overall wasteful transactions. The single machine which can strand the wire and apply PVC coating on them can be found to be a better solution for this problem, what we are trying to infer from this discussion is that we need to infuse the parameters in the systems and this methodology can bring upon the reasons of low productivity in the system. This is one of the major advantages of such a system.

Hence in the end we can see that the parameters P1 – P6 can be very well simulated with the help of Petri .net and it is n particularly very efficient in dealing with the distributed assembly line systems in our case three different sub sections are analyzed and it was found that as the production time will be going to be increased the utilization will be increasing.

In this way the central server can calculate the percentage utilization of sensitive resources and along with this the output of each parameter is also defined. In the output we can say that certain parameters are showing a higher value in the starting but as the time passes by with the production cycle the value of these parameters is lowering. These parameters can be found very easily from the diagram of systems S1 and S2. We have also found that P2 and P3 are showing a lower value and hence on analyzing we found that P2 is the part of the central process of stranding and finally the PVC coated conductors are built at the P3, this means that the process is facing delays and are less utilized due to distributed production and hence the manufacturing process can be speeded up at the S1 system which will reduce this problem. Hence this technique is very easy to apply and it has clearly found the underutilized sections in our case study of wire manufacturing unit. In this case we have utilized the P2 and P3 parameters by increasing the production rate at P2 by increasing the number of achiness and this output increase will reduce the delay in transitions and the main systems containing P3 will also be improved. So a simple application has resulted in saving the precious production resources. The technique is utilized in saving resources and more over the training of such technique is very easy and can be easily applied to any manufacturing firm. The study is hence proving the applicability of this technique and it has been proved by validating it on a real time basis on a distributed production system of a wire manufacturing firm.

The application of this technique is shown in this study and a system is developed, this system is traced and utilized in more efficient manner in this study by better utilizing resources, upgraded the parameter's performance and the transition times in between this distributed process is also reduced. The system is very helpful in those production lines where the modern production techniques are very difficult to employ due to different production sites producing different sections of same product. In this case the central monitoring systems are developed without much cost involved. This system can be very easily used by middle and lower level firms due to lower cost of investment. This technique also allows us to create a strategy framework for these distributed systems by real time sharing of production unit's data among the different production sites. In future it can be used to implement data analytics on a centralized server.

REFRENCES

Abdullah, A. A., & Rahman, H. A. (2012). Identification of relevant risks in abandoned housing projects in Malaysia: A qualitative study. *Procedia: Social and Behavioral Sciences, 62,* 1281–1285. doi:10.1016/j.sbspro.2012.09.219

Akyuz, G. A., & Erkan, T. E. (2010). Supply chain performance measurement: A literature review. *International Journal of Production Research, 48*(17), 5137–5155. doi:10.1080/00207540903089536

Alawamleh, M., & Popplewell, K. (2011). Interpretive structural modelling of risk sources in a virtual organisation. *International Journal of Production Research, 49*(20), 6041–6063. doi:10.1080/00207543.2010.519735

Alias, Z., Baharum, Z. A., & Idris, M. F. M. (2012) Project Management towards Best Practice. *Procedia - Social and Behavioral Sciences, 68,* 108 – 120.

Alketbi, S., & Gardiner, P. (2014). Top Down Management An approach In Project Portfolio management. *Procedia: Social and Behavioral Sciences, 119,* 611–614. doi:10.1016/j.sbspro.2014.03.068

Aloini, D., Dulmin, R., & Mininno, V. (2012). Risk assessment in ERP projects. *Information Systems, 37*(3), 183–199. doi:10.1016/j.is.2011.10.001

Audy, J., Lehoux, N., DAmours, S., & Ronnqvist, M. (2012). A framework for an efficient implementation of logistics collaborations. *International Transactions in Operational Research, 19*(5), 633–657. doi:10.1111/j.1475-3995.2010.00799.x

Aurich, J. C., & Barbian, P. (2004). Production projects – designing and operating lifecycle-oriented and flexibility-optimized production systems as a project. *International Journal of Production Research, 42*(17), 3589–3601. doi:10.1080/00207 540410001696348

Baccarini, D., & Archer, R. (2001). The risk ranking of projects: A methodology. *International Journal of Project Management, 19*(3), 139–145. doi:10.1016/S0263-7863(99)00074-5

Bergqvist, R., & Pruth, M. (2006). Public/Private Collaboration in Logistics: An Exploratory Case Study, Supply Chain Forum -. *International Journal (Toronto, Ont.), 7*(1), 106–118.

Binder, J., Aillaud, L. I. V., & Schilli, L. (2014). The project management cocktail model: An approach for balancing agile and ISO 21500. *Procedia: Social and Behavioral Sciences, 119,* 182–191. doi:10.1016/j.sbspro.2014.03.022

Black, J. T. (2007). Design rules for implementing the Toyota Production System. *International Journal of Production Research*, *45*(16), 3639–3664. doi:10.1080/00207540701223469

Bouras, V. K. (2013). A Method for the Evaluation of Project Management Efficiency in the Case of Industrial Projects Execution. *Procedia: Social and Behavioral Sciences*, *74*, 285–294. doi:10.1016/j.sbspro.2013.03.008

Boute, R., Demeulemeester, E., & Herroelen, W. (2004). A real options approach to project management. *International Journal of Production Research*, *42*(9), 1715–1725. doi:10.1080/00207540310001639946

Canbolat, Y. B., Gupta, G., Matera, S., & Chelst, V. (2008). Analysing risk in sourcing design and manufacture of components and sub-systems to emerging markets. *International Journal of Production Research*, *46*(18), 5145–5164. doi:10.1080/00207540701266807

Cantor, D., Bolumole, Y., Coleman, B. J., & Frankel, R. (2010). An examination of trends and impact of authorship Collaboration in logistics research. *Journal Of Business Logistics*, *31*(1), 197–217. doi:10.1002/j.2158-1592.2010.tb00135.x

Chan, F. T. S., Bhagwat, R., & Wadhwa, S. (2006). Increase in flexibility: Productive or counterproductive? A study on the physical and operating characteristics of a flexible manufacturing system. *International Journal of Production Research*, *44*(7), 1431–1445. doi:10.1080/00207540500398959

Chen, J. (2015) Synchronisation of production scheduling and shipment in an assembly flowshop. *International Journal of Production Research*. doi:10.1080/002 07543.2014.994075

Chen, J., Sohal, A. S., & Prajogo, D. I. (2013). Supply chain operational risk mitigation: A collaborative approach. *International Journal of Production Research*, *51*(7), 2186–2199. doi:10.1080/00207543.2012.727490

Chen, Z., Li, H., Ren, H., Xu, Q., & Hong, J. (2011). A total environmental risk assessment model for international hub airports. *International Journal of Project Management*, *29*(7), 856–866. doi:10.1016/j.ijproman.2011.03.004

Choudhary, A., Sarkar, S., Settur, S., & Tiwari, M. K. (2014). A carbon market sensitive optimization model for integrated forward-reverse logistics. *International Journal of Production Economics*. doi:10.1016/j.ijpe.2014.08.015

Choy, K. L., Chow, H. K. H., Tan, K. H., Chan, C., Mok, E. C. M., & Wang, Q. (2008). Leveraging the supply chain flexibility of third party logistics - Hybrid knowledge-based system approach. *Expert Systems with Applications, 35*(4), 1998–2016. doi:10.1016/j.eswa.2007.08.084

Christoph, A. J., & Konrad, S. (2014). Project complexity as an influence factor on the balance of costs and benefits in project management maturity modeling. *Procedia: Social and Behavioral Sciences, 119*, 162–171. doi:10.1016/j.sbspro.2014.03.020

Clifton, C., Iyer, A., Jiang, R.C.W., Kantarcoglu, M., & Vaidya, J. (2008). An Approach to Securely Identifying Beneficial Collaboration in Decentralized Logistics Systems. *Manufacturing & Service Operations Management, 10*(1), 108-125.

Dawei, L., & Xuefeng, Z. (2012). Research on the Application of Life Cycle Cost Management in the Civil Aircraft Assembly Line Project. *Physics Procedia, 25*, 443–451. doi:10.1016/j.phpro.2012.03.109

Denant-Boèmont, L., & Hammiche, S. (2010). Flexibility of Transport Choice in a Real-Option Setting: An Experimental Case Study. *Journal of Intelligent Transportation Systems: Technology, Planning, and Operations, 14*(3), 140–153. doi:10.1080/15472450.2010.484742

Dey, P. (2001). Decision support system for risk management: A case study. *Management Decision, 39*(8), 634–649. doi:10.1108/00251740110399558

Dey, P. (2010). Managing project risk using combined analytical hierarchy process and risk map. *Applied Soft Computing, 10*(4), 990–100. doi:10.1016/j.asoc.2010.03.010

Diabat, A., Govindan, K., & Panicker, V. V. (2012). Supply chain risk management and its mitigation in a food industry. *International Journal of Production Research, 50*(11), 3039–3050. doi:10.1080/00207543.2011.588619

Fan, M., Lin, N., & Sheu, C. (2007). Choosing a risk handling strategy: An analytical model. *International Journal of Production Economics, 112*(2), 700–713. doi:10.1016/j.ijpe.2007.06.006

Fang, C., & Marle, F. (2012). A simulation based risk network model for decision support in project risk management. *Decision Support Systems, 52*(3), 635–644. doi:10.1016/j.dss.2011.10.021

Favari, E. (2012). Reducing complexity in urban infrastructure projects. *Procedia: Social and Behavioral Sciences, 53*, 9–15. doi:10.1016/j.sbspro.2012.09.855

Gong, Z. (2008). An economic evaluation model of supply chain flexibility. *European Journal of Operational Research, 184*(2), 745–758. doi:10.1016/j.ejor.2006.11.013

Gosling, J., Purvis, L., & Naim, M. M. (2010). Supply chain flexibility as a determinant of supplier selection. *International Journal of Production Economics, 128*(1), 11–21. doi:10.1016/j.ijpe.2009.08.029

Harik, R. (2015) Towards a holistic sustainability index for measuring sustainability of manufacturing companies. *International Journal of Production Research*. doi:10.1080/00207543.2014.993773

Herroelen, W., & Leus, R. (2004). Robust and reactive project scheduling: A review and classification of procedures. *International Journal of Production Research, 42*(8), 1599–1620. doi:10.1080/00207540310001638055

Hillson, D. (2001). Extending risk process to manage opportunities. *International Journal of Project Management, 20*(3), 235–240. doi:10.1016/S0263-7863(01)00074-6

Hussein, B. A., & Klakegg, O. J. (2014). Measuring the impact of risk factors associated with project success criteria in early phase. *Procedia. Social and Behavioral Sciences, 119*, 711–718. doi:10.1016/j.sbspro.2014.03.079

Ishfaq, R. (2012). Resilience through flexibility in transportation operations. *International Journal of Logistics Research and Applications: A Leading Journal of Supply Chain Management, 15*(4), 215-229. DOI: 10.1080/13675567.2012.709835

Ismail, F., Yusuwan, N. M., & Baharuddin, H. E. A. (2012). Management Factors for Successful IBS Projects Implementation. *Procedia: Social and Behavioral Sciences, 68*, 99–107. doi:10.1016/j.sbspro.2012.12.210

Ivanov, D., & Sokolov, B. (2013). Control and system-theoretic identification of the supply chain dynamics domain for planning, analysis and adaptation of performance under uncertainty. *European Journal of Operational Research, 224*(2), 313–323. doi:10.1016/j.ejor.2012.08.021

Iyer, K. C., & Sagheer, M. (2010). Hierarchical Structuring of PPP Risks Using Interpretative Structural Modeling. *Journal of Construction Engineering and Management, 136*(2), 151–159. doi:10.1061/(ASCE)CO.1943-7862.0000127

Jayaram, J., & Tan, K. (2010). Supply chain integration with third-party logistics providers. *International Journal of Production Economics, 125*(2), 262–271. doi:10.1016/j.ijpe.2010.02.014

Johansen, A., Halvorsen, S. B., Haddadic, A., & Langlo, J. A. (2014). Uncertainty Management – A Methodological Framework Beyond The Six Ws. *Procedia: Social and Behavioral Sciences, 119*, 566–575. doi:10.1016/j.sbspro.2014.03.063

Jr, B. (2009). A tutorial on project management from a theory of constraints perspective. *International Journal of Production Research, 47*(24), 7029–7046. doi:10.1080/00207540802392551

Kähkönen, K., Keinänen, M., & Naaranoja, M. (2013). Core Project Teams as an Organizational Approach for Projects and Their Management. *Procedia: Social and Behavioral Sciences, 74,* 369–376. doi:10.1016/j.sbspro.2013.03.010

Kolisch, R. (2010). Managing risk in projects–fundamentals of project management, by D. Hillson. *International Journal of Production Research, 48*(18), 5547–5548. doi:10.1080/00207543.2010.484187

Kuchta, D. (2014). Information Technology and Quantitative Management (ITQM 2014) A new concept of project robust schedule – use of buffers. *Procedia Computer Science, 31,* 957–965. doi:10.1016/j.procs.2014.05.348

Lee, C. K. M., Lv, Y., & Hong, Z. (2013). Risk modelling and assessment for distributed manufacturing system. *International Journal of Production Research, 51*(9), 2652–2666. doi:10.1080/00207543.2012.738943

Liedtke, G., & Schepperle, H. (2004). Segmentation of the transportation market with regard to activity-based freight transport modelling. *International Journal of Logistics Research and Applications: A Leading Journal of Supply Chain Management, 7*(3), 199-218.

Lin, S.-W., & Ying, K.-C. (2015). A multi-point simulated annealing heuristic for solving multiple objective unrelated parallel machine scheduling problems. *International Journal of Production Research, 53*(4), 1065–1076. doi:10.1080/002075 43.2014.942011

Lindkvist, C., Stasis, A., & Whyte, J. (2013). Configuration management in complex engineering projects. *Procedia CIRP, 11,* 173–176. doi:10.1016/j.procir.2013.07.046

Liu, Y., & Liang, L. (2015). Evaluating and developing resource-based operations strategy for competitive advantage: An exploratory study of Finnish high-tech manufacturing industries. *International Journal of Production Research, 53*(4), 1019–1037. doi:10.1080/00207543.2014.932936

Lockamy, I. I. I. III, & McCormack, K. (2010). Analysing risks in supply networks to facilitate outsourcing decisions. *International Journal of Production Research, 48*(2), 593–611. doi:10.1080/00207540903175152

López, C., & Salmeron, J. L. (2012). Monitoring software maintenance project risks. *Procedia Technology, 5,* 363–368. doi:10.1016/j.protcy.2012.09.040

Lummus, R. R., Vokurka, R. J., & Duclos, L. K. (2005). Delphi study on supply chain flexibility. *International Journal of Production Research, 43*(13), 2687–2708. doi:10.1080/00207540500056102

Maravas, A., & Pantouvakis, J. P. (2013). Guidelines for Modelling Time and Cost Uncertainty in Project and Programme Management. *Procedia: Social and Behavioral Sciences, 74*, 203–211. doi:10.1016/j.sbspro.2013.03.045

Marques, A., Varajão, J., Sousa, J., & Peres, E. (2013). Project Management Success I-C-E model – a work in progress. *Procedia Technology, 9*, 910–914. doi:10.1016/j.protcy.2013.12.101

Mehrjoo, M., & Pasek, Z. J. (2015). Risk assessment for the supply chain of fast fashion apparel industry: A system dynamics framework. *International Journal of Production Research.* doi:10.1080/00207543.2014.997405

Meixell, M., & Norbis, M. (2012). Integrating carrier selection with supplier selection decisions to improve supply chain security. *International Transactions in Operational Research, 19*(5), 711–732. doi:10.1111/j.1475-3995.2011.00817.x

Micheli, G. J. L., Mogre, R., & Perego, A. (2014). How to choose mitigation measures for supply chain risks. *International Journal of Production Research, 52*(1), 117–129. doi:10.1080/00207543.2013.828170

Nahod, M. M., Vukomanovi, M., & Radujkovi, M. (2013). The Impact of ICB 3.0 Competences on Project Management Success. *Procedia: Social and Behavioral Sciences, 74*, 244–254. doi:10.1016/j.sbspro.2013.03.014

Naim, M., Aryee, G., & Potter, A. (2010). Determining a logistics providers flexibility capability. *International Journal of Production Economics, 127*(1), 39–45. doi:10.1016/j.ijpe.2010.04.011

Naim, M., & Gosling, J. (2011). On leanness, agility and leagile supply chains. *International Journal of Production Economics, 131*(1), 342–354. doi:10.1016/j.ijpe.2010.04.045

Ng, S. C. H., Rungtusanatham, J. M., Zhao, X., & Ivanova, A. (2015). TQM and environmental uncertainty levels: Profiles, fit, and firm performance. *International Journal of Production Research, 53*(14), 4266–4286. doi:10.1080/00207543.2014.994076

Nof, S. Y., Morel, G., Monostori, L., Molina, A., & Filip, F. (2006). From plant and logistics control to multi-enterprise collaboration. *Annual Reviews in Control, 30*(1), 55–68. doi:10.1016/j.arcontrol.2006.01.005

Olaru, M., Sandru, M., & Pirnea, I. C. (2014). Monte Carlo method application for environmental risks impact assessment investment projects. *Procedia: Social and Behavioral Sciences, 109*, 940–943. doi:10.1016/j.sbspro.2013.12.568

Papadaki, M., Gale, A. W., Rimmer, J. R., Kirkham, R. J., Taylor, A., & Brown, M. (2014). Essential factors that increase the effectiveness of project/programme risk management. *Procedia: Social and Behavioral Sciences, 119*, 921–930. doi:10.1016/j. sbspro.2014.03.103

Pinheiro, P. R., Machado, T. C. S., & Tamanini, I. (2013). Dealing the Selection of Project Management through Hybrid Model of Verbal Decision Analysis, Procedia. *Computer Science, 17*, 332–339.

Pinto, R., & Dominguez, C. (2012). Characterization of the practice of project management in 30 Portuguese metalworking companies. *Procedia Technology, 5*, 83–92. doi:10.1016/j.protcy.2012.09.010

Purnus, A., & Bodea, C. N. (2013). Considerations on Project Quantitative Risk Analysis. *Procedia: Social and Behavioral Sciences, 74*, 144–153. doi:10.1016/j. sbspro.2013.03.031

Purvis, L., Gosling, J., & Naim, M. (2014). The development of a lean, agile and leagile supply network taxonomy based on differing types of flexibility. *International Journal of Production Economics, 151*, 100–111. doi:10.1016/j.ijpe.2014.02.002

Rajesh, R., Ravi, V., & Venkata Rao, R. (2015). Selection of risk mitigation strategy in electronic supply chains using grey theory and digraph-matrix approaches. *International Journal of Production Research, 53*(1), 238–257. doi:10.1080/0020 7543.2014.948579

Richey, R. J., Adams, F., & Dalela, V. (2012). Technology and Flexibility: Enablers of Collaboration and Time-Based Logistics Quality. *Journal of Business Logistics, 33*(1), 34–49. doi:10.1111/j.0000-0000.2011.01036.x

Rolfe, B. (2013). Doing Project Management Ironically. *Procedia: Social and Behavioral Sciences, 74*, 264–273. doi:10.1016/j.sbspro.2013.03.022

Šalkovska, J., Ribakova, N., & Danovics, V. (2014). Marketing and logistics cooperation problems in Latvian companies. *Procedia: Social and Behavioral Sciences, 110*, 390–397. doi:10.1016/j.sbspro.2013.12.883

Samvedi, A., Jain, V., & Chan, F. T. S. (2013). Quantifying risks in a supply chain through integration of fuzzy AHP and fuzzy TOPSIS. *International Journal of Production Research, 51*(8), 2433–2442. doi:10.1080/00207543.2012.741330

Sato, T. (2014). Risk-based project value – the definition and applications to decision making. *Procedia: Social and Behavioral Sciences, 119*, 152–161. doi:10.1016/j.sbspro.2014.03.019

Savci, S., & Kayis, B. (2006). Knowledge elicitation for risk mapping in concurrent engineering projects. *International Journal of Production Research, 44*(09), 1739–1755. doi:10.1080/00207540500445321

Schwind, M., Gujo, O., & Vykoukal, J. (2009). A combinatorial intra-enterprise exchange for logistics services. *Information System E-Business Management, 7*(4), 447–471. doi:10.1007/s10257-008-0102-4

Shariff, S. M., Johan, Z. J., & Jamil, N. A. (2013). Assessment of Project Management Skills and Learning Outcomes in Students Projects. *Procedia: Social and Behavioral Sciences, 90*, 745–754. doi:10.1016/j.sbspro.2013.07.148

Sheykh, M. J., Azizi, M., & Sobhiyah, M. H. (2013). How Can the Trade off between Corporate Business Strategy and Project Risk be Optimized? *Procedia: Social and Behavioral Sciences, 74*, 134–143. doi:10.1016/j.sbspro.2013.03.012

Sidawi, B., & Al-Sudairi, A. A. (2014). The Use of Advanced Computer Based Management Systems by Large Saudi Companies for Managing Remote Construction Projects. *Procedia Engineering, 77*, 161–169. doi:10.1016/j.proeng.2014.07.013

Singh, A. (2014). Resource Constrained Multi-Project Scheduling with Priority Rules & Analytic Hierarchy Process. *Procedia Engineering, 69*, 725–734. doi:10.1016/j.proeng.2014.03.048

Smitha, P. (2014). Project Cost Management – Global Issues and Challenges. *Procedia: Social and Behavioral Sciences, 119*, 485–494. doi:10.1016/j.sbspro.2014.03.054

Souza, R., Goh, M., Lau, H., Ng, W., & Tan, P. (2014). Collaborative Urban Logistics - Synchronizing the Last Mile A Singapore Research Perspective. *Procedia: Social and Behavioral Sciences, 125*, 422–431. doi:10.1016/j.sbspro.2014.01.1485

Spiegler, V.L.M., & Naim, M.M. (2014). The impact of freight transport capacity limitations on supply chain dynamics. *International Journal of Logistics Research and Applications: A Leading Journal of Supply Chain Management, 17*(1), 64-88. DOI: 10.1080/13675567.2013.838012

Stare, A. C. S. P. M. (2014). Agile Project Management in Product Development Projects. *Procedia: Social and Behavioral Sciences, 119*, 295–304. doi:10.1016/j.sbspro.2014.03.034

Tang, C., & Tomlin, B. (2008). The power of flexibility for mitigating supply chain risks. *International Journal of Production Economics, 116*(1), 12–27. doi:10.1016/j.ijpe.2008.07.008

Thevendran, V., & Mawdesley, M. J. (2004). Perception of human risk factors in construction Projects: An exploratory study. *International Journal of Project Management, 22*(2), 131–137. doi:10.1016/S0263-7863(03)00063-2

Tohidi, H., & Jabbari, M. M. (2012). Role of human aspects in project management. *Procedia: Social and Behavioral Sciences, 31*, 837–840. doi:10.1016/j.sbspro.2011.12.152

Vanichchinchai, A., & Igel, B. (2011). The impact of total quality management on supply chain management and firms supply performance. *International Journal of Production Research, 49*(11), 3405–3424. doi:10.1080/00207543.2010.492805

Vasiliauskas, A. V. (2002). Modelling of freight flows that consist of multiple products transported by different modes of transport in a multimodal network. *Transport, 17*(5), 194–200.

Wagner, S. M., Padhi, S. S., & Zanger, I. (2014). A real option-based supply chain project evaluation and scheduling method. *International Journal of Production Research, 52*(12), 3725–3743. doi:10.1080/00207543.2014.883473

Wang, Y., Caron, F., Vanthienen, J., Huang, L., & Guo, Y. (2014). Acquiring logistics process intelligence: Methodology and an application for a Chinese bulk port. *Expert Systems with Applications, 41*(1), 195–209. doi:10.1016/j.eswa.2013.07.021

Weerakkody, V., & Irani, Z. (2010). A value and risk analysis of offshore outsourcing business models: An exploratory study. *International Journal of Production Research, 48*(2), 613–634. doi:10.1080/00207540903175160

Wyk, R. V., Bowen, P., & Akintoye, A. (2007). Project risk management practice: The case of a South African utility company. *International Journal of Project Management, 26*, 149–163.

Yanwen, W. (2012). The Study on Complex Project Management in Developing Countries. *Physics Procedia, 25*, 1547–1552. doi:10.1016/j.phpro.2012.03.274

Yu, V. F., Hu, K.-J., & Chang, A.-Y. (2015). An interactive approach for the multi-objective transportation problem with interval parameters. *International Journal of Production Research, 53*(4), 1051–1064. doi:10.1080/00207543.2014.939236

ADDITIONAL READING

Barad, M., & Sapir, D. (2003). Flexibility in logistic systems-modeling and performance evaluation. *International Journal of Production Economics*, *85*(2), 155–170. doi:10.1016/S0925-5273(03)00107-5

Carvalho, M. M., & Rabechini Junior, R. (2015). Impact of risk management on project performance: The importance of soft skills. *International Journal of Production Research*, *53*(2), 321–340. doi:10.1080/00207543.2014.919423

Dikmen, I., Birgonul, M. T., Anac, C., Tah, J. H. M., & Aouad, G. (2008). Learning from risks: A tool for post-project risk assessment. *Automation in Construction*, *18*(1), 42–50. doi:10.1016/j.autcon.2008.04.008

Erickson, J. M., & Evaristo, R. (2006) Risk Factors in Distributed Projects.*Proceedings of the 39th Hawaii International Conference on System Sciences IEEE.*

Gösling, H., & Geldermann, J. (2014). A framework to compare OR models for humanitarian logistics, Humanitarian Technology: Science, Systems and Global Impact 2014, HumTech 2014. *Procedia Engineering*, *78*, 22–28.

Kaynak, R., & Tuger, A. T. (2014). Coordination and collaboration functions of disaster coordination centers for humanitarian logistics. *Procedia: Social and Behavioral Sciences*, *109*, 432–437. doi:10.1016/j.sbspro.2013.12.486

Mason, R., & Nair, R. (2013). Strategic flexibility capabilities in the container liner shipping sector, Production Planning & Control. *The Management of Operations*, *24*(7), 640–651. doi:10.1080/09537287.2012.659873

Regos, G. (2012). Comparison of power plants risks with multi criteria decision Models. *Central European Journal of Operations Research*, *21*(4), 845–865. doi:10.1007/s10100-012-0257-4

Vidal, L., & Marle, F. (2012). A system thinking approach for project vulnerability management. *Kybrnetes*, *41*(1), 206–228. doi:10.1108/03684921211213043

Wright, S. (2013). Designing flexible transport services: Guidelines for choosing the vehicle type. *Transportation Planning and Technology*, *36*(1), 76–92. doi:10.1080/03081060.2012.745757

Compilation of References

Aamodt, A., & Plaza, E. (1994). Case-based reasoning: Foundational issues, methodological variations, and system approaches. *AI Communications, 7*(1), 39–59.

Abdullah, A. A., & Rahman, H. A. (2012). Identification of relevant risks in abandoned housing projects in Malaysia: A qualitative study. *Procedia: Social and Behavioral Sciences, 62,* 1281–1285. doi:10.1016/j.sbspro.2012.09.219

Adamopoulos, P. (2014). *On Discovering Non Obvious Recommendations: Using Unexpectedness and Neighborhood Selection Methods in Collaborative Filtering Systems.* ACM. doi:10.1145/2556195.2556204

Agarwal, A. (2009). *Web 3.0 concepts explained in plain English.* Retrieved June 12,fromhttp://www.labnol.org/internet/web-3-concepts-explained/8908/

Agrawal, A., Catalini, C., & Goldfarb, A. (2015). Crowdfunding: Geografy, social networks, and the timing of investment decisions. *Journal of Economics & Management Strategy, 24*(2), 253–274. doi:10.1111/jems.12093

Aickelin, U., & Cayzer, S. (2002). The Danger Theory and itts Application to Artificial Immune Systems. *Proceedings of The First International Conference on Artificial Immune Systems (ICARIS 2002),* 141–148.

Ainin, S., Lim, C. H., & Wee, A. (2005). Prospects and challenges of E-Banking in Malaysia. *Electronic Journal of Information Systems in Developing Countries, 22,* 1–110.

Ainscough, T., & Luckett, M. (1996). The Internet for the rest of us: Marketing on the World Wide Web. *Journal of Consumer Marketing, 13*(2), 36–47. doi:10.1108/07363769610115393

Akyuz, G. A., & Erkan, T. E. (2010). Supply chain performance measurement: A literature review. *International Journal of Production Research, 48*(17), 5137–5155. doi:10.1080/00207540903089536

Alama, M., & Sadafa, K. (2014). *Labeling of Web Search Result Clusters using Heuristic Search and Frequent Itemset. In ICICT, Procedia Computer Science, Science Direct* (pp. 216–222). Elsevier.

Compilation of References

Alawamleh, M., & Popplewell, K. (2011). Interpretive structural modelling of risk sources in a virtual organisation. *International Journal of Production Research, 49*(20), 6041–6063. doi:10 .1080/00207543.2010.519735

Algoet, P. H., & Cover, T. M. (1991). Asymptotic optimality and asymptotic equip-partition properties of log-optimum investment. *Annals of Probability*, 876–898.

Ali, A. F. (2014). *Genetic local search algorithm with self-adaptive population resizing for solving global optimization problems*. I.J. Information Engineering and Electronic Business.

Alias, Z., Baharum, Z. A., & Idris, M. F. M. (2012) Project Management towards Best Practice. *Procedia - Social and Behavioral Sciences, 68*, 108 – 120.

Ali, J., & Kumar, S. (2011). Information and communication technologies (ICTs) and farmers decision-making across the agricultural supply chain. *International Journal of Information Management, 31*(2), 149–159. doi:10.1016/j.ijinfomgt.2010.07.008

Alketbi, S., & Gardiner, P. (2014). Top Down Management An approach In Project Portfolio management. *Procedia: Social and Behavioral Sciences, 119*, 611–614. doi:10.1016/j.sb-spro.2014.03.068

Aloini, D., Dulmin, R., & Mininno, V. (2012). Risk assessment in ERP projects. *Information Systems, 37*(3), 183–199. doi:10.1016/j.is.2011.10.001

Alrifai, M., & Risse, T. (2009). Combining global optimization with local selection for efficient QoS -aware service composition. *Proceedings of the 18th International conference on world wide web*, 881-890. doi:10.1145/1526709.1526828

Alrifai, M., Skoutas, D., & Risse, T. (2010). Selecting skyline services for QoS-based web services composition.*Proceedings of the 19th International conference on World Wide Web*, 11-20. doi:10.1145/1772690.1772693

Alsaidi, M., & Mo, J. P. T. (2014). System Support Engineering Framework: A Tool to Achieve Strategy Transformation. *Technology and Investment, 5*(1), 32–44. doi:10.4236/ti.2014.51005

Althoff, T., & Leskovec, J. (2015). Donor retention in online crowdfunding communities: A case study of donorschoose.org.*Proceedings of the 24th International Conference on World Wide Web*, 34-44. doi:10.1145/2736277.2741120

ANACOM. (2012). InformaçãoEstatística do Serviço de Acesso à Internet: Vol. 3. *Trimestre de 2012*. Lisboa: ANACOM.

Andreas, B., & Andreas, G. H. (2001). A Framework for Internet-Based Distributed Learning. Academic Press.

Antonio, P.J., Fernandez, P., & Cortes, A.R. (2008). QoS-aware services composition using Tabu search and hybrid genetic algorithms. *Actas de Tallers de Ingeniera del software y Bases de Datos, 2*(1), 55-66.

239

Aoki, Y., Koshijima, R., & Toyama, M. (2015). *Automatic Determination of Hyperlink Destination in Web Index.* ACM. doi:10.1145/2790755.2790784

Appei, M. (2009). *Investing with exchange trade funds made easy: A start to finish plan to reduce costs and achieve higher returns* (2nd ed.). Upper Saddle River, NJ: Pearson Education Inc.

Ardagna, D., & Pernici, B. (2007). Adaptive service composition in flexible processes. *IEEE Transactions on Software Engineering*, *33*(6), 369–384. doi:10.1109/TSE.2007.1011

Audy, J., Lehoux, N., DAmours, S., & Ronnqvist, M. (2012). A framework for an efficient implementation of logistics collaborations. *International Transactions in Operational Research*, *19*(5), 633–657. doi:10.1111/j.1475-3995.2010.00799.x

Aurich, J. C., & Barbian, P. (2004). Production projects – designing and operating lifecycle-oriented and flexibility-optimized production systems as a project. *International Journal of Production Research*, *42*(17), 3589–3601. doi:10.1080/00207540410001696348

Baccarini, D., & Archer, R. (2001). The risk ranking of projects: A methodology. *International Journal of Project Management*, *19*(3), 139–145. doi:10.1016/S0263-7863(99)00074-5

Badjonski, M., Ivanovic, M., & Budimac, Z. (1997). Intelligent tutoring system as multi-agent system. *IEEE International Conference on Intelligent Processing Systems (ICIPS '97)*, *1*, 871-875,

Bahdori, S., Kafi, S., Zamani, K., & Khayyambashi, M. R. (2009). Optimal web service composition using hybrid GA-TABU search. *Journal of Theoretical and Applied Information Technology*, *9*(1), 10–15.

Barnard, J. (2012). *ZenithOptimedia releases September 2012 advertising expenditure forecast.* Retrieved January 4, 2013, from http://www.zenithoptimedia.com/zenith/zenithoptimedia-releases-september-2012-advertising-expenditure-forecasts/

Bayo-Moriones, A., & Lera-López, F. (2007). A firm-level analysis of determinants of ICT adoption in Spain. *Technovation*, *27*(6-7), 352–366. doi:10.1016/j.technovation.2007.01.003

Benklifa, M., & Olmstead, W. (2013). *Learn how to trade options (Collection).* Upper Saddle River, NJ: Pearson Education.

Bentley, P. J., Greensmith, J., & Ujjin, S. (2005). Two Ways to Grow Tissue for Artificial Immune Systems. *Proceedings of the Fourth International Conference on Artificial Immune Systems (ICARIS 2005)*, 139-152.

Bergqvist, R., & Pruth, M. (2006). Public/Private Collaboration in Logistics: An Exploratory Case Study, Supply Chain Forum -. *International Journal (Toronto, Ont.)*, *7*(1), 106–118.

Berthon, P. R., Pitt, L. F., Plangger, K., & Shapiro, D. (2012). Marketing meets Web 2.0, social media, and creative consumers: Implications for international marketing strategy. *Business Horizons*, *55*(3), 261–271. doi:10.1016/j.bushor.2012.01.007

Compilation of References

Berthon, P., Pitt, L. F., & Watson, R. T. (1996). The World Wide Web as an advertising medium. *Journal of Advertising Research*, *36*(1), 43–54.

Bezerra, G. B., Barra, T. V., de Castro, L. N., & Von Zuben, F. J. (2005). Adaptive Radius Immune Algorithm for Data Clustering. *LNCS*, *3627*, 290–303.

Bhama, S. (2011). Realizing the need for similarity based reasoning of cloud service. *International Journal of Engineering Science and Technology*, *3*(12).

Binder, J., Aillaud, L. I. V., & Schilli, L. (2014). The project management cocktail model: An approach for balancing agile and ISO 21500. *Procedia: Social and Behavioral Sciences*, *119*, 182–191. doi:10.1016/j.sbspro.2014.03.022

Bishara, R. H. (2006). *Cold chain management-an essential component of the global pharmaceutical supply chain*. American Pharmaceutical Review.

Black, J. T. (2007). Design rules for implementing the Toyota Production System. *International Journal of Production Research*, *45*(16), 3639–3664. doi:10.1080/00207540701223469

Blanchard, D. (2007). *Supply chain management best practices*. John Wiley & sons, Inc.

Blanco, A. M., Masini, G., Petracci, N., & Bandoni, J. A. (2005). Operations management of a packaging plant in the fruit industry. *Journal of Food Engineering*, *70*(3), 299–307. doi:10.1016/j.jfoodeng.2004.05.075

Bo, C., & Mei, L. (2014). *Design and Development of Semantic based Search engine Model*. IEEE.

Bogataj, M., Bogataj, L., & Vodopivec, R. (2005). Stability of perishable goods in cold logistic chains. *International Journal of Production Economics*, *93*(8), 345–356. doi:10.1016/j.ijpe.2004.06.032

Borodin, A., Roberts, G. O., Rosenthal, J. S., & Tsaparas, P. (2001). Finding authorities and hubs from link structures on the world wide web. World Wide Web, 415–429. doi:10.1145/371920.372096

Bouras, V. K. (2013). A Method for the Evaluation of Project Management Efficiency in the Case of Industrial Projects Execution. *Procedia: Social and Behavioral Sciences*, *74*, 285–294. doi:10.1016/j.sbspro.2013.03.008

Bourlakis, C., & Bourlakis, M. (2005). Information technology safeguards, logistics asset specificity and fourth-party logistics network creation in the food retail chain. *Journal of Business and Industrial Marketing*, *20*(2), 88–98. doi:10.1108/08858620510583687

Boute, R., Demeulemeester, E., & Herroelen, W. (2004). A real options approach to project management. *International Journal of Production Research*, *42*(9), 1715–1725. doi:10.1080/0020754031000163994

Boyd, S. L., Hobbs, J. E., & Kerr, W. A. (2003). The impact of customs procedures on business to consumer e-commerce in food products. *Supply Chain Management: An International Journal*, *8*(3), 195–200. doi:10.1108/13598540310484591

Broder, A. (2002). *A taxonomy of web search, Technical report*. IBM Research.

Brown, J., Broderick, A. J., & Lee, N. (2007). Word of mouth communication within online communities: Conceptualizing the online social network. *Journal of Interactive Marketing, 21*(3), 2–20. doi:10.1002/dir.20082

Bruntje, D., & Gajda, O. (2016). *Crowdfunding in Europe. State of the art in theory and practice*. Berlin, Germany: Springer. doi:10.1007/978-3-319-18017-5

Brusilovski, P. (1999). Adaptive and Intelligent Technologies for Web-based Education. *Kustliche Intelligence, 4*, 19–25.

Brusilovsky, P., Schwarz, E., & Weber, G. (1996), ELM-ART: An Intelligent Tutoring System on World Wide Web. In C. Frasson, G. Gauthier,, & A Lesgold (Eds.), *Proc. of 3rd International Conference on Intelligent Tutoring Systems, ITS-96*. Springer Verlag. doi:10.1007/3-540-61327-7_123

Budden, C. B., Anthony, J. F., Budden, M. C., & Jones, M. A. (2011). Managing the evolution of a revolution: Marketing implications of Internet media usage among college students. *College Teaching Methods & Styles Journal, 3*(3), 5–10. doi:10.19030/ctms.v3i3.5283

Buisson, B., & Silberzahn, P. (2010). Blue Ocean Or Fast-Second Innovation? A Four-Breakthrough Model To Explain Successful Market Domination. *International Journal of Innovation Management, 14*(03), 359–378. doi:10.1142/S1363919610002684

Burger, C., & Rotherme, K. (2001). *A Framework to Support Teaching in Distributed Systems*. University of Stuttgart.

Burke & Van Stel. (2009). *Blue Ocean versus Competitive Strategy: Theory and Evidence*. Academic Press.

Burns, H. L., & Capps, C. G. (1988). Foundations of intelligent tutoring systems: an introduction. In M. C. Polson & J. J. Richardson (Eds.), *Foundations of Intelligent Tutoring Systems*. Hillsdale, NJ: Lawrence Frlbaum.

Business Review Australia. (n.d.). Retrieved from: http://www.businessreviewaustralia.com

Cacheda, F., Carneiro, V., Fernandez, D., & Formso, V. (2011). Comparison of Collaborative FilteringAlgorithms: Limitations of Current Techniques and Proposal for Scalable, High Performance Recommender Systems. *ACM Transactions, 5*(1), 2:1-2:32.

Canbolat, Y. B., Gupta, G., Matera, S., & Chelst, V. (2008). Analysing risk in sourcing design and manufacture of components and sub-systems to emerging markets. *International Journal of Production Research, 46*(18), 5145–5164. doi:10.1080/00207540701266807

Cantor, D., Bolumole, Y., Coleman, B. J., & Frankel, R. (2010). An examination of trends and impact of authorship Collaboration in logistics research. *Journal Of Business Logistics, 31*(1), 197–217. doi:10.1002/j.2158-1592.2010.tb00135.x

Compilation of References

Cardellini, V., Casalicchio, E., Grassi, V., & Lo, F. (2007) Flow-Based Service Selection for Web Service Composition Supporting Multiple QoS Classes. *Proceedings of the 5th IEEE International Conference on Web Services (ICWS)*, 743-750. doi:10.1109/ICWS.2007.91

Carol, M. C., & Prodeus, A. P. (1998). Linkages of Innate and Adaptive Immunity. *Current Opinion in Immunology*, *10*(1), 36–40. doi:10.1016/S0952-7915(98)80028-9 PMID:9523108

Castro, L. N., & Von Zuben, F. J. (1999). Artificial Immune Systems: Part I – basic theory and applications. Technical Report No. DCA-RT 01/99. School of Computing and Electrical Engineering, State University of Campinas. Retrieved from ftp://ftp.dca.fee.unicamp.br/pub/docs/ vonzuben/tr_dca/ trdca0199.pdf

Castro, L. N., & Von Zuben, F. J. V. (2000). *Artificial Immune Systems: Part II – a survey of applications*. Retrieved from www.dca.fee.unicamp.br/~vonzuben/research/lnunes.../ rtdca0200.pdf

Castro, P. A. D., & Von Zuben, F. J. (2010). GAIS: A Gaussian Artificial Immune System for Continuous Optimization. ICARIS 2010, LNCS 6209. Springer. doi:10.1007/978-3-642-14547-6_14

Castro, L. N., & Von Zuben, F. J. (2002). Learning And Optimization Using The Clonal Selection Principle. *IEEE Transactions on Evolutionary Computation*, *6*(3), 239–251. doi:10.1109/ TEVC.2002.1011539

Castro, P. A. D., & Von Zuben, F. J. (2008). MOBAIS: A Bayesian Artificial Immune System For Multi-Objective Optimization. *LNCS*, *5132*, 48–59.

Castro, P. A. D., & Von Zuben, F. J. (2009). BAIS: A Bayesian Artificial Immune System for the effective handling of building blocks. *Information Sciences*, *179*(10), 1426–1440. doi:10.1016/j. ins.2008.11.040

Chan, F. T. S., Bhagwat, R., & Wadhwa, S. (2006). Increase in flexibility: Productive or counterproductive? A study on the physical and operating characteristics of a flexible manufacturing system. *International Journal of Production Research*, *44*(7), 1431–1445. doi:10.1080/00207540500398959

Chang, S. C. (2010). Bandit cellphones: A blue ocean strategy. *Technology in Society*, *32*(3), 219–223. doi:10.1016/j.techsoc.2010.07.005

Chappell, A. R., & Mitchell, C. M. (1997). The Case Based Intelligent Tutoring System: An Architecture for Developing and Maintaining Operator Expertise. *Proceedings of the 1997 IEEE International Conference on Systems, Man, and Cybernetics*, 308-318. doi:10.1109/ ICSMC.1997.638311

Chavan, J. (2013). Internet banking - Benefits and challenges in an emerging economy. *International Journal of Research in Business Management*, *1*, 19–26.

Chen, A., Hsu, Y., & Hu, K. A (2008). Hybrid Forecasting Model for Foreign Exchange rate Based on a Multi-neural network. *ICNC'08: Fourth International Conference on Natural Computation*. Jinan: IEEE.

Chen, J. (2015) Synchronisation of production scheduling and shipment in an assembly flowshop. *International Journal of Production Research*. doi:10.1080/00207543.2014.994075

Chen, J., Sohal, A. S., & Prajogo, D. I. (2013). Supply chain operational risk mitigation: A collaborative approach. *International Journal of Production Research*, *51*(7), 2186–2199. doi:10.1080/00207543.2012.727490

Chen, Z., Li, H., Ren, H., Xu, Q., & Hong, J. (2011). A total environmental risk assessment model for international hub airports. *International Journal of Project Management*, *29*(7), 856–866. doi:10.1016/j.ijproman.2011.03.004

Cho, J., Ya-Molina, H. G., & Page, L. (1998). Efficient crawling through URL ordering. *Computer Networks and ISDN Systems, 30*(1–7), 161–172.

Chopra, S., & Meindl, P. (2007). *Supply Chain Management: Strategy, Planning and Operation* (3rd ed.). Upper Saddle River, NJ: Prentice Hall.

Choudhary, A., Sarkar, S., Settur, S., & Tiwari, M. K. (2014). A carbon market sensitive optimization model for integrated forward-reverse logistics. *International Journal of Production Economics*. doi:10.1016/j.ijpe.2014.08.015

Choy, K. L., Chow, H. K. H., Tan, K. H., Chan, C., Mok, E. C. M., & Wang, Q. (2008). Leveraging the supply chain flexibility of third party logistics - Hybrid knowledge-based system approach. *Expert Systems with Applications*, *35*(4), 1998–2016. doi:10.1016/j.eswa.2007.08.084

Christoph, A. J., & Konrad, S. (2014). Project complexity as an influence factor on the balance of costs and benefits in project management maturity modeling. *Procedia: Social and Behavioral Sciences*, *119*, 162–171. doi:10.1016/j.sbspro.2014.03.020

Chulis, K. (2012). Optimal segmentation approach and application- Clustering vs. classification trees. *IBM developerWorks*. Retrieved from http://www.ibm.com/developerworks/library/ba-optimal-segmentation/

Clifton, C., Iyer, A., Jiang, R.C.W., Kantarcoglu, M., & Vaidya, J. (2008). An Approach to Securely Identifying Beneficial Collaboration in Decentralized Logistics Systems. *Manufacturing & Service Operations Management, 10*(1), 108-125.

Colaco, C. (1998). Acquired Wisdom in Innate Immunity. *Imm. Today, 19*(1).

Collins, A., Henchion, M., & OReilly, P. (1999). The impact of couple deconsolidation: Experiences from the Irish food industry. *Supply Chain Management: An International Journal, 4*(2), 102–111. doi:10.1108/13598549910264789

Corbett, K. (2005). *Anderson*. Intelligent Tutoring System.

Cover, T. M. (1991). Universal portfolios. *Mathematical Finance, 1*(1), 1–29. doi:10.1111/j.1467-9965.1991.tb00002.x

Compilation of References

Craven, M. (1998). Learning to Extract Symbolic Knowledge From the World Wide Web. *Proceedings of the Fifteenth National Conference on Artificial Intellligence (AAAI'98)*, 509-516.

Cristea, A., & Okamoto, T. (2002), Student model-based, agent-managed, adaptive Distance Learning Environment for Academic English Teaching. *IWALT 2002 Proceedings*, 159-162.

Cunningham, D. C. (2001). The distribution and extent of agri-food chain management research in the public domain. *Supply Chain Management: An International Journal, 6*(5), 212–218. doi:10.1108/EUM0000000006040

Damos, M. (2014). *Online crowdfunding platforms*. Frankfurt, Germany: Epubli.

Dastjerdi, A. V., Garg, S., Rana, O. F., & Buyaa, R. (2014). Cloud Pick: A Framework for QoS -aware and ontology- based service deployment across Clouds. *Software, Practice & Experience, 00*, 1–34.

Dawei, L., & Xuefeng, Z. (2012). Research on the Application of Life Cycle Cost Management in the Civil Aircraft Assembly Line Project. *Physics Procedia, 25*, 443–451. doi:10.1016/j.phpro.2012.03.109

Denant-Boèmont, L., & Hammiche, S. (2010). Flexibility of Transport Choice in a Real-Option Setting: An Experimental Case Study. *Journal of Intelligent Transportation Systems: Technology, Planning, and Operations, 14*(3), 140–153. doi:10.1080/15472450.2010.484742

Dey, P. (2001). Decision support system for risk management: A case study. *Management Decision, 39*(8), 634–649. doi:10.1108/00251740110399558

Dey, P. (2010). Managing project risk using combined analytical hierarchy process and risk map. *Applied Soft Computing, 10*(4), 990–100. doi:10.1016/j.asoc.2010.03.010

Diabat, A., Govindan, K., & Panicker, V. V. (2012). Supply chain risk management and its mitigation in a food industry. *International Journal of Production Research, 50*(11), 3039–3050. doi:10.1080/00207543.2011.588619

Ding, C., He, X., Husbands, P., Zha, H., & Simon, H. (2001). *Link analysis: Hubs and authorities on the world*. Technical report:47847,

Dinov, I. D. (2008). Expectation Maximization and Mixture Modeling Tutorial. *Statistics Online Computational Resource*. Retrieved from http://repositories.cdlib.org/socr/EM_MM

Donk, D. P. V., Akkerman, R., & Vaart, T. V. (2008). Opportunities and realities of supply chain integration: The case of food manufacturers. *British Food Journal, 110*(2), 218–235. doi:10.1108/00070700810849925

Donselaar, K., Woensel, T., Broekmeulen, R., & Fransoo, J. (2006). Inventory control of perishables in supermarkets. *International Journal of Production Economics, 104*(2), 462–472. doi:10.1016/j.ijpe.2004.10.019

Douw, S. (2012). *Crowdfunding*. Haarlem, Netherlands: SBP Editorial.

245

Duhan, N., Sharma, A. K., & Bhatia, K. K. (2009). Page Ranking Algorithms: A Survey. *IEEE International Advance Computing Conference (IACC 2009)*. doi:10.1109/IADCC.2009.4809246

Dunne, A. J. (2008). The impact of an organizations collaborative capacity on its ability to engage its supply chain partners. *British Food Journal*, *110*(4/5), 361–375. doi:10.1108/00070700810868906

Dzever, S., Merdji, M., & Saives, A.-L. (2001). Purchase decision making and buyer-seller relationship development in the French food processing industry. *Supply Chain Management: An International Journal*, *6*(5), 216–229. doi:10.1108/13598540110407769

Eid, R., & El-Gohary, H. (2011). The impact of E-marketing use on small business enterprises marketing success. *Service Industries Journal*, *33*(1), 31–50. doi:10.1080/02642069.2011.594878

Ellison, N. B., Steinfield, C., & Lampe, C. (2007). The benefits of Facebook friends: Social capital and college students use of online social network sites. *Journal of Computer-Mediated Communication*, *12*(4), 1143–1168. doi:10.1111/j.1083-6101.2007.00367.x

Fabiano, A., Dorca, C. R., Lopes, M. A., & Fernandez. (2003). A Multi agent architecture for Distance Education Systems. *Proceedings of the 3rd IEEE International Conference on Advanced Learning Technologies*.

Fang, C., & Marle, F. (2012). A simulation based risk network model for decision support in project risk management. *Decision Support Systems*, *52*(3), 635–644. doi:10.1016/j.dss.2011.10.021

Fan, M., Lin, N., & Sheu, C. (2007). Choosing a risk handling strategy: An analytical model. *International Journal of Production Economics*, *112*(2), 700–713. doi:10.1016/j.ijpe.2007.06.006

Favari, E. (2012). Reducing complexity in urban infrastructure projects. *Procedia: Social and Behavioral Sciences*, *53*, 9–15. doi:10.1016/j.sbspro.2012.09.855

Fearne, A., Barrow, S., & Schulenberg, D. (2006). Implanting the benefits of buyer-supplier collaboration in the soft fruit sector. *Supply Chain Management: An International Journal*, *11*(1), 3–5. doi:10.1108/13598540610642402

Fearne, A., & Hughes, D. (2000). Success factors in the fresh produce supply chain: Insights from the UK. *British Food Journal*, *102*(10), 760–772.

Fearon, D. T., & Locksley, R. M. (1996). The Instructive Role of Innate Immunity in the Acquired Immune Response. *Science*, *272*(5258), 50–53. doi:10.1126/science.272.5258.50 PMID:8600536

Fisher, T. (2009). ROI in social media: A look at the arguments. *Journal of Database Marketing & Customer Strategy Management*, *16*(3), 189–195. doi:10.1057/dbm.2009.16

Folinas, D., Manikas, L., & Manos, B. (2006). Traceability data management for food chains. *British Food Journal*, *108*(8), 622–633. doi:10.1108/00070700610682319

Fontanills, G., & Cawood, R. (2009). *Trade options online*. Hoboken, NJ: Wiley.

Fraley, C., & Raftery, A. E. (2000). *Model-Based Clustering, Discriminant Analysis, and Density Estimation*. Technical Report no. 380, Dept. of Statistics, University of Washington.

Compilation of References

Fraley, C., Raftery, A. E., Murphy, T. B., & Scrucca, L. (2012). *mclust Version 4 for R: Normal Mixture Modeling for Model-Based Clustering, Classification, and Density Estimation.* Technical Report No. 597. Department of Statistics, University of Washington. Retrieved from my.ilstu. edu/~mxu2/mat456/mcluster.pdf

Fraley, C., & Raftery, A. E. (2002). Model-based Clustering, Discriminant Analysis and Density Estimation. *Journal of the American Statistical Association, 97*(458), 611–631. doi:10.1198/016214502760047131

Freedman, D. M., & Nutting, M. R. (2015). *The foundations of online crowdfunding, in equity crowdfunding for investors: A guide to risks, returns, regulations, funding portals, due diligence, and deal terms.* Hoboken, NJ: Wiley. doi:10.1002/9781118864876

Friedman, B. M. (2000). Decoupling at the margin: The threat to monetary policy from the electronic revolution in banking. *International Finance, 3*(2), 261–272. doi:10.1111/1468-2362.00051

Gebara, F., Hofstee, H., & Nowka, K. (2015). Second Generation Big Data Systems. *IEEE Computers & Society, 48*(1), 36–41. doi:10.1109/MC.2015.25

Ghani, R., & Fano, A. (2002) Building Recommender Systems Using a Knowledge Base of Product Semantics.*Proceedings of the Workshop on Recommendation and Personalization in E-Commerce, at the 2nd International Conference on Adaptive Hypermedia and Adaptive Web Based Systems (AH2002)*, 11-19.

Gong, Z. (2008). An economic evaluation model of supply chain flexibility. *European Journal of Operational Research, 184*(2), 745–758. doi:10.1016/j.ejor.2006.11.013

Gonzalez, F. (2003). *A Study of Artificial Immune Systems Applied to Anomaly Detection* (Doctoral Thesis). University of Memphis. Retrieved from dis.unal.edu.co/~fgonza/papers/gonzalez03study.pdf

Goscinski, A., & Brock, M. (2010). Toward dynamic and attribute based publication, discovery and selection for cloud computing. *Future Generation Computer Systems, 26*(7), 947–970. doi:10.1016/j.future.2010.03.009

Gosling, J., Purvis, L., & Naim, M. M. (2010). Supply chain flexibility as a determinant of supplier selection. *International Journal of Production Economics, 128*(1), 11–21. doi:10.1016/j.ijpe.2009.08.029

Greensmith, J., Whitbrook, A., & Aickelin, U. (2010). Artificial Immune Systems. Handbook of Metaheuristics. Springer US.

Guy, I., Jaimes, A., Agullo, P., Moore, P., Nandy, P., Nastar, C., & Schinzel, H. (2010). *Will Recommenders Kill Search? Recommender Systems – An Industry Perspective.* ACM.

Hahn, K. H., Hwant, H., & Shinn, S. W. (2004). A returns policy for distribution channel coordination of perishable items. *European Journal of Operational Research, 152*(3), 770–780. doi:10.1016/S0377-2217(02)00753-1

Handfield, R. B., Monczka, R. M., Giunipero, L. G., & Patterson, J. L. (2014). *Sourcing and Supply Chain Management* (5th ed.). Cengage Learning.

Härdle, W., Müller, M., Sperlich, S., & Werwatz, A. (2004). *Nonparametric and Semiparametric Models: An Introduction*. Retrieved from http://sfb649.wiwi.hu-berlin.de/fedc_homepage/xplore/ebooks/html/spm/

Harik, R. (2015) Towards a holistic sustainability index for measuring sustainability of manufacturing companies. *International Journal of Production Research*. doi:10.1080/00207543.2014.993773

Hart, C. M. (2005). *I want to make money in the stock market: Learn to begin investing without losing your life savings*. Denver, CO: Outskirts Press.

Herroelen, W., & Leus, R. (2004). Robust and reactive project scheduling: A review and classification of procedures. *International Journal of Production Research, 42*(8), 1599–1620. doi:10.1080/00207540310001638055

Hillson, D. (2001). Extending risk process to manage opportunities. *International Journal of Project Management, 20*(3), 235–240. doi:10.1016/S0263-7863(01)00074-6

His ham, A.K. (2015). QoS Optimization for Cloud Service Composition Based on Economic Model. *Lecture Notes of the Institute for Computer Sciences, Social Informatics and Telecommunications Engineering, 150*, 355-366.

Hobson, R. (2012). *The dividend investor: A practical guide to building a share portfolio designed to maximise income*. Hampshire, UK: Harriman House Ltd.

Hoffman, D. L., & Fodor, M. (2010). Can you measure the ROI of your social media marketing? *MIT Sloan Management Review, 52*(1), 41–49.

Holt, P., Dubs, S., Jones, M., & Greer, J. (1991). The state of Student Modeling. In *Student Modelling: The Key to Individualizes Knowledge-Based Instruction, NATO ASI Series, 125* (pp. 3–35). London, UK: Springer verlag.

Huertas, J. C. G., & González, F. A. (2008). INDIE: An Artificial Immune Network for online Density Estimation. *MICAI, 2008*, 254–265.

Hussein, B. A., & Klakegg, O. J. (2014). Measuring the impact of risk factors associated with project success criteria in early phase. *Procedia: Social and Behavioral Sciences, 119*, 711–718. doi:10.1016/j.sbspro.2014.03.079

Hutchings, C. (2012). Commercial use of Facebook and Twitter–risks and rewards. *Computer Fraud & Security, 2012*(6), 19–20. doi:10.1016/S1361-3723(12)70065-9

Hwang, S.Y., Lim, E.P., Lee, C.H., & Chen, C.H. (2008). Dynamic Web service selection for reliable web service composition. *IEEE Transactions on Services Computing, 1*, 104-116.

Impact of Technology on Marketing. (2016, May 26). Boundless Marketing. *Boundless*.

Ishfaq, R. (2012). Resilience through flexibility in transportation operations. *International Journal of Logistics Research and Applications: A Leading Journal of Supply Chain Management, 15*(4), 215-229. DOI: 10.1080/13675567.2012.709835

Ismail, F., Yusuwan, N. M., & Baharuddin, H. E. A. (2012). Management Factors for Successful IBS Projects Implementation. *Procedia: Social and Behavioral Sciences, 68,* 99–107. doi:10.1016/j.sbspro.2012.12.210

Ivanov, D., & Sokolov, B. (2013). Control and system-theoretic identification of the supply chain dynamics domain for planning, analysis and adaptation of performance under uncertainty. *European Journal of Operational Research, 224*(2), 313–323. doi:10.1016/j.ejor.2012.08.021

Iyer, K. C., & Sagheer, M. (2010). Hierarchical Structuring of PPP Risks Using Interpretative Structural Modeling. *Journal of Construction Engineering and Management, 136*(2), 151–159. doi:10.1061/(ASCE)CO.1943-7862.0000127

Jackson, V., Blair, I. S., McDowell, D. A., Kennedy, J., & Bolton, D. J. (2007). The incidence of significant foodborne pathogens in domestic refrigerators. *Food Control, 18*(4), 346–351. doi:10.1016/j.foodcont.2005.10.018

Jaeyong, K. (2011). Towards Agents and Ontology for Cloud Service Discovery. *Proceedings of the International Conference on Cyber- Enabled Distributed Computing and Knowledge Discovery.* IEEE Computer Society.

Jahre, M., & Hatteland, C. J. (2004). Packages and physical distribution: Implications for integration and standardization. *International Journal of Physical Distribution & Logistics Management, 34*(2), 123–139. doi:10.1108/09600030410526923

Jain, A. K. (2009). Data Clustering: 50 Years Beyond K-Means. *Pattern Recognition.*

Janeway, C. A. Jr. (1992). The Immune System Evolved to Discriminate Infectious Nonself from Noninfectious Self. *Immunology Today, 13*(1), 11–16. doi:10.1016/0167-5699(92)90198-G PMID:1739426

Janeway, C. A. Jr. (1993). How the Immune System recognizes Invaders. *Scientific American, 269*(3), 72–79. doi:10.1038/scientificamerican0993-72 PMID:8211093

Janeway, C. A. Jr, & Travers, P. (1997). *Immunobiology The Immune System in Health and Disease* (2nd ed.). Artes Médicas. (in Portuguese)

Jang, J. H., Shin, D. H., & Lee, K. H. (2006). Fast quality driven selection of composite web services. *Proceedings of the 4th European Conference on Web Services,* 87-96. doi:10.1109/ECOWS.2006.21

Jayaram, J., & Tan, K. (2010). Supply chain integration with third-party logistics providers. *International Journal of Production Economics, 125*(2), 262–271. doi:10.1016/j.ijpe.2010.02.014

Johansen, A., Halvorsen, S. B., Haddadic, A., & Langlo, J. A. (2014). Uncertainty Management – A Methodological Framework Beyond The Six Ws. *Procedia: Social and Behavioral Sciences, 119*, 566–575. doi:10.1016/j.sbspro.2014.03.063

Jose, M., & Gascuena, A. F-C. (2005). *An Agent-based Intelligent Tutoring System for Enhancing E-Learning/ E-Teaching*. Academic Press.

Joshi, R., Banwet, D. K., & Shankar, R. (2009). Indian cold chain: Modeling the inhibitors. *British Food Journal. Emerald Publishing, 111*(11), 1260–1283.

Jr, B. (2009). A tutorial on project management from a theory of constraints perspective. *International Journal of Production Research, 47*(24), 7029–7046. doi:10.1080/00207540802392551

Jung, S., Harris, K., Webster, J., & Herlocker, J. (2004). *SERF: Integrating Human Recommendations with Search*. ACM. doi:10.1145/1031171.1031277

Kähkönen, K., Keinänen, M., & Naaranoja, M. (2013). Core Project Teams as an Organizational Approach for Projects and Their Management. *Procedia: Social and Behavioral Sciences, 74*, 369–376. doi:10.1016/j.sbspro.2013.03.010

Kaplan, A. M., & Haenlein, M. (2010). Users of the world, unite! The challenges and opportunities of social media. *Business Horizons, 53*(1), 59–68. doi:10.1016/j.bushor.2009.09.003

Khan, A. U. (2005). *The domestic food market: Is India ready for food processing?* Conference on SPS towards Global Competitiveness in the Food Processing Sector, Pune, India.

Khurana, A. (2014). Bringing Big Data Systems to the Cloud.what's trending? Column. *IEEE Computers & Society*, 72–75.

Kim, J., Bentley, P., Aickelin, U., Greensmith, J., Tedesco, G., & Twycross, J. (2007). Immune System Approaches to Intrusion Detection - A Review. *Journal of Natural Computing, Springer, 6*(4), 413–466. doi:10.1007/s11047-006-9026-4

Kim, W. C., & Mauborgne, R. (2008). *Blue ocean strategy: How to create uncontested market space and make the competition irrelevant*. Harvard Business School Press.

Kleinberg, J. (1998). Authoritative Sources in a Hyperlinked Environment.*Proceeding of 9th ACM-SIAM Symposium on Discrete Algorithms*, 668-677.

Kolisch, R. (2010). Managing risk in projects–fundamentals of project management, by D. Hillson. *International Journal of Production Research, 48*(18), 5547–5548. doi:10.1080/0020 7543.2010.484187

Kolodner, J. L. (1993). *Case-Based Reasoning*. San Mateo, CA: Morgan Kaufmann. doi:10.1016/ B978-1-55860-237-3.50005-4

Kondopoulos, D. (2011). Internet marketing advanced techniques for increased market share. *ChimicaOggi-Chemistry Today, 29*(3), 9–12.

Krantz, M. (2013). *Investing online for dummies*. Hoboken, NJ: Wiley.

Compilation of References

Kuchta, D. (2014). Information Technology and Quantitative Management (ITQM 2014) A new concept of project robust schedule – use of buffers. *Procedia Computer Science, 31*, 957–965. doi:10.1016/j.procs.2014.05.348

Kumar, R., Novak, J., & Tomkins, A. (2010). Structure and evolution of online social networks. In P. S. Yu, J. Han, & C. Faloutsos (Eds.), *Link mining: Models, algorithms, and applications* (pp. 337–357). New York: Springer. doi:10.1007/978-1-4419-6515-8_13

Kumar, S. (2008). A study of the supermarket industry and its growing logistics capabilities. *International Journal of Retail & Distribution Management, 36*(3), 192–211.

Kuppusamy, K. S., & Aghila, G. (2013). CaSePer: An Efficient Model for Personalized Web Page Change Detection Based on Segmentation. *Journal of King Saud University, 26*, 19–27.

Lampe, C. A. C., Ellison, N., & Steinfield, C. (2007). A familiar face(book): Profile elements as signals in an online social network.*Proceedings of the SIGCHI Conference on Human Factors in Computing Systems.* doi:10.1145/1240624.1240695

Laopodis, N. (2013). *Understanding investments: Theories and strategies.* New York, NY: Routledge.

Lassar, P., Lambert, L., Woodford, C., & Moschovitis, C. J. P. (2005). *The internet: A historical encyclopedia.* Santa Barbara, CA: ABC-CLIO.

Lee, C. K. M., Lv, Y., & Hong, Z. (2013). Risk modelling and assessment for distributed manufacturing system. *International Journal of Production Research, 51*(9), 2652–2666. doi:10.1080/00207543.2012.738943

Liao, S., Pu, S., Yuan, W. H., & Chen, A. (1999). The adoption of virtual banking: An empirical study.*PERGAMON International Journal of Information Management, 19*(1), 63–74. doi:10.1016/S0268-4012(98)00047-4

Liedtke, G., & Schepperle, H. (2004). Segmentation of the transportation market with regard to activity-based freight transport modelling. *International Journal of Logistics Research and Applications: A Leading Journal of Supply Chain Management, 7*(3), 199-218.

Limbu, D., Conor, A., Pears, R., & Mac Donell, S. (2006). *Contextual Relevance Feedback in Web Information Retrieval.* ACM.

Lindkvist, C., Stasis, A., & Whyte, J. (2013). Configuration management in complex engineering projects. *Procedia CIRP, 11*, 173–176. doi:10.1016/j.procir.2013.07.046

Lin, F. O. (2005). Designing Distributed Learning Environments with Intelligent Software Agents. *Journal of Educational Technology & Society, 8*(1), 132–133.

Lin, S.-W., & Ying, K.-C. (2015). A multi-point simulated annealing heuristic for solving multiple objective unrelated parallel machine scheduling problems. *International Journal of Production Research, 53*(4), 1065–1076. doi:10.1080/00207543.2014.942011

Liu, Y., & Liang, L. (2015). Evaluating and developing resource-based operations strategy for competitive advantage: An exploratory study of Finnish high-tech manufacturing industries. *International Journal of Production Research, 53*(4), 1019–1037. doi:10.1080/00207543.2014.932936

Lockamy, I. I. I. III, & McCormack, K. (2010). Analysing risks in supply networks to facilitate outsourcing decisions. *International Journal of Production Research, 48*(2), 593–611. doi:10.1080/00207540903175152

López, C., & Salmeron, J. L. (2012). Monitoring software maintenance project risks. *Procedia Technology, 5*, 363–368. doi:10.1016/j.protcy.2012.09.040

Lummus, R. R., Vokurka, R. J., & Duclos, L. K. (2005). Delphi study on supply chain flexibility. *International Journal of Production Research, 43*(13), 2687–2708. doi:10.1080/00207540500056102

Maheshwar, C., & Chanakwa, T. S. (2006). Post-harvest losses due to gaps in cold chain in India-a solution. *ISHS Acta Horticulturae 712: IV International Conference on Managing Quality in Chains - The Integrated View on Fruits and Vegetables Quality.*

Malhotra, D., & Verma, N. (2013). An Ingenious Pattern Matching Approach to Ameliorate Web Page Rank. *International Journal of Computer Applications,* 33-39.

Malhotra, D. (2014). *Intelligent Web mining to Ameliorate Web Page Rank using Back propagation Neural Network. In Confluence: The Next Generation Information Technology Summit* (pp. 77–81). IEEE.

Malhotra, D., & Rishi, O. P. (2016, August). IMSS-E: An Intelligent Approach to Design of Adaptive Meta Search System for E Commerce Website Ranking. In *Proceedings of the International Conference on Advances in Information Communication Technology & Computing* (p. 3). ACM. doi:10.1145/2979779.2979782

Mangold, W. G., & Faulds, D. J. (2009). Social media: The new hybrid element of the promotion mix. *Business Horizons, 52*(4), 357–365. doi:10.1016/j.bushor.2009.03.002

Maravas, A., & Pantouvakis, J. P. (2013). Guidelines for Modelling Time and Cost Uncertainty in Project and Programme Management. *Procedia: Social and Behavioral Sciences, 74*, 203–211. doi:10.1016/j.sbspro.2013.03.045

Marina, K. (2009). *Reference in the e-banking*. Cairo, Egypt: The Publisher of the Universities.

Marques, A., Varajão, J., Sousa, J., & Peres, E. (2013). Project Management Success I-C-E model – a work in progress. *Procedia Technology, 9*, 910–914. doi:10.1016/j.protcy.2013.12.101

Massolution. (2014). *Crowdfunding industry report*. Author.

Mattila, E. (2008). *Behavioral Segmentation of Telecommunication Customers* (Master of Science Thesis). TRITA-CSC-E 2008:075 ISRN-KTH/CSC/E--08/075--SE ISSN-1653-5715.

Matzinger, P. (2002). The danger model: A renewed sense of self. *Science, 296*(5566), 301–305. doi:10.1126/science.1071059 PMID:11951032

Compilation of References

McCalla, G. I., & Greer, J. E. (1991). *Granularity-Based Reasoning and Belief Revision in Student Models, In the Key to Individualised Knowledge-Based Instruction.* NATO ASI Series.

Medzhitov, R., & Janeway, C. A., Jr. (1998). Innate Immune Recognition and Control of Adaptive Immune Responses. *Seminars in Imm., 10.*

Mehrjoo, M., & Pasek, Z. J. (2015). Risk assessment for the supply chain of fast fashion apparel industry: A system dynamics framework. *International Journal of Production Research.* doi:1 0.1080/00207543.2014.997405

Meixell, M., & Norbis, M. (2012). Integrating carrier selection with supplier selection decisions to improve supply chain security. *International Transactions in Operational Research, 19*(5), 711–732. doi:10.1111/j.1475-3995.2011.00817.x

Mell, P., and Grance, T. (2011). *The NIST definition of cloud computing (draft).* NIST special publication, vol. 800, pp. 145.

Micheli, G. J. L., Mogre, R., & Perego, A. (2014). How to choose mitigation measures for supply chain risks. *International Journal of Production Research, 52*(1), 117–129. doi:10.1080/00 207543.2013.828170

Mobasher, B., Dai, H., Luo, T., & Nakagawa, M. (2002). Discovery and Evaluation of Aggregate Usage Profiles for Web Personalization. *Data Mining and Knowledge Discovery, 6*(1), 61–82. doi:10.1023/A:1013232803866

Mollick, E. (2014). The dynamics of crowdfunding: An exploratory study. *Journal of Business Venturing, 29*(1), 1–16. doi:10.1016/j.jbusvent.2013.06.005

Montanari, R. (2008). Cold chain tracking: A managerial perspective. *Trends in Food Science & Technology, 19*(8), 425–431. doi:10.1016/j.tifs.2008.03.009

Nahod, M. M., Vukomanovi, M., & Radujkovi, M. (2013). The Impact of ICB 3.0 Competences on Project Management Success. *Procedia: Social and Behavioral Sciences, 74*, 244–254. doi:10.1016/j.sbspro.2013.03.014

Naim, M., Aryee, G., & Potter, A. (2010). Determining a logistics providers flexibility capability. *International Journal of Production Economics, 127*(1), 39–45. doi:10.1016/j.ijpe.2010.04.011

Naim, M., & Gosling, J. (2011). On leanness, agility and leagile supply chains. *International Journal of Production Economics, 131*(1), 342–354. doi:10.1016/j.ijpe.2010.04.045

Nasraoui, O., Gonzalez, F., Cardona, C., Rojas, C., & Dasgupta, D. (2003). A scalable artificial immune system model for dynamic unsupervised learning. *Genetic and Evolutionary Computation—GECCO 2003*, 219-230.

Nasraoui, O., Gonzlez, F., Cardona, C., Rojas, C., & Dasgupta, D. (2003). A Scalable Artificial Immune System Model for Dynamic Unsupervised Learning. *LNCS, 2723*, 219–230.

Nasraoui, O., Cerwinske, J., Rojas, C., & Gonzalez, F. (2007). Performance of Recommendation Systems in Dynamic Streaming Environments.*Proceedings of the 2007 SIAM International Conference on Data Mining.* doi:10.1137/1.9781611972771.63

Ng, S. C. H., Rungtusanatham, J. M., Zhao, X., & Ivanova, A. (2015). TQM and environmental uncertainty levels: Profiles, fit, and firm performance. *International Journal of Production Research*, *53*(14), 4266–4286. doi:10.1080/00207543.2014.994076

Nielsen, D. (n.d.). Retrieved from: http://www.nielsen.com/us/en/insights/news/2011/how-social-media-impacts-brandmarketing.html

Nieto, E., & Roman, F. (2013). Similarity Preserving Snippet Based Visualization of Web Search Results. *IEEE Transactions on Visualization and Computer Graphics*, 1–14.

Nof, S. Y., Morel, G., Monostori, L., Molina, A., & Filip, F. (2006). From plant and logistics control to multi-enterprise collaboration. *Annual Reviews in Control*, *30*(1), 55–68. doi:10.1016/j.arcontrol.2006.01.005

Northcott, A. (2009). *The mutual funds book: How to invest in mutual funds and earn high rates of returns safely.* Ocala, FL: Atlantic Publishing *Group*.

Novel Guide. (n.d.) Retrieved from: http://www.novelguide.com

Olaru, M., Sandru, M., & Pirnea, I. C. (2014). Monte Carlo method application for environmental risks impact assessment investment projects. *Procedia: Social and Behavioral Sciences*, *109*, 940–943. doi:10.1016/j.sbspro.2013.12.568

Owens, N. D. L., Greensted, A., Timmis, J., & Tyrrell, A. (2009). T Cell Receptor Signalling Inspired Kernel Density Estimation and Anomaly Detection. *LNCS*, *5666*, 122–135.

Page, L., Brin, S., Motwani, R., & Winograd, T. (1999). *The pagerank citation ranking: Bringing order to the Web.* Technical report, Stanford Digital Libraries SIDL-WP- 1999- 0120.

Papadaki, M., Gale, A. W., Rimmer, J. R., Kirkham, R. J., Taylor, A., & Brown, M. (2014). Essential factors that increase the effectiveness of project/programme risk management. *Procedia: Social and Behavioral Sciences*, *119*, 921–930. doi:10.1016/j.sbspro.2014.03.103

Pardo, R. (2008). *The evaluation and optimization of trading strategies.* Hoboken, NJ: Wiley.

Parish, C. R., & ONeill, E. R. (1997). Dependence of the Adaptive Immune Response on Innate Immunity: Some Questions Answered but New Paradoxes Emerge. *Immunology and Cell Biology*, *75*(6), 523–527. doi:10.1038/icb.1997.83 PMID:9492188

Pathak, V., Dhyani, P., & Mahanti, P. (2011). Data Clustering with Artificial Innate Immune System Adding Probabilistic Behaviour. *International Journal of Data Mining and Emerging Technologies*, *1*(2), 77–84. doi:10.5958/j.2249-3212.1.2.5

Pinheiro, P. R., Machado, T. C. S., & Tamanini, I. (2013). Dealing the Selection of Project Management through Hybrid Model of Verbal Decision Analysis, Procedia. *Computer Science, 17*, 332–339.

Pinto, R., & Dominguez, C. (2012). Characterization of the practice of project management in 30 Portuguese metalworking companies. *Procedia Technology, 5*, 83–92. doi:10.1016/j.protcy.2012.09.010

Pitt, L., Berthon, P., Watson, R., & Zinkhan, G. (2002). The Internet and the birth of real consumer power. *Business Horizons, 45*(4), 7–14. doi:10.1016/S0007-6813(02)00220-3

Pokorny, J., & Smizansky J. (n.d.). *Page Content Rank: An Approach to the Web Content Mining*. Academic Press.

Porzak, J. (2008). Using R for Customer Segmentation. *useR! 2008*. Retrieved from https://ds4ci.files.wordpress.com/.../user08_jimp_custseg_revnov08.pdf

Prabha, D., & Ilango, K. (2014). A Rough Set Approach for Customer Segmentation. *Arabian Journal for Science and Engineering, 39*(6), 4565–4576. doi:10.1007/s13369-014-1013-y

Purnus, A., & Bodea, C. N. (2013). Considerations on Project Quantitative Risk Analysis. *Procedia: Social and Behavioral Sciences, 74*, 144–153. doi:10.1016/j.sbspro.2013.03.031

Purvis, L., Gosling, J., & Naim, M. (2014). The development of a lean, agile and leagile supply network taxonomy based on differing types of flexibility. *International Journal of Production Economics, 151*, 100–111. doi:10.1016/j.ijpe.2014.02.002

Rajesh, R., Ravi, V., & Venkata Rao, R. (2015). Selection of risk mitigation strategy in electronic supply chains using grey theory and digraph-matrix approaches. *International Journal of Production Research, 53*(1), 238–257. doi:10.1080/00207543.2014.948579

Rasekh, I. (2015). *A New Competitive Intelligence based Strategy for Web Page Search*. IEEE.

Reed. (2005). Cold Chains are Hot! - Mastering the Challenges of Temperature-Sensitive Distribution in Supply Chains. *Chain Link Research*.

Revilla, E., & Seenz, M. J. (2014). Supply chain disruption management: Global convergence vs national specificity. *Journal of Business Research, 67*(6), 1123–1135. doi:10.1016/j.jbusres.2013.05.021

Richey, R. J., Adams, F., & Dalela, V. (2012). Technology and Flexibility: Enablers of Collaboration and Time-Based Logistics Quality. *Journal of Business Logistics, 33*(1), 34–49. doi:10.1111/j.0000-0000.2011.01036.x

Ridings, C., & Shishigin, M. (2002). *Pagerank uncovered*. Technical report.

Riesbeck, C., & Schank, R. (1989). *Inside Case-Based Reasoning*. Hillsdale, NJ: Lawrence Erlbaum.

Rinaldo, A., & Wasserman, L. (2010). Generalized density clustering. *Annals of Statistics, 38*(5), 2678–2722. doi:10.1214/10-AOS797

Rishi, Rekha, Govil, & Madhavi. (2007). Agent Based student Modeling in Distributed CBR based Intelligent Tutoring System. *Proceedings of the World Congress on Engineering and Computer Science.*

Rizzotti, S., & Burkhart, H. (2010). useKit: a step towards the executable web s3.0.*Proceedings of the 19th International Conference on Worldwide Web.* doi:10.1145/1772690.1772861

Rodríguez-Ardura, I., Ryan, G., & Gretzel, U. (2012). Special issue on qualitative approaches to E-marketing and online consumer behaviour: Guest editors' introduction. *Journal of Theoretical and Applied Electronic Commerce Research*, (August), 2012.

Roebuck, K. (2011). *Crowdfunding: High impact strategies-what you need to know.* Amsterdam, Netherlands: Tebbo Publisher.

Rolfe, B. (2013). Doing Project Management Ironically. *Procedia: Social and Behavioral Sciences, 74*, 264–273. doi:10.1016/j.sbspro.2013.03.022

Safiye, T. (2005). *A Multi Agent system Approach For Distance Learning Architecture.* TOJET.

Salin, V., & Nayga, R. M. Jr. (2003). A cold chain network for food exports to developing countries. *International Journal of Physical Distribution & Logistics Management, 33*(10), 918–933. doi:10.1108/09600030310508717

Šalkovska, J., Ribakova, N., & Danovics, V. (2014). Marketing and logistics cooperation problems in Latvian companies. *Procedia: Social and Behavioral Sciences, 110*, 390–397. doi:10.1016/j.sbspro.2013.12.883

Samvedi, A., Jain, V., & Chan, F. T. S. (2013). Quantifying risks in a supply chain through integration of fuzzy AHP and fuzzy TOPSIS. *International Journal of Production Research, 51*(8), 2433–2442. doi:10.1080/00207543.2012.741330

Sarlak, M. A., & Astiani, A. A. (2011). *E-banking and emerging multidisciplinary processes: Social, economical, and organizational models.* Hershey, PA: IGI Global. doi:10.4018/978-1-61520-635-3

Sato, T. (2014). Risk-based project value – the definition and applications to decision making. *Procedia: Social and Behavioral Sciences, 119*, 152–161. doi:10.1016/j.sbspro.2014.03.019

Savci, S., & Kayis, B. (2006). Knowledge elicitation for risk mapping in concurrent engineering projects. *International Journal of Production Research, 44*(09), 1739–1755. doi:10.1080/00207540500445321

Schwartz, R. A. (2010). *Micro markets: A market structure approach to microeconomic analysis.* Hoboken, NJ: Wiley. doi:10.1002/9781118268131

Schwind, M., Gujo, O., & Vykoukal, J. (2009). A combinatorial intra-enterprise exchange for logistics services. *Information System E-Business Management, 7*(4), 447–471. doi:10.1007/s10257-008-0102-4

Compilation of References

Self, J. A. (1991). Formal Approaches to Student Modelling.GREE91, 295-352.

Sembiring, R. W., & Zain, J. M. (2010). Cluster Evaluation of Density Based Subspace Clustering. *Journal of Computing, 2*(1).

Seybert, H. (2012). *Internet use in households and by individuals 2012*. Retrieved January 25, 2013, from http://epp.eurostat.ec.europa.eu/cache/ITY_OFFPUB/KS-SF-12-050/EN/KS-SF12-050-EN.PDF

Shang, Shi, & Chen. (2001). An Intelligent Distributed Environment for Active Learning. University of Missouri-Columbia.

Shariff, S. M., Johan, Z. J., & Jamil, N. A. (2013). Assessment of Project Management Skills and Learning Outcomes in Students Projects. *Procedia: Social and Behavioral Sciences, 90*, 745–754. doi:10.1016/j.sbspro.2013.07.148

Sheykh, M. J., Azizi, M., & Sobhiyah, M. H. (2013). How Can the Trade off between Corporate Business Strategy and Project Risk be Optimized? *Procedia: Social and Behavioral Sciences, 74*, 134–143. doi:10.1016/j.sbspro.2013.03.012

Shi, S. M., Yu, J., Yang, G. W., & Wang, D. X. (2003). Distributed Page Ranking in Structured P2P Networks. *Proceedings of the International Conference on Parallel Processing (ICPP'03)*.

Shou, G., Bai, K., Chan, K., & Chen, G. (2014). Supporting privacy protection in personalized web search. *IEEE Transactions on Knowledge and Data Engineering, 26*(2), 453–467. doi:10.1109/TKDE.2012.201

Sidawi, B., & Al-Sudairi, A. A. (2014). The Use of Advanced Computer Based Management Systems by Large Saudi Companies for Managing Remote Construction Projects. *Procedia Engineering, 77*, 161–169. doi:10.1016/j.proeng.2014.07.013

Silva, J. M., MahfujurRahman, A. S. M., & El Saddik, A. (2008). Web 3.0: a vision for bridging the gap between real and virtual. *Proceeding of the 1st ACM International Workshop on Communicability Design and Evaluation in Cultural and Ecological Multimedia Systems*.

Silvana, A., & Karim, D. (2012). A QoS Optimization Model for Service Composition. *The Fourth International Conference on Adaptive and Self-Adaptive Systems and Applications*, 24-29.

Singh, D., & Reddy, C.K. (2014). A Survey on Platforms for Big Data Analytics. *Journal of Big Data*, 1-20.

Singh, M. K., & Sharma, D. K. (2012). Page Ranking Algorithm based number of link visits: An implementation. *National Conference NCETIT-2012*.

Singh, M. K., Akhtar, Z., & Begam, N. (2012). Challenges and Research Issues in Association Rule Mining. IJECSE, 1(2), 767-774.

Singh, A. (2014). Resource Constrained Multi-Project Scheduling with Priority Rules & Analytic Hierarchy Process. *Procedia Engineering, 69*, 725–734. doi:10.1016/j.proeng.2014.03.048

Singh, A., & Velez, H. (2014). Hierarchical Multi-Log Cloud-Based Search Engine.*IEEE International Conference on Complex, Intelligent and Software Intensive Systems, IEEE CPS* (pp. 212–219). IEEE.

Smitha, P. (2014). Project Cost Management – Global Issues and Challenges. *Procedia: Social and Behavioral Sciences*, *119*, 485–494. doi:10.1016/j.sbspro.2014.03.054

Social Media Today. (n.d.). Retrieved from: http://www.socialmediatoday.com/content/impact-social-media-marketing-trendsdigital-marketing

Souza, R., Goh, M., Lau, H., Ng, W., & Tan, P. (2014). Collaborative Urban Logistics - Synchronizing the Last Mile A Singapore Research Perspective. *Procedia: Social and Behavioral Sciences*, *125*, 422–431. doi:10.1016/j.sbspro.2014.01.1485

Spiegler, V.L.M., & Naim, M.M. (2014). The impact of freight transport capacity limitations on supply chain dynamics. *International Journal of Logistics Research and Applications: A Leading Journal of Supply Chain Management, 17*(1), 64-88. DOI: 10.1080/13675567.2013.838012

Srivastava, J., Cooley, R., Deshpande, M., & Tan, P.-N. (2000). Web Usage Mining: Discovery and Applications of Usage Patterns from Web Data. *SIGKDD Explorations*, *1*(2), 12–23. doi:10.1145/846183.846188

Stank, T., Crum, M., & Arango, M. (1999). Benefits of inter-firm coordination in food industry supply chains. *Journal of Business Logistics*, *20*(2), 21–41.

Stare, A. C. S. P. M. (2014). Agile Project Management in Product Development Projects. *Procedia: Social and Behavioral Sciences*, *119*, 295–304. doi:10.1016/j.sbspro.2014.03.034

Stein, B., & Busch, M. (2005). Density-based Cluster Algorithms in Low-dimensional and High-dimensional Applications. *Second International Workshop on Text-Based Information Retrieval (TIR 05), Fachberichte Informatik*, 45-56.

Steinberg, D. (2012). *The Kickstarter handbook: real-life crowdfunding success stories*. Philadelphia, PA: Quirk Books.

Stepney, S., Smith, R. E., Timmis, J., Tyrrell, A. M., Neal, M. J., & Hone, A. N. W. (2005). Conceptual Frameworks for Artificial Immune Systems. *Int. Journal of Unconventional Computing*, *1*, 315–338.

Stoica, P., & Moses, R. (2005). *Spectral Analysis of Signals*. Prentice Hall.

Sugiyama, K., Hatano, K., & Yoshikawa, M. (2004). *Adaptive Web Search Based on User Profile Constructed without any Effort from Users*. ACM.

Su, J. H., Wang, B. W., & Tseng, V. S. (2008). Effective Ranking and Recommendation on Web Page Retrieval by Integrating Association Mining and PageRank. *IEEE/WIC/ACM International Conference on Web Intelligence and Intelligent Agent Technology*. doi:10.1109/WIIAT.2008.49

Compilation of References

Tanapaiankit, P., Versterre, L., & Song, M. (2012). *Personalized Query Expansion in the QIC System*. ACM.

Tang, C., & Tomlin, B. (2008). The power of flexibility for mitigating supply chain risks. *International Journal of Production Economics*, *116*(1), 12–27. doi:10.1016/j.ijpe.2008.07.008

Taylor, D. (2006). *Global Cases in logistics and Supply Chain Management*. Thompson, South Western.

Taylor, D. (n.d.). *Behavioral Segmentation*. Fuzzy Logix White paper series, Fuzzy Logix, LLC. Retrieved from http://www.fuzzyl.com/wp-content/uploads/Behavioral-Segmentation-Paper.pdf

Tesai, C-W., Lai, C-F., Chao, H-C., & Vasilakos, A. V. (2015). Big Data Analytics: A Survey. *Journal of Big Data,* 1-32.

Thevendran, V., & Mawdesley, M. J. (2004). Perception of human risk factors in construction Projects: An exploratory study. *International Journal of Project Management*, *22*(2), 131–137. doi:10.1016/S0263-7863(03)00063-2

Timmis, J., Neal, M., & Hunt, J. (2000). An Artificial Immune System for Data Analysis. *Bio Systems*, *55*(1-3), 143–150. doi:10.1016/S0303-2647(99)00092-1 PMID:10745118

Tohidi, H., & Jabbari, M. M. (2012). Role of human aspects in project management. *Procedia: Social and Behavioral Sciences*, *31*, 837–840. doi:10.1016/j.sbspro.2011.12.152

Tomczak, A., & Brem, A. (2013). A conceptualized investment model of crowdfunding. *Venture Capital*, *15*(4), 335–359. doi:10.1080/13691066.2013.847614

Tome, T., & de Felício, J. R. D. (1996). Probabilistic cellular automaton describing a biological immune system. *Physical Review E: Statistical Physics, Plasmas, Fluids, and Related Interdisciplinary Topics*, *53*(4), 3976–3981. doi:10.1103/PhysRevE.53.3976 PMID:9964709

Trippi, R. R., & Lee, J. K. (1996). *Artificial Intelligence in Finance and Investing*. Irwin.

Tulsian, M., & Saini, N. (2014). Market-driven innovations in rural marketing in India. *International Journal of Scientific & Engineering Research*, *5*(5), 1439–1445.

Union, I. T. (2009). *Media statistics: Mobile phone subscribers (most recent) by country*. Retrieved December 6, from http://www.NationMaster.com/graph/med_mob_pho-media-mobile-phones 17

Van Belleghem, S., Thijs, D., & De Ruyck, T. (2012). *Social Media around the World 2012*. Retrieved November 3, from http://www.slideshare.net/InSitesConsulting/social-media-around-the-world-2012-by-insites-consulting

Vanichchinchai, A., & Igel, B. (2011). The impact of total quality management on supply chain management and firms supply performance. *International Journal of Production Research*, *49*(11), 3405–3424. doi:10.1080/00207543.2010.492805

Vasiliauskas, A. V. (2002). Modelling of freight flows that consist of multiple products transported by different modes of transport in a multimodal network. *Transport*, *17*(5), 194–200.

Verma, N., & Singh, J. (2015). Improved web mining for e-commerce website restructuring. In *Computational Intelligence & Communication Technology,2015 IEEE International Conference*. IEEE.

Verma, N., Malhotra, D., Malhotra, M., & Singh, J. (2015). E Commerce Web Site Ranking using Semantic Web Mining and Neural Computing. *Science Direct*, *45*, 42–51.

Vijiyarani, S., & Suganya, E. (2015). Research Issues in Web Mining. *International Journal of Computer-Aided Technologies, 2*(3), 55-64.

Vinay, V., Wood, K., Frayling, N., & Cox, I. (2005). *Comparing Relevance Feedback Algorithms for Web Search*. ACM.

Viswanadham, N. (2006). *Can India be the food basket for the world?* Available at: www.isb.edu/faculty/Working_Papers_pdfs/Can_India_be_the_Food_Basket_for_the_World.pdf

Wagner, S. M., Padhi, S. S., & Zanger, I. (2014). A real option-based supply chain project evaluation and scheduling method. *International Journal of Production Research*, *52*(12), 3725–3743. doi:10.1080/00207543.2014.883473

Wang, H., & Wong, K. (2014). Personalized Search: An Interactive and Iterative Approach. *IEEE 10th World Congress on Services*, (pp. 3-10). IEEE.

Wang, S., Zheng, Z., Sun, Q., Zou, H., & Yang, F. (2011). Cloud Model for Service Selection, Workshop on Cloud Computing. *IEEE INFOCOM*, 677 - 682.

Wang, Y., Xu, K., & Zhang, Y. (2011). Search engine optimization based on algorithm of BP neural networks. *IEEE International conference on computational intelligence and security* (pp. 390–394). IEEE.

Wang, Y., Caron, F., Vanthienen, J., Huang, L., & Guo, Y. (2014). Acquiring logistics process intelligence: Methodology and an application for a Chinese bulk port. *Expert Systems with Applications*, *41*(1), 195–209. doi:10.1016/j.eswa.2013.07.021

Wasid, M., & Kant, V. (2015). A Particle Swarm Approach to Collaborative Filtering based Recommender Systems through Fuzzy Features. *Science Direct*, *54*, 440–448.

Weerakkody, V., & Irani, Z. (2010). A value and risk analysis of offshore outsourcing business models: An exploratory study. *International Journal of Production Research*, *48*(2), 613–634. doi:10.1080/00207540903175160

Weinberg, B. D., & Pehlivan, E. (2011). Social spending: Managing the social media mix. *Business Horizons*, *54*(3), 275–282.

Weiss, G. (1999). Multiagent Systems: A Modern Approach to Distributed Artificial Intelligence. Cambridge, MA: MIT Press.

Wenger, E. (1987). *Artificial Intelligence & Tutoring System*. Los Altos, CA: Morgen Kaufman. doi:10.1016/B978-0-934613-26-2.50013-X

Compilation of References

Wenying, Z. (2009). *Cloud Service and Service Selection Algorithm Research. In GEC Summit* (pp. 1045–1048). ACM.

Whitla, P. (2009). Crowdsourcing and its application in marketing activities. *Contemporary Management Research, 5*(1), 15–28.

Williamson, D. G. (2006). Enhanced authentication in online banking. *Journal of Economic Crime Management, 4*, 1–42.

Witten, I. H., & Frank, E. (2005). *Data Mining- Practical Machine Learning Tools and Techniques.* Morgan Coffman Publishers.

Wyk, R. V., Bowen, P., & Akintoye, A. (2007). Project risk management practice: The case of a South African utility company. *International Journal of Project Management, 26*, 149–163.

Xing, W., & Ghorbani, A. (2004). Weighted PageRank Algorithm. *Proceedings of the Second Annual Conference on Communication Networks and Services Research (CNSR'04).* IEEE. doi:10.1109/DNSR.2004.1344743

Xu, M. X., Wikes, S., & Shah, M. H. (2006). *E-Banking application and issues in Abbey National PLC. E-Technologies. In Encyclopedia of E-Commerce, E-Government, and Mobile Commerce.* Hershey, PA: IGI Global.

Yanwen, W. (2012). The Study on Complex Project Management in Developing Countries. *Physics Procedia, 25*, 1547–1552. doi:10.1016/j.phpro.2012.03.274

Yao, Z. (2013). Visual Customer Segmentation and Behavior Analysis A SOM-Based Approach. Retrieved from http://www.doria.fi/bitstream/handle/10024/92542/yao_zhiyuan.pdf

Yazdani, M. (1987). Intelligent Tutoring Systems: An Overview. In R. Lawler (Ed.), *Artificial Intelligence and Education* (pp. 183–201). *Ablex Publishing Corp.*

Young, T. E. (2013). *The everything guide to crowdfunding: learn how to use social media for small-business funding: understand crowd psychology: gain an online presence: create a successful crowdfunding campaign: promote your campaign to reach hidden funding sources.* Avon, MA: Adams Media.

Youssif, A., Ghalwash, A., & Amer, E. (2011). *HSWS: Enhancing Efficiency of Web Search Engine Via Semantic Web.* ACM. doi:10.1145/2077489.2077530

Yu, S., & Dasgupta, D. (2008). Conserved Self Pattern Recognition Algorithm. *Proceedings of the 7th International Conference in Artificial Immune System (ICARIS).*

Yu, T., Zhang, Y., & Lin, K.J. (2007). Efficient algorithm for web service selection with end-to-end QoS constraints. *ACM Transactions on the Web, 1*, 1-26.

Yu, M., & Nagurney, A. (2013). Competitive food supply chain networks with application to fresh produce. *European Journal of Operational Research, 224*(2), 273–283. doi:10.1016/j.ejor.2012.07.033

Yu, V. F., Hu, K.-J., & Chang, A.-Y. (2015). An interactive approach for the multi-objective transportation problem with interval parameters. *International Journal of Production Research*, *53*(4), 1051–1064. doi:10.1080/00207543.2014.939236

Zhang, G., Li, C., & Xing, C. (2012). A Semantic++ Social Search Engine Framework in the Cloud. *IEEE International Conference on Semantics, Knowledge and Grids, IEEE CPS*, (pp. 277–278). IEEE. doi:10.1109/SKG.2012.9

Zhang, Y., Yu, J. X., & Hou, J. (2006). *Web Communities: Analysis and Construction*. Berlin: Springer.

About the Contributors

Om Prakash Rishi is an Associate Professor at University of Kota. His research area of interests include Artificial Intelligence, Big Data Analytics, Cloud Computing, and Information Security.

Anukrati Sharma is currently Associate Professor in the Faculty of Commerce and Management, University of Kota, Kota Rajasthan, India. Dr. Sharma has worked as an internal trainer and teacher in the management arena. In the year 2015 she got a Research Award by UGC, New Delhi on the topic of Analysis of the Status of Tourism in Hadoti and Shekhawati Region/Circuit (Rajasthan):Opportunities, Challenges and Future Prospectus. Her doctorate degree is in Tourism Marketing from University of Rajasthan and she completed her dissertation research on the topic of Tourism in Rajasthan Progress & Prospects. She has two postgraduate degree specialties-one in International Business (Masters of International Business) and another in Business Administration (Masters of Commerce). Her core subjects are Tourism, Strategic Management, Law, General Management and International Business Management. She has written 10 books on different subjects titled -Tourism Marketing, Organizational Behavior, Principles and Practices.

* * *

Zaved Akhatar works as an Associate Prof. in Department of Computer Science & Engineering. Research areas are Link Mining, Semantic Web, Web Mining.

Stelios Bekiros is a Research Professor at IPAG Business School, Professor at European University Institute (EUI) and Associate Professor at the Athens University of Economics and Business (AUEB). He was a faculty member at many distinguished universities and research institutions, mainly in the Netherlands, Italy, France, UK and Greece. He has participated in numerous conferences and academic seminars and has been an invited speaker in many prestigious universities and institutions. He has served as principal investigator and project manager in many European and national research projects. He is expert evaluator/vice-chair for the European Commission (EU-REA Panels, Horizon 2020, Brussels), expert evaluator for the Swiss National Science Foundation (SNF), a WES expert for Ifo Institute (Leibniz Institute for Economic Research, University of Munich), expert evaluator for the NSERC (Natural Sciences and Engineering Research Council of Canada) and the NSF (USA), while he is a regular evaluator of Hellenic national research bodies. He is currently associate editor for 7 Journals in Economics & Finance. Among other Associations and Societies, Professor Bekiros is Senior Fellow at the RCEA and member of the Faculty Row the official home of America's Top Professors. His work has been published in many well-known academic journals and in books and proceedings in many scientific fields. For a detailed resume visit his web-page http://www.mwpweb.eu/SteliosBekiros/

Praveen Dhyani is working as Executive Director, Banasthali University- Jaipur Campus. Looking after academic administration at Jaipur Campus of Banasthali University. Involved in process of developing academic and administrative systems as also educational reforms along with guiding students in their research work for Ph.D. degree. Member of two academic bodies, namely, Research Board and Academic Council of the University.

Vivek Gaur received a M.E. degree from Birla Institute of Technology and Science (BITS), Pilani, India in December 2001 and pursuing a Ph.D. degree from the Banasthali University, Jaipur, India, since May 2011. Currently, he is an Assistant Professor of Computer Science Department at the BIT, Mesra, Ranchi, India. Mr. Gaur's major research interest lies in cloud and grid computing, distributed systems, social networking, and web mining technologies.

Santosh Kumar, an expert in Financial Management, Managerial Economics and International Business, is presently associated as Assistant Professor in SOM, IMS Unison University, Dehradun. He was associated with the Birla Institute of Technology, Mesra, Jaipur Campus as a Full time Research Scholar in the Department of Management Studies. He has held manager and administrative positions in several organizations of good repute in his career. He has worked with ICIC bank Ltd and Reliance Capital in Mumbai region. In his academic profile, he is pursuing M.Phil and Ph.D from Birla Institute of Technology in Finance domain after completion of his MBA in Finance. As a dedicated researcher and scholar, he has published many research papers in reputed journals and seminars. He has participated and presented research papers in the national and international conferences. He is one of the resource persons of DST sponsored Refresher Courses organized by Birla

Institute of Technology in June 2013. He is a regular trainer for Financial market and Banking domain of India and organized many training programs.

Shweta Mahlawat has a Masters of Computer Application from Maharshi Dayanand University, Rohtak in 2004. She has been working as Associate Lecturer with Birla Institute of Technology, Mesra, Ranchi extension center at Jaipur for last 7 yrs. Presently she is doing her research in Agent Based Distributed Intelligent Tutoring System using Case Based Reasoning from Banasthali University, Jaipur, Rajasthan, India.

Dheeraj Malhotra is an Asst. Professor in IT at Vivekananda Institute of Professional Studies, GGS IP University. He is research scholar at University of Kota. His area of interests include Big Data Analytics, Web personalization, Semantic Web. He has number of International publications to his credit with reputed publishers like IEEE, Elsevier, Springer, ACM, FCS (USA).

Vishwambhar Pathak is an Asst. Professor in Department of CSE, Birla Institute of Technology, MESRA, Jaipur Campus, Rajasthan, India. Areas of interest include data analytics, statistical pattern recognition, Medical Image Mining, computer vision, and parallel computing.

Roopali Sharma, an expert in Managerial Economics and International Business, is presently associated with the Birla Institute of Technology, Mesra, Jaipur Campus as an Associate Professor and Head of the Management Department. She has held faculty and administrative positions in several institutions of higher learning in her career. In her academic profile, she has an MBA (International Business), M.A. (Economics), M. Phil and Ph.D. degrees. She is a Rajasthan University gold medalist in M. Phil. She has been conducting courses in Economics, International Business and Finance for post graduate and graduate management students. She has received the "Indo-Nepal Gold Star Award" in recognition of sterling merit, excellent performance & outstanding contribution to the progress of the nation and worldwide. The award has been given by the Economic Growth Society of India in Kathmandu, Nepal on April 20, 2013. A dedicated researcher and scholar, she has published 17 research papers in reputed journals and seminars. She has participated and presented a research paper in the international conference on "Sustainable Decision-Making in a Time of Crisis: Public and Private Perspectives", organized by the United Nations University's Institute for Sustainability and Peace (UNU-ISP) and the Asia Pacific Academy of Business in Society (APABIS). The conference held on 4 - 5 November 2010, at the United Nations University headquarters in Tokyo, Japan. She has also written one book on "India and SAARC – New Vistas in Regional Trade", and a monograph on "Indian Banking Sector – Reforms Owing To Globalization And Its Implication".

Jatinder Singh received his M.Tech degree from Punjabi University, Patiala with 84% marks and Ph.D. from the same university in Computer Engineering with specialization in Wireless Network Security. He has 3 years of industrial and 15 years of teaching, research and administrative experience to his credit. He is a prolific author in the field of Computer Engineering. He has published more than 100 research papers in International & National journals of repute. Apart from that, he has 22 highly acclaimed text/research to his oeuvre which are recommended as text books in many Indian and foreign universities. He is also a life member of several professional scientific organizations (ISTE, CSI, IETE etc) and has lectured widely at academic institutions. He got many National and International awards including Best Research Scholar Award by UGC in 2007, Excellence Service Award by PB. Govt. in 2008, R&D Gem of DBIEM, Vigyan Ratna Award by Honorable Governor of Punjab in 2012, Bharat Gaurav Award by AITMC 2013 and many more awards by the different organization.

Neha Verma is Research Scholar at IK Gujral Punjab Technical University, India. Her area of interest includes Data Mining, Big Data, OOP etc. She has many international publications to her credit.

Javier Vidal is an Assistant Professor of Finance, University of Valladolid. Spain. He graduated with a BSc in Management from Queen´s University Belfast, MSc in Finance from Aston Business School, MA in Economics from Autonomous University of Madrid, Phd in Financial Economics from Complutense University of Madrid and has been postdoctoral fellow at the Harvard Business School.

Marta Vidal has a BSc and MBA from ESADE Business School, PhD student in Management at Complutense University, Assistant Professor of Management at European University of Madrid.

Index

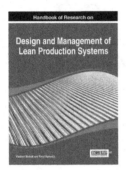
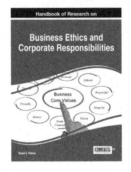

Stay Current on the Latest Emerging Research Developments

Become an IGI Global Reviewer for Authored Book Projects

Premier Reference Source

Solutions for High-Touch Communications in a High-Tech World

Premier Reference Source

Advanced Research on Biologically Inspired Cognitive Architectures

Premier Reference Source

Workforce Development Theory and Practice in the Mental Health Sector

Premier Reference Source

Resource Management and Efficiency in Cloud Computing Environments

The overall success of an authored book project is dependent on quality and timely reviews.

In this competitive age of scholarly publishing, constructive and timely feedback significantly decreases the turnaround time of manuscripts from submission to acceptance, allowing the publication and discovery of progressive research at a much more expeditious rate. Several IGI Global authored book projects are currently seeking highly qualified experts in the field to fill vacancies on their respective editorial review boards:

Applications may be sent to:
development@igi-global.com

Applicants must have a doctorate (or an equivalent degree) as well as publishing and reviewing experience. Reviewers are asked to write reviews in a timely, collegial, and constructive manner. All reviewers will begin their role on an ad-hoc basis for a period of one year, and upon successful completion of this term can be considered for full editorial review board status, with the potential for a subsequent promotion to Associate Editor.

If you have a colleague that may be interested in this opportunity, we encourage you to share this information with them.

Printed in the United States
By Bookmasters